Anne Ridler

MEMOIRS

Anne in the late 1930s, photographed by Vivian.

Anne Ridler
MEMOIRS

THE PERPETUA PRESS
OXFORD

Anne Ridler
Born Rugby, 30 July 1912
Died Oxford, 15 October 2001

ISBN 1 870882 18 0

Further copies of these memoirs may be obtained from:
Orchard Close, Top Lane,
Wootton, Woodstock, Oxon, OX20 IDP

Set by Neil Scott, Wootton, Woodstock
Printed and bound in Great Britain by Biddles Limited
Kings Lynn, Norfolk

CONTENTS

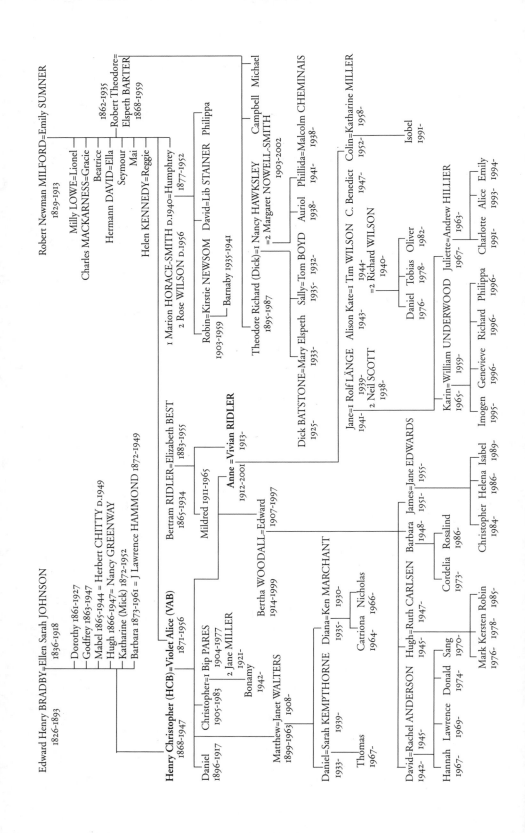

Robert Newman MILFORD=Emily SUMNER
1829-1913

Edward Henry BRADBY=Ellen Sarah JOHNSON
1826-1893 / 1836-1918

Milly LOWE=Lionel
Charles MACKARNESS=Gracie
Beatrice
Hermann DAVID=Ella
Seymour
1862-1935
Robert Theodore=Elspeth BARTER
Mai
Helen KENNEDY=Reggie
1868-1959

Dorothy 1861-1927
Godfrey 1863-1947
Mabel 1865-1944 = Herbert CHITTY D.1949
Hugh 1866-1947= Nancy GREENWAY
Katharine (Mick) 1872-1952
Barbara 1873-1961 = J Lawrence HAMMOND 1872-1949

Henry Christopher (HCB)=Violet Alice (VAB)
1868-1947 / 1871-1956

1 Marion HORACE-SMITH D.1940=Humphrey   2 Rose WILSON D.1956
1877-1952

Robin=Kirstie NEWSOM   David-Lib STAINER   Philippa
1903-1959
Barnaby 1935-1941

Theodore Richard (Dick)=1 Nancy HAWKSLEY
=2 Margaret NOWELL-SMITH
1895-1987 / 1903-2002

Campbell   Michael

Sally=Tom BOYD   Auriol   Phillida=Malcolm CHEMINAIS   Colin=Katharine MILLER
1935- 1932-   1938-   1941- 1938-   1952- 1958-
Isobel 1991-

Dick BATSTONE=Mary Elspeth
1925- 1933-

Jane=1 Rolf LÄNGE   Alison   Kate=1 Tim WILSON   C. Benedict
2 Neil SCOTT   1943-   =2 Richard WILSON   1947-
1941- 1939-   1944-
1938-   1940-
Daniel 1976-   Tobias 1978-   Oliver 1982-

Bertram RIDLER=Elizabeth BEST
1865-1934 / 1883-1955
Mildred 1911-1965
Anne = Vivian RIDLER
1912-2001 / 1913-

Bertha WOODALL=Edward
1914-1999 / 1907-1997

Daniel
1896-1917
Christopher=1 Bip PARES
2 Jane MILLER
1905-1983 / 1904-1977 / 1921-
Bonamy 1942-
Matthew=Janet WALTERS
1899-1963 / 1908-

Karin=William UNDERWOOD   Juliette=Andrew HILLIER
1965- 1959-   1967- 1963-
Imogen 1995-   Genevieve 1996-   Richard 1996-   Philippa 1996-
Charlotte 1991-   Alice 1993-   Emily 1994-

Daniel=Sarah KEMPTHORNE   Diana=Ken MARCHANT
1933- 1939-   1935- 1930-
Thomas 1967-   Catriona 1964-   Nicholas 1966-

David=Rachel ANDERSON   Hugh=Ruth CARLSEN   Barbara   James=Jane EDWARDS
1942- 1945-   1945- 1947-   1948-   1951- 1955-
Cordelia 1973-   Rosalind 1986-
Christopher 1984-   Helena 1986-   Isabel 1989-
Hannah   Lawrence   Donald   Sang
1967-   1969-   1974-   1970-
Mark 1976-   Kersten 1978-   Robin 1985-

CHAPTER I

Face to face with an infant, one is treated to an intent and piercing gaze which seems to register the essential being of the person looked at. Yet is anything of the sort stored in the infant's memory? Not, at any rate, in any accessible part. This is why I hesitate to record that my earliest memory is of lying on my back in a pram that is being wheeled along by... not an identifiable person but a shape, behind which is the sky. Moreover, this is confused with what must have been a much later memory of walking with a nurse on the Hillmorton Road in Rugby, along which some cattle are being driven, and there is a cow whose damaged eye is like a huge and revolting strawberry.

Otherwise, I can date my fragmentary visual memories by checking them with the dates so faithfully recorded by my mother in a notebook, and they do not begin until my third year.

I was born at 10.30 pm on 30 July 1912, on the last day of the summer term at Rugby School, in the house, School Field, where my father was housemaster. I arrived early, so that he had to cast around for a nurse in the midst of the end-of-term bustle. Presumably I was born in my parents' large double bed where I later so often snuggled for early-morning comforts. Mother recorded that she saw her first aeroplane from the bathroom window that day, 'winging its way across the Close like a bird of ill omen'.

My father, who had been educated at Rugby, had returned there as an assistant master in 1893, after Oxford and a sojourn abroad to learn German, and had taken over the boys' boarding house called School Field on the death of Rupert Brooke's father, two years before my birth. My parents were delighted when School Field fell to their lot, for it was much the most attractive of the boarding houses, overlooking the school playing field (the Close), and with a large garden, which Rupert Brooke had loved just as we did. It must have been built during the expansion of the school in the mid-nineteenth century, and was of red brick with a blue brick patterning in the style of Butterfield, architect of the school chapel. The front, overlooking the drive, was covered with a lovely old wisteria. The dormitories and studies for the fifty-five boys were at the back, and below stairs was their large dining-hall, which we took over as our living room at Christmas time, and the semi-basement kitchen, scullery and pantry. A hand-operated lift for food trays ran up to the front hall, out of which opened the drawing room and back drawing room, the dining room and Father's study. The stairs and landings were lit by gas. Upstairs we had a nursery (later the schoolroom) and night-nursery, apart from bedrooms and a large chilly bathroom. Here my parents took a daily cold bath, and here I used to imagine with a shudder the murder of Marat in his bath by Charlotte Corday. On the top floor were more bedrooms, some belonging to the maids, with washstands smelling of soapy flannels.

It was a sunny house, with many large chests and cupboards excellent for hide-and-seek – which could extend into the boys' part during the holidays. My mother, strongly influenced by the William Morris movement, chose white wallpapers and Morris chintzes: the dining-room wallpaper, however, which I specially loved, was not (she told me) a Morris design. It had a pattern of arbutus berries, which I took to be strawberries. The floor of that room was covered with a large Turkey carpet, over which I used to crawl, rolling a crystal ball to magnify the pattern.

The drawing room, which had a large bow window looking west over the tennis court, had blue velvet curtains and Persian rugs, and there was room for the Broadwood piano, a small grand bought by my parents for £100 when they married; the grandfather clock they had then acquired for £3; and the long sofa covered with blue linen of the kind worn by Egyptian donkey-boys, and favoured by the more artistic of the Rugby ladies.

Among the pictures (oil paintings and engravings, some of which you children will remember as my inheritance) the most valuable was a large 'Canaletto' of the Campanile at Venice (later pronounced to be by his brother-in-law Belotto), which hung in Father's study. There were also a number of Arundel prints of Italian Renaissance masterpieces, fashionable among Victorian art lovers, but travesties of the originals.

Fond as I was of the house, it was the garden which played the most important part in my early life and, I believe, in that of my two youngest brothers. I suppose it was not much more than an acre, but it was on two levels, and was so divided as to seem much larger. A bank and ivy-covered hedge separated the grass tennis court from the gravel drive, and a rambling sunken path overarched by creepers led to another path between herbaceous borders, ending in a seat under a weeping-ash tree. Behind the kitchen garden and greenhouse was a two-storey coach house, with two small rooms on the upper floor (which we used as dens), and a wide opening where hay for the horses had presumably been lowered, now overlooking the vast stores of coal needed for heating and cooking. At either end of the tennis lawn were a wooden summerhouse and a swing on a wooden frame, where my nursemaids used to swing while I waited for a turn. (But I couldn't swing for long before feeling sick.) Dotted about the garden were the trees that provided another dimension to my existence, for I was an inveterate climber. The queen of these was a large cedar on the bank above the tennis court, in front of which I and other children who did lessons with me acted scenes from Shakespeare. At the top of the cedar my brothers had built a platform, and once when I had climbed up to it with Father I remember our moving slowly round the trunk, to keep out of sight of a Parent seen approaching up the drive. Other large trees were a wych-elm (unclimbable), a deodar, and an ash so wreathed with ivy that in climbing it you had to battle through dusty choking stalks, to reach a pleasantly soft but brittle perch.

Here with my companions, the children of other masters and of our family doctor, I played endless games of make-believe, based on the books I had been reading. By comparison, the walks we were occasionally compelled to make ('To the water tower and back', or 'The Retreat from Moscow', across uninteresting fields) were boring indeed.

To return to my infant self, left mewling and puking in the double bed. A girl had been hoped for, after four boys, and I must have been much petted, to judge by one of my brother Dan's comic drawings entitled 'Worship of Anne'. My early infancy seems to have proceeded smoothly, and Mother (who was nearly forty-one) fed me entirely for two months, and partially for six. The trouble began with the introduction of cow's milk, diluted but unpasteurized: like two of my contemporaries I was infected with bovine tuberculosis, and the glands in my neck swelled. At ten months old I was operated on by our (then) family doctor, Dr Dukes, and four months later by a specialist at Kingsgate. (I also remember being taken somewhere for X-ray treatment, when I had to lie still under a lamp, but that must have been a year or two later.) I was half an hour under the anaesthetic, and the surgeon told Mother that he found it unnerving to operate on such a young baby. But the experience evidently did nothing to halt my development in talking and walking, nor was I shy as a young child. Timorous I certainly was, and I wonder what effect the long separation from my mother may have had, with only my nurse Lucy as a familiar presence for many weeks, in the nursing home and at the seaside.

Lucy, however, must have been a benign mother-substitute. I don't remember her face except from photographs, for she left to get married when I was two years old, but Christopher and Edward, who had had her as their nurse, were devoted to her, and in her old age we used to exchange letters at Christmas. 'Our marshes are all white with water' she wrote once from her Norfolk home, and (in answer to some comment of mine): 'Your face never looked screwed-up to me, dear.'

The nursery I remember as a cosy place, with a blazing coal fire (behind a fireguard) on which we could make toast to be spread with delicious beef dripping; and I have a dim memory of being bathed in a hip bath near the fire. This bath later did duty as an imaginary boat in our games. The rocking-horse, High Flyer, which had belonged to Matt, stood in front of the window, and here I would ride for half-hours at a time, telling myself stories.

After Lucy I was in the charge of a young woman who is designated in VAB's notes as 'stupid Rhoda', and after a year, of an apple-cheeked 'Trissie', who later became our housemaid. VAB noted that I was 'much better and happier' in her charge, and I was certainly fond of her, but I have a bad memory of some violence from her, which my parents were unaware of. This took the form of a prolonged shaking, after which I would be flung into a chair, and I remember vividly the sensation of powerlessness during a crescendo of shaking. I don't think this can have happened more than three or four times, but I was sufficiently afraid of Trissie to keep the promise she exacted that I should not tell my mother of these episodes.

After Trissie, I had a succession of teenage nursemaids, until, aged seven, I had a governess. Of course, this was the usual regime for children of the middle classes in those days, and my mother's time was fully occupied with her duties as a conscientious housemaster's wife. There were fifty-five or fifty-six boys in the house, with a staff of seven, so that with the family at home she was catering for a household of about seventy people. She was also responsible for 'seeing that the bills were sent out with the half-term reports', and for such details as that the boys' top-hats (in pre-war days) were regularly ironed, but not unnecessarily often. When boys were ill she sent daily reports to their parents, and she or my father visited them daily in the San; the new boys were invited to tea and games each Sunday during their first term, and other groups of boys, masters or Old Rugbeians were regularly entertained. She played her violin in the school orchestra, and trained quartet and chorus for the house singing competitions, unless a boy was competent to do it. There were also many charitable calls on her time. Nevertheless, we children did see a good deal of our mother. She taught us all to read, from a book called *Reading without Tears* (on the cover of which I raised a blister with a large hot tear), and gave Christopher and Edward their first lessons, before they started at a kindergarten. After tea, I always had some time with her in the drawing room, singing or playing games, and when one of her children's stories was in progress, she would read it aloud.

What daily contacts did I have with my father in those early years? In her notes VAB wrote that during term-time, when he was not teaching or seeing parents, he was in his study most of the day or, after supper, strolling round the passages or visiting the boys' studies to make sure that no bullying was going on. (He used to say of the small boys that he spent their first fortnight in fear of their being sat upon, and the next in fear that they wouldn't be.) I remember his being sometimes in the garden with me, as on the above-mentioned episode at the top of the cedar tree, and on Sunday mornings after chapel, looking for a snail to put out 'for a thrush's Sunday dinner'. Two more memories of him are somewhat guilty ones. A certain Mademoiselle Guibert visited our house to give a weekly French lesson to me and a couple of other masters' children, which bored me very much. (Edward, who was also taught by her, records similar boredom.) I remember her personality only dimly, but I recall that she bounced on her toes as she walked. One day when the lesson was due I hid behind the enormous heap of coal which was stored below the old coach-house, and remained there while I heard my father calling my name all over the garden, till eventually he found me. I don't remember his scolding me, and I felt remorseful in relation to him, though not particularly distressed at the large black square against my name in Mlle Guibert's notebook.

The other memory concerns the day, soon after my sixth birthday, when I was to start daily lessons in a class kept by the sister of one of the masters, Miss Rhoades. I refused to go, and my father carried me weeping, pick-a-back through the local streets to her house. (I remember from this and other journeys the pleasant smell of tweed from his Norfolk jacket under my nose.)

Normally I used to walk to this class with another housemaster's daughter rather older than me, Rosamond Hawkesworth, who bullied me slightly. I think I quite enjoyed the lessons, but I remember shedding tears at my inability to understand how six taken from seven left one: of course we were given no concrete objects to clarify the terms.

I remember Father's reading aloud of *Uncle Remus* (as he did in his old age to Jane and Kate), with lively imitations of the characters, but most recollections of his reading are of later date.

By the time I started with Miss Rhoades, Christopher and Edward were well into their schooldays, so I chiefly remember them in the holidays. I was sometimes allowed on sufferance in their den constructed of boards in the garden, or to watch them manipulate the cut-out figures in their toy theatre. They seemed enviably grown-up to me, as they sat on the sofa reading bound volumes of *Punch*, and I looked forward to being able to do the same. I suppose they were role models, for I certainly wanted very much to be a boy. My friends and I used to dress up in their outgrown grey flannel jackets and shorts, but I wasn't allowed these as everyday wear, which I should have liked. Mother recorded my saying, soon after Dan's death: 'If I pray Jesus, will he make me a boy? Then you'd have four boys again.'

Although I remember School Field as a happy place, those years of 1914–18 must have been ones of great anxiety for our parents – 'the older boys [in the House] leaving and being swallowed up by the Army, as VAB put it in her *Reminiscences*, 'writing us pencilled notes from France, coming down on leave and then, too often, their names read out by the

Headmaster in the Memorial Services in Chapel.' I remember one of these boys in particular, Jim Dowson, coming into the nursery one day with a doll for me under each arm – a boy and a girl, whom I named John and Betty. I knew that he was on leave and was going 'out to France', and later, that he had been killed. The dolls therefore had an emotional importance for me, as I shall describe later.

Then there was the departure of our brother Dan for the Army soon after the outbreak of war, and to France in December 1915, when he was just nineteen. He was in the Rifle Brigade, which suffered badly in the Somme offensive: he had been at Brigade Headquarters as Intelligence Officer during the battle, and was promoted as Captain of the remnants of one of the companies thereafter. He came home on leave three times, the last time in early October 1916. It is probably from the leave before that, in May 1916, when I was three and three-quarters, that I have my only conscious memory of him, though reported sayings of mine show that he often played with me, and a letter of his from France says 'Please thank Anne [I being three and a half] for her long and interesting letter.' My clear visual memory is of his figure, striking a tennis ball from near the back line of the School Field grass court, and calling out in answer to my enquiry (as I was being taken off to bed): 'It's on the table in the drawing room.' It was a box made out of a fragment of a shell, which was full of chocolates, and miraculously refilled every time you took the last one out. This I remember his demonstrating to me as I sat next to him on the drawing-room sofa.

He should again have been safely at HQ during the battle of Arras on Easter Monday, 9 April 1917, but he had persuaded the authorities to let him stay with his battalion. He led his company into the attack, and had gained their first objective, when a bullet through his heart killed him instantly. A week later my parents received the dreaded telegram from the War Office, and next morning I was called into bed beside my mother, who said: 'Dan's gone to live with Jesus.'

Our parents did not let us see their tears, but I remember standing horror-struck on the stairs as Maggie, our parlour-maid, was supported past me by one of the other maids on the way up to her bedroom, wailing and crying 'Ahh-aha-O dear': she had just received the news of her fiancé's death at the front.

13

'People change and smile, but the agony abides', as Eliot put it in 'The Dry Salvages', and we children could not but be aware that there was a gap in the family which none of us could fill. About nine months after Dan's death, when Dr David the Headmaster's baby daughter had died, I said (as VAB recorded): 'It does seem puzzlin' to me Elizabeth being dead. I shan't ever be as happy as I was – you aren't as happy as you were because Dan's dead.'

Just at the time of Dan's death, our parents had to see their second son claimed for war service. Matt had left school and joined up for the Navy early in 1917, and became a midshipman in a battleship, HMS *Revenge*. He later witnessed the scuttling of the German fleet in Scapa Flow. By Christmas 1918, having been awarded an MBE for his war service, he was in HMS *Delhi* in the Baltic, where Britain was supporting the White Russians against the Bolsheviks. (I then began to knit him a long woolly scarf, which was not finished until he had gone out to India and presumably had little need of it.) He was a brilliant games-player, and played Rugby football for the Navy and for England, but after the war there seemed little prospect for him in the Navy, and in 1922 he decided to join the firm of Shaw Wallace, which offered him a job as a tea-planter in Assam.

In that unhappy spring of 1917, my younger brothers and I had measles, the memory of which is a blank for me, though I do remember the earlier chickenpox and whooping-cough. 'A choice was killed by every childish illness' wrote Auden, but this was only true for me with a later illness. I do remember, though, that the summer holidays of that year were unhappy for me, though not altogether for the others, it seems. VAB records that the place, Rhos Neigr in Anglesey, was a great success: her brother Humphrey Milford and his family were there, and Matt came on leave, complete with sea-chest. But the weather was wet and windy; I had a dislikable maid, shared with my cousin Patty Chitty, who was eight years older than me, and I must have been so fractious that it left an impression on my Milford cousins which was quite hard to live down later on.

I don't remember any food restrictions because of the war, except that we gave up sugar in our nursery tea, and had margarine ('Blue Band') instead of butter. Rationing was not introduced until spring 1918, and

VAB notes that it was a welcome remedy for food scarcities and queuing. The boys in the House then had 6oz of sugar (of which 2oz were kept back for cooking), 4oz of margarine and 4 meat coupons worth 1s 3d each. Celebrations at the end of the war were marked for me by my being whisked out of bed at night and carried up to the leads on the roof, where a number of the boys were assembled, to watch a display of fireworks let off in the town recreation ground.

It was at this time that reading to myself began to be my greatest resource (I had actually learnt to read some while earlier), and to be the basis of my imaginative life – not quite yet the novels of Sir Walter Scott, but VAB's own books (particularly *The Enchanted Forest* and *The Happy Families*, based on the famous card characters) and Victorian classics such as *Holiday House, The Cuckoo Clock, The Princess and Curdie,* and so on. When I was tall enough to climb on to the midway ledge of the double bookcase in the hall, it became a favourite place, for here were stored a mass of books which had belonged to my brothers and to Mother herself: Captain Marryatt, Anthony Hope, R. L. Stevenson, Rudyard Kipling, Mark Twain, Rider Haggard, F. Hodgson Burnett, Mrs Ewing, Mrs Molesworth, George Macdonald, Charlotte Yonge, and of course Fenimore Cooper, whose hero Hawk-Eye I pretended to be, patrolling the garden with one of our stilts held to my shoulder, to represent the rifle with which Hawk-Eye could kill two birds as they crossed in the sky with a single shot. The only boys' writer I could not stomach was G. A. Henty. Louisa May Alcott, E. Nesbitt and Talbot Baines Reed ('Adventures of a Five-Guinea Watch' etc) were I think additions made to the list for me: Nesbitt's *The Magic City*, where constructions of toy bricks become real, peopled cities, I found a seminal book. I was first introduced to Scott and Dickens by Father's reading aloud in the holidays, but I soon devoured them for myself.

Books rather than toys fed my imaginative life, though I continued to cherish the boy doll given me by Jim Dowson, until one day he was left out in the rain and my nurse Trissie refused to countenance him in the nursery in his damaged state. Before this, I had really murdered the girl doll, Betty, besmirching her with mud. I cannot analyse the impulse behind this, but I remember the feeling of guilt that accompanied it. I derived a good deal of pleasure from those paper dolls on to whose shoulders one could fix different sets of clothes; and I had a teddy-bear, bought one Christmas in Bournemouth, named by the grown-ups Edward Bruin, and by me, Teddy. I later invented a character for him with which I used to amuse my governess, Miss Ohlson. Before Edward Bruin there was a soft toy monkey whom I wished to call Pimp, and I was puzzled when Mother forbade this name, suggesting Pimpo as a substitute, which was not the right name at all.

To return to 1918: it was in that year that our summer holidays were spent at Aisholt, in the Somerset Quantocks, a place that was to mean so much to me later on. We took a night train to Bridgewater, which was very exciting, and saw a shooting star as we waited on the platform at Rugby's Great Central station. We had rented a farmhouse, French's, on the opposite side of the valley to Olive Willis's Aisholt cottage, and took a cook and housemaid – the bereaved Maggie – with us. I remember that the farmhouse had a brick bread-oven built into its wall: loaves are baked in such ovens from the heat that remains after a conflagration has died out, and I was allowed to knead and bake my own small loaf with the rest. As very often happened, we had relations and friends staying near by: Humphrey and Marion Milford and their three children; Father's eldest brother, Uncle Godfrey; Uncle Herbert Chitty and his daughter Letty who was Dan's contemporary. I have a memory of cousin Robin which is very uncharacteristic of him, at a picnic on the Quantock moors, where he pointed out an inviting-looking green mound for me to sit on and it proved to be a gorse bush. Perhaps he didn't expect me to be such an idiot as to follow the suggestion.

This may be a convenient point to describe the pattern of our holidays. In those expansive days we generally went away for six weeks in the summer to lodgings 'all found' or to a rented house taking maids with us, and for two at Easter. At Christmas the Milfords came to stay with us, and afterwards we went to Granny Milford and aunts Mai and Beatrice at 2 Richmond Gardens, Bournemouth for about a week, and often to the Chittys (Father's sister Mabel) in Hampstead for some days. We had no car of course, but took bicycles away with us sometimes, and did much walking, with the occasional trip by pony and trap. Being the youngest by five years, I found some of the walks a trial, especially in Cornwall, where we tramped through the lanes to meet friends along the coast, or to church at Gorran Churchtown. I regularly developed hiccups on the way to that after a large breakfast, for which a supposed cure was devised by Mother: the 'hiccup herb' found in the hedge, which was I believe wood-sage and tasted bitter. According to Edward, it generally worked.

It seems surprising that we were all happy for so long in cramped lodgings, with no radio, television or cinema, but bathing, exploring, the companionship of friends and cousins, books, and reading aloud from Father in the evenings, seemed all we needed. Also, we explored a different place each year, except for Tregavarras, where we went for three consecutive summers. That was not only because we liked the coast so much, but also because we had made great friends with a family, the Phippses, who used to stay near by at Gorran Haven. We later went on holiday with them to St David's in Wales, twice to France, and to Mount Grace in Yorkshire.

Our first French holiday, in 1923 when I was just eleven, was to a convent in Brittany which took in visitors, St Gildas de Rhuys. (Mother has described it in her story *A Summer Friendship*.) It was a picturesque place with lovely old (climbable) trees in the grounds, and a coast-line somewhat like Cornwall, though Nicholas and I compared it unfavourably with the Dodman and Greeb Point. On Sundays the peasants came in to the Convent church wearing their traditional costumes – one of the fringed shawls is still in our dressing-up chest. I was excited by a visit to a well-preserved castle, Suscinio, but did not accompany the rest to Carnac. The food was dismal, with either vermicelli or tapioca soup each day and no fruit – except on fast days when we had grapes – and we ate in a stifling dining room with the hundred or so other guests: if we opened a window one of the nuns would rush in to shut it, exclaiming 'Courant d'air!'.

At St David's in 1924, we Bradbys took a house, Twr y Felin Cottage, and the Phippses were at the hotel next door. The Cathedral and ruins were romantic places to explore, and the coast and bathing were almost as good as Cornwall, we thought – especially with a picnic on Ramsey Island to enhance the pleasure. At the end of this holiday we saw, in London, Cedric Hardwicke in his celebrated comic part as Churdles Ash in *The Farmer's Wife* by Eden Philpotts, and Sybil Thorndike in Shaw's *St Joan*.

At Christmas when the Milfords came, the party staying with Uncle Godfrey always visited on Christmas Day or Boxing Day. After his retirement, when he went to live at 80 Dunchurch Road, this consisted of Aunt Dolly (Dorothy), the third Bradby brother Uncle Hugh and his wife Nancy, and a rather bizarre character known to us as Old Mo. I quote from VAB's description of him.

Mr Benham, stout and very Jewish, was the butt of all three Bradby brothers, and certainly he laid himself out to be teased and laughed at. He was very amusing sometimes and was devoted to Godfrey; but he was very egotistical and incurably greedy. He had all the passionate love of sweet things which schoolboys have, and which most people outgrow or become ashamed of in later years. Old Mo never either outgrew or was ashamed of this relish, and would frankly overeat himself whenever he got the chance. He worked as a legal reader on the *Daily Mail* practically all his life, and was immensely pleased when Lord Northcliff left him a small legacy. Mrs Bradby [HCB's mother], who was the soul of courtesy, used to lament the way her sons made fun of poor old Mo; but he much preferred being 'ragged' and being the centre of attention, to being ignored, which would have hurt him much more.

My most vivid memory of him is of a charade where he was acting the part of Lady Macbeth, and terrifyingly advancing across the floor with closed eyes, rubbing his hands.

Uncle Hugh invariably greeted me as Sister Anne, often followed by a quotation from the story of Bluebeard, where Bluebeard's imprisoned wife reiterates her cry for help: 'Sister Anne, Sister Anne, is there anybody coming?' Both the Bradby uncles seemed very remote to me, chiefly because they did not know how to get on terms with a small girl – the boys fared much better – but it was on more than one of their visits that we played a game which I enjoyed. The grown-ups all sat round in their easy-chairs in the drawing room (a satisfactory arrangement for them no doubt), and I in the middle with closed eyes was lifted up on a stool 'higher and higher', and set down again, to find myself in a strange country. No one could recognize me, and they would question me as to who I was and where I came from. How the game ended is a blank in my mind, but I entered into it in that state of half-belief, or suspension of disbelief, which children so easily adopt.

The arrival of the Milfords was always a festive moment, and it was delightful to move down to the House dining-hall with its blazing fire. Although it was not until my adolescence that I grew close to Uncle Humphrey, he was always an enlivening presence, and there was perfect sympathy between him and Aunt Marion and our parents. Aunt Marion was gentle and sympathetic to everybody. Pippa, their youngest child, was three years older than me, but I enjoyed having someone in the party younger than my brothers: we shared a small dormitory (perhaps it was the House sickroom), and opened our Christmas stockings together.

Presents we had on the breakfast table, with no elaborate gift-wrappings, and the only Christmas tree I remember, a large one in the corner of the hall, was there for the Boys' Brigade who were invited to tea on Boxing Day, either with us or with Uncle Godfrey. I can still see my father wheeling a scooter into the hall when I was about six – my 'biggest present', and on it I used to tear down the pavement of the short hill near our house (it was outside the hospital!), until one day the front and back came asunder and I had a nasty fall.

Church in the holidays was rather dreary, either at the Parish Church or Holy Trinity for mattins, with pompous settings of the Te Deum, and sermons so boring (until the arrival of Dr, later Bishop, Hunkin, but that was after we had left School Field) that there was competition among the grown-ups as to who should lead out the youngest and so escape. (VAB recorded my saying, aged five, after a Whitsunday reading: 'I don't care much for that about the Holy Ghost.') In term time I attended mattins in the school chapel, where the seats for the families were opposite a stained-glass window of Christ preaching, in a red robe. I enjoyed the hymns, so lustily sung, and the sermons were generally mercifully short. Carols at home we used to sing, in parts, round the drawing room Broadwood, and I especially remember the singing at our last School Field Christmas in 1924, when Cousin Robin was engaged to Kirstie and she came with the Milfords, wearing a beautiful green velvet dress: Robin had composed a hymn for the new 'Songs of Praise', and she sang it to his accompaniment.

A propos of the fantasy game described earlier, I remember that in 'Animula' Eliot says that the small child

Confounds the actual and the fanciful,
Content with playing cards and kings and queens,
What the fairies do and what the servants say...

'What the au pairs say' might be truer of the contemporary child, but certainly the numerous servants at School Field were prominent in the landscape of my early world, and that includes Enticott, the elderly gardener, who would sit on a bench, leaning over a frame containing early strawberries, and hold one up between finger and thumb as I ran (generally barefoot) along the path behind him. For the household work we had a cook, kitchenmaid, housemaid, parlourmaid, boys-man and bootboy (who pulled the mowing machine steered by Enticott, and worked the circular knife-grinder), also a matron, Annie Haggar in the years that I remember, and always a friendly presence. Her father had I think been a railwayman, and owned an old railway carriage at the bottom of his garden. This seemed to me a priceless possession, and I enjoyed the occasional treat of an invitation to tea there.

The knife-grinder was in the boys-man's pantry – still in use during the war years, for stainless steel was not introduced in England until 1917. The servants' hall was in the dark semi-basement, and I have no idea how much time off they had; I expect they were glad of our many weeks away. Unless the maids got married, they stayed with us, and Annie I think never married.

Also peopling the landscape were figures connected with the school, notably Rupert Brooke's mother, whose face was quite remarkably seamed with wrinkles. She had been an alarming figure in earlier years to the other school ladies, as she was a great gossip and censorious, but by the time of my childhood her bereavements had, as Mother said, softened her. Mother thought that although Mrs Brooke was immensely proud of Rupert, she was always a little puzzled and uneasy over his career. 'It was a little bit like a hen having hatched a peacock, and finding its bright tail feathers rather an embarrassment.'

A child's eye exaggerates physical peculiarities, and I am sure there cannot have been so many odd-looking people as I remember. One lady had a goitre and another a head that shook with palsy, and an elderly retired master (Mr Stokes) would offer me his hand to shake – or 'Would you like to shake my bunny-glove?' an unwelcome invitation, for his fingers were alarmingly purple and dead-looking. I thought of him when I first read John Crowe Ransom's poem 'Winter Remembered':

> ...ten poor frozen fingers not worth much,
> Ten frozen parsnips hanging in the weather.

Mr Highton was stately on a tricycle, and Greville Augustus Frederick Mason Chatwin, who took a middle form and was much mimicked by my brothers, resembled a bird not only in name.

If I was walking with Mother when boys were on the move, we passed along a ripple of raised straw boaters – or boaters chased along the pavement if a wind was blowing, A striking figure was Mrs Vaughan, wife of the headmaster, who wore a hat crowned with a veil which flowed out behind her as she strode along. She was the daughter of John Addington Symonds, critic and aesthete, and was inclined to look down on the provinciality of Rugby as compared with Clifton, where they had previously lived. Witty and astringent, she did not spare the schoolboys her mockery. When Edward was in the Sixth Form and found himself sitting next to her at lunch, he tried to make conversation about George Meredith's novels which he much enjoyed. 'O, you like that tedious *Diana of the Crossways*?' was her response. 'I far prefer *Tarzan of the Apes*.'

As I grew older, I became more aware of the goings-on of the school, and shared in some of the excitements of competition between the houses in music and acting, though I don't remember watching their Cock House matches with any great enthusiasm. Christopher and Edward were both in the School House, run by the Headmaster, and I watched the plays in which they took part with intense interest – and distress when Edward died on stage as Duff Penner in Drinkwater's *Robert E. Lee*. They were both in Yeats's *On Baile's Strand*, but I don't remember their being in another School House play, Shaw's *Captain Brassbound's Conversion*, in which the name part was taken by Alexander MacLehose, to whom I briefly lost my heart, though I never exchanged a word with him.

Although our garden adjoined the school racquets and fives courts, where Father coached the racquets pairs, and our cousin David Milford will often have played there on the way to his career of glory (he was several times world champion, continuing into his 'fifties), I don't remember watching any matches. But I do remember the excitement of the centenary Rugger match in 1923, celebrating the achievement of William Webb Ellis who (as the plaque in the Close phrased it, apparently innocent of irony) 'with a fine disregard for the rules of the game, first picked up the ball and ran with it'. Davies and Kershaw, captain and vice-captain of the England Fifteen of which Matt was a member, stayed with us for it, but Matt had by then left for India.

Edward has recorded his bitter disappointment at being dropped without explanation from the School House First Fifteen. I knew nothing of that, but I well remember the excitement of waiting with Mother at the finishing point in the Hillmorton Road when he was running in the twelve-mile cross-country run called The Crick, and seeing him come in first.

Edward and I were both grounded in the piano by a Miss Daisy Stevens, whom we visited in her small house. Not only was she a very kind teacher, she also (as Edward writes) 'managed to make the early stages of piano-playing both attractive and systematic'. And she taught me Sol-Fa, which is an excellent foundation for sight-reading in singing. (Once she invited me to her house when she had 'the Peppin twins' staying: I played them one of my pieces, and then they played theirs. They were a couple of years older than me, and immeasurably more accomplished: they became quite well known as professionals, playing piano duets.)

Edward went on to become a really good player, and I, though I never acquired much technique, was given the experience of joy which Yehudi Menuhin says is the essential ingredient for the education of any player. I remember the delight with which I played some of my early pieces – an easy Bach arrangement, and a Beethoven Bagatelle. Later on, I would take the bass part in duets with Edward or my Milford aunts – and with Alice Stainer.

When I was seven, my parents engaged a Belgian lady as governess, in the hope that I should acquire fluent French by the companionship of a French speaker at this early age. She was to live with us in term time, and four or five other children would share my daily lessons. Miss Ghysen had been a refugee pupil at the local girls' school, The Laurels, and I imagine that it was on their recommendation that she came to us. As far as I was concerned, the experiment was a failure. Miss Ghysen, being quite at home in English, found it much too boring to talk French with a beginner, and I can't remember her ever doing so except in the context of a lesson. She was preoccupied with her engagement to a Belgian officer called Muskamp, who once came to stay, and I remember that on a walk with him she suddenly berated me for walking on a ledge above a small brook, which I had often done before, unreproved. I was quite aware that she was 'showing off' in front of her fiancé, and when teatime came and she offered me some cake, I sullenly reminded her that she had told me I wasn't to have any as a punishment.

Miss Ghysen left after about a year, and I don't remember that we kept up with her later, though I must have continued to wear to chapel the 'little French hat' that she made for me, which I found embarrassingly conspicuous.

Our next governess, Miss Ohlson, was much beloved. She was middle-aged, and daughter of the captain of a P & O liner, known by us in the schoolroom for his prohibition of beginning a sentence with a conjunction. Moly, as we soon came to call her, was homely in looks, and wore her darkish hair swept up from her high forehead by a tortoise-shell comb. A life spent in looking after children had not killed her love for them, and she entered into all our interests and make-believe. I don't remember her ever being out of temper, yet it must sometimes have happened, for Mother recorded my saying: 'Moly, I can't bear to think of you sitting in the schoolroom with a growly face.'

The last family Moly had lived with had been higher up the social scale than we were. John and Diana, children of the Earl and Countess of Ellesmere, were vivid to us in her stories of their doings, but we never felt they were preferred to us – rather the opposite, in fact.

Moly was certainly not an intellectual: her newspaper was the *Daily Mail*, and Uncle Godfrey remarked (as I learnt long after she had left us) that in her the line between goodness and goosiness was hard to determine. But for us her sympathy was nourishing, and her lessons, based on the PNEU syllabus, were never boring. We started each day with a hymn, accompanied by her on the schoolroom piano – on which, by the way, she would sometimes agree to perform a song about snobbery among toys, entitled 'I was walking one day down the Lowther Arcade', that ended

> And it's so in this world, for I'm in love With a maiden of high
> degree,
> But I am only marked one and nine, while the other chap's
> two and three.

Elementary arithmetic, spelling and 'Prayer-book finding' were tested in verbal competition. Prayer books or Bibles in front of us, the first person to find, say, the Collect for the second Sunday after Trinity, or the answer to twelve times twelve, would gain a mark. My India-paper Bible was quite a handicap, I remember. Maths meant simply arithmetic, and elementary at that, for when later I did the entrance paper for Downe House, I was found to be behindhand in this; not in other subjects however, although I think we only had formal lessons in the morning. For exercise we played in the garden or in the quiet roads near the house: we climbed the trees, walked on stilts, bowled our hoops (iron ones, made by the local blacksmith) or whipped our tops. A trapeze was hung in the doorway between my bedroom (formerly the night nursery) and the schoolroom, on which we practised somersaults.

The other children who came to share lessons, sitting round the oak gate-legged table, were eventually all girls, though at first Dr David's son John was one of them. They were Mary Evers, Elizabeth and Jossett Odgers, daughters of housemasters, and Audrey Wheeler, daughter of our family doctor; also for a time Angela Culme-Seymour and May Lennox-Conyngham, whose widowed mother lived near by but was not, I think, connected with the school. Mary Evers fell ill with tuberculosis and had to leave the class – much regretted, for she was very good-looking and good-natured. Audrey, of course, was the best companion any child could have, and apart from the years when we were both at boarding school and college, we have been in close touch ever since. When she first began with us, though, she was delicate and inclined to be tearful, and I know I was not at all welcoming. She must soon have settled down and earned her cheerful nickname of Pinky Perkins, which was somehow connected with the two pigtails in which she wore her dark hair.

In the summer term before my ninth birthday, and during the three following summers, Mother produce d us in Scenes from Shakespeare on the grassy space in front of the cedar tree, the audience (of senior boys and neighbours) being disposed on the tennis lawn below. She imported adults to act in some of the scenes: in *As You Like It,* where I was Rosalind, Audrey Celia and Mary Evers Orlando, Christopher was the melancholy Jaques and Edward Old Adam, and Father looked so impressive as Duke Senior that a local lady said gushingly after the performance: 'O Mr Bradby, now I know why Mrs Bradby married you!' (An ambiguous compliment, whichever way you look at it.) John Christie, the House Tutor (of whom more anon) also took part – I suppose he must have been the wicked Duke.

Mother had seen Ellen Terry as Rosalind, and I remember that she tried (probably unsuccessfully) to persuade me to run backwards to the cedar tree as I exclaimed, 'O coz, coz, coz, my pretty little coz, thou canst not know how deep I am in love!' Father had written a Prologue in case of chilly weather for me to recite, which ended: 'And often clap your hands to keep them warm.'

In *A Midsummer Night's Dream* I was Puck, and in *The Tempest* Ariel, Edward being Caliban, but I think we must have omitted much of the plot in that. Finally we did Martin Shaw's musical play derived from *The Winter's Tale,* entitled *The Pedlar,* and had a small string ensemble on stage behind a screen to accompany us. I was Autolycus and Audrey Mopsa, and I don't remember that we were nervous at having to sing, though our small voices cannot have carried very far.

During one winter term, Moly produced us in a version of Longfellow's *Hiawatha,* acted in front of a wigwam in the back drawing room, the audience of parents in the main room. Perhaps 'in front of' is not quite correct, for VAB's account implies that much of the action took place *inside* the wigwam, and the rest in semi-darkness. Moly, she writes, had invested in a wonderful costume from Hamley's for me as Hiawatha; she herself played Old Nokomis, and took so long in darkening her face before the play began that the patience of a less indulgent audience might have been exhausted.

It was in her last winter with us that Moly's generosity again provided me with a fancy dress – this time a page's costume of blue velvet tunic and cap to wear at the fancy-dress dance Mother and Father gave in the

Christmas holidays for about seventy people, using one of the boys' dormitories, with a small band of piano and violins. The Milfords were with us, and VAB records that Uncle Humphrey went as St Francis (perhaps because he had a brown dressing-gown?), and she herself as a Romney portrait 'in a lovely hired white wig'. David Milford was a Yahoo, and Edward a Prince to my Page. Father was Lawrence Sheriff, the founder of the school.

I think this was the only dance I have ever really enjoyed, for the children's dances to which we were invited were generally a pain, and I remember sitting out with Christopher because waltzing made us both giddy. 'Sir Roger de Coverley' and the gallop with which the dance generally ended were fun, of course, and so were the little books with pencil attached in which we recorded our engagements.

Another winter treat was the regular visit to the pantomime at Bournemouth when we stayed there after Christmas, and there I remember seeing Charlie Chaplin with Jackie Coogan in *The Kid*. Rugby itself provided a theatre visited by travelling companies, and I remember seeing Frank Benson's company act *The Tempest*, where he as Caliban, old and rather heavy, struggled to climb up a pole, stage centre. We also occasionally went to the cinema, where I saw Douglas Fairbanks in *The Thief of Baghdad*, and Mary Pickford as little Lord Fauntleroy *and* his mother.

We had plenty of tobogganning in the winter, down a short slope at the far end of the Close or in various fields, but only once do I remember our getting to a frozen lake a few miles away for skating on two consecutive days – not long enough to learn properly. On Guy Fawkes Night we had a bonfire and fireworks on the gravel. I used to skulk indoors when the bangers were let off, to be greeted with 'Well, Lionheart' by Mother as I came out again to roast a potato in the ashes.

In summer we could picnic by the canal. It seems to me that we walked through the buttercup fields to get there, for though I learned to ride a bicycle quite early, I rode it chiefly in the neighbouring streets, and when away on holiday. We were occasionally allowed to use the school swimming bath, but it was in Cornwall that I learnt to swim.

Another school amenity was the carpentry workshop, where Elizabeth Odgers and I were supervised by a gentle Scot whose name I remember as pronounced McGorley – was it really Macauley? Here little Miss Odgers was a good deal more 'andy than little Miss Bradby, whose chiselled grooves he used to look at and say sadly: 'O Miss Bradby, it looks as though a lot of 'ens 'ad been pecking at it.' I did manage to make a miniature mahogany chest of drawers to hold Father's blue marking-pencils and paper-clips – for the wood of which he received a surprisingly large bill.

Mother always gave a garden party on the first day of the cricket match between the school and the Old Rugbeians, captained by Father. She writes that I and my friends 'flitted about, doing full justice to the strawberry and vanilla ices, made with real cream' which came in huge pails of ice chunks from Hobleys, the town confectioner. Six gallons were required, for the party and the boarding boys' supper, and certainly those ices were the best I have ever tasted.

Tennis I think I only played with the family, during the last summer or two before we left School Field, but our class all attended Miss Smythe's weekly dancing class. We wore dancing sandals, but I remember her as always in high-heeled shoes: how, I wonder, did she demonstrate the steps to us? She occasionally aired her pupils in displays with an instrumental accompaniment, and once I was required to do a solo dance with cymbals. Just as I left the platform, to friendly applause, up rushed Mother saying urgently: 'May she do it again, as her father wasn't there?' Miss Smythe politely acceded, and I started again, with rather a feeling of anti-climax.

Father had been a cricket Blue at Oxford, and coached the school First Eleven as well as the House teams. We always went to London for the two days of the Rugby and Marlborough match at the end of the summer term, and even after Father's retirement, when the fortunes of the Rugby Eleven were no longer so important, these were pleasant social occasions for him and Mother, when Old Rugbeians would seek them out. As a child I should have been very bored with the long days of watching, if I had not been allowed to bring a parcel of books to read. Even so, the best year for me was when the game had to be called off because of rain, and our family party adjourned to the Coliseum where Grock was performing. We were entranced as he turned his top hat into a concertina, or solved the problem of distance between the piano stool and the keyboard by heaving the grand piano to the stool, or nimbly kicked a ball away from his outstretched fingers each time he bent to pick it up. We did not realize how lucky we were to catch him, for soon afterwards he quarrelled with the theatre management and never played in England again. (Vivian saw him at that time in Bristol, and remembers his playing a violin while disappearing into the piano-stool until only the fiddle and his feet were showing.)

For the match we generally stayed with the Chittys at 24 East Heath Road, Hampstead – a desirable position, but somehow an uncomfortable house, where the chair-backs were bolt upright like Aunt Mabel's rigid poise, and the Arundel prints closely packed frame to frame upon the walls. Aunt Mabel was kind, and planned outings for us children, but she was rather forbidding, and it was Cousin Letty who made us feel at home. We could not enter into her mathematical researches, but she had many other talents, and was a reassuring bedtime companion for me, in the dark, chilly house – especially when I had been reading about Macbeth in *Lamb's Tales from Shakespeare,* and shivered at the thought of the hour 'when only the wolf and the murderer are abroad'.

(This absence from Rugby always coincided with my birthday on 30 July, and I can't remember celebrating it as a child. One year, indeed, we all forgot it until after breakfast, when I was told to listen to a street-crier. On my looking puzzled, they said that he was shouting 'Many happy returns of the day'. Our parents' birthdays were on equally inconvenient dates, Father's on 28 December, and Mother's on Boxing Day, when all our ideas for presents had been exhausted.)

Another excellent person with whom to discuss Shakespeare was John Christie, who was Father's House Tutor during the School Field years that I remember, and was always invited to dinner on a Friday evening, when he supervised Prep in the Hall. He became a lifelong friend of the family, and wrote a warm appreciation of Mother for me after her death – now to be found among my papers. He took an entirely unpatronizing interest in me, and I found him the most delightful sharer in my love of the novels of Sir Walter Scott: he could always remember the details and names of the characters in any which I happened to be reading. When I went away to school he gave me a writing case, and later I became godmother to his daughter Jane, and he godfather to our Benedict.

Although I was I suppose quite precocious in my novel-reading, my love of poetry came later, and my early attempts at writing poetry show no promise whatever. Words however retained their picture-properties for me from the time when I first learned them. I tried to express this to Mother when I was about seven, in a remark which she recorded. 'Some words *resemble* what they mean: Innocent, Adventurous, Bold.' I can only describe the quality as a fleeting glimpse of a gesture made by a human figure, which must be derived from a combination of meaning, sound and the shape of a mouth speaking. It is not coloured, as are the days of the week, also months and numbers, in my mind's eye, as they are for many people.

I do not remember learning poetry by heart (except for Shakespeare, of course) or hearing it read aloud to any extent, until I went for weekly literature lessons to Aunt Dolly at 80 Dunchurch Road. Here she read me Milton's *L'Allegro* and *Il Penseroso*, Scott's *Marmion* and Gray's *The Bard*— this last with a dramatic relish of the curses. I enjoyed this, but the complicated chronology of the poem baffled me, and I think the lessons seem more important to me in retrospect, now that I have come to know Aunt Dorothy through her letters, than they did at the time.

The tenure set for Rugby housemasters was fifteen years, and we knew that beloved School Field was not ours to keep. Nineteen twenty-five was the year when we should have to leave it, and this would be a turning-point in other ways, as Edward would then leave school and go up to Oxford, and I should go to boarding school. I could have gone as a day girl to The Laurels, the school mentioned earlier, but its character can be guessed from its name, and my parents thought that I should be more likely to flourish at a less conventional school, such as Olive Willis's Downe House, which had recently moved to a breezy site near Newbury in Berkshire.

They had come to know Olive through Aunt Marion, who had been a close friend since Somerville College days, and in 1916 our family and the Milfords had been lent the premises of the earlier Downe House, near Orpington in Kent (formerly Charles Darwin's home) for a summer holiday. They had enjoyed Olive's company for part of the time, and the boys had helped the eccentric Miss Nickel mix cement for her perpetual building works. To send me to Downe involved some financial sacrifice for my parents, even when Olive had reduced the fees for me (as in fact she did for so many that I wonder how the school was made to pay). For my part, I had no desire to go to boarding school, and was delighted when I heard Mrs Vaughan volubly urging Mother not to send me away – 'Not till she is sixteen; not till her character is formed.' They were not persuaded however, and away I was to go, for the summer term of 1925, which was Edward's last at school.

At the end of the Lent term, our class said a tearful farewell to Miss Ohlson, and she helped us move our belongings to the house known as Hillbrow, a short distance away down the Barby Road. Moly then retired to her flat in Eastbourne, where she lived for the rest of her life with her cat Tiger. I only saw her again once, when she took me to see *The Ghost Train* in London, but we always kept in touch by letter.

Hillbrow had housed the prep school attended by my brothers. It was now to be made into a new boarding house for Rugby School, and we were to rent the private part pro tem. Mother describes it as 'sunny and spacious, though icily cold in winter', and that is how I remember it, so it came as a surprise when I read John Christie's description of it (in his memoir of Mother) as 'ugly and uncompromising'. Mother set about transforming the rooms with her usual enthusiasm, and had been going there to paint the walls with Walpamure for some months past. The garden was on a slope (for the house really was on the brow of what passed for a hill in Rugby), and had a lawn big enough for a nine-hole putting-course, planned by Father, though not enough for tennis. Its chief glory was a tall magnolia (soulangeana I suppose), covered with glistening white blossoms in the spring. This was to be our home for the next four years, until Father retired at the age of sixty. He was now Second Master, and in charge of the school when Dr Vaughan was absent for a term or two.

He and Mother had determined that they would not continue to live in Rugby after his retirement, 'like an extinct volcano', and had been looking around for possible places to settle in. They had been attracted to the idea of converting an old barn which was for sale at Fairlight in Sussex, near the celebrated gorse-covered cliffs known as the Fire Hills: they had bought it for £600, and had commissioned plans from an architect friend for its conversion. The young Milfords and Stainers had camped there and loved it; now, however, we learnt that all the surrounding farm land had been bought by a Dutchman, who intended to develop it. Accordingly, as soon as the move to Hillbrow had been achieved, we booked rooms in the hotel in Fairlight and went down to investigate.

We found that the Dutchman did indeed intend to build a bungalow town on the land surrounding the barn, and our parents regretfully decided that they must accept his offer to buy it for £200, and cut their losses.

My heart was in my boots as we walked about the Sussex hills in damp spring weather, for apart from this disappointment, I dreaded the prospect of boarding school, and took no encouragement from Cowper's hymn which we sang in church on the Sunday:

> Ye fearful saints, fresh courage take,
> The clouds ye so much dread
> Are big with mercy, and shall break
> In blessings on your head.

The one cheerful aspect for me was our purchase of the school uniform, bought from Portrush in Ireland: a green tunic (called a djibbah) worn over a white blouse; a purple blazer and beret and purple winter coat; three cotton tunics for summer which could be made at home in any colour you liked, and a purple straw hat for expeditions outside the school. This last could I think be bought at school, and Mother decided that it was not necessary to buy it beforehand – indeed it was only worn for the journeys to and from school and was a waste of money. However, her decision was a pity from my point of view, for I proved to be the only child in the crowd waiting on the platform at Paddington to catch the Newbury train who was wearing not a hat but a beret.

CHAPTER II

The school my parents had chosen for me took its character from that of its founder and headmistress, Olive Willis. I have written at length about it in my biography of her, but I will briefly set the scene here. Olive had not been happy at her own boarding school, Roedean, and had dreamed from those early days that she might start a school of her own, 'where life would be normal, and relations between people would be easy'. She fulfilled the dream at the age of thirty when she opened a school at Charles Darwin's old home in Kent, with a staff of five and one pupil – increasing at the end of two years to the intended number of thirty girls. From then on, her problem was always to keep the numbers to a manageable size, and by 1920 it was clear that a larger house must be found. A couple of years later she had found an ideal place at Cold Ash near Newbury in Berkshire, and moved in there in the summer of 1922 with eighty-three girls.

The house was out of the ordinary, like Olive's school. It had been built during the 1914 war for an eccentric organization, the 'Ladies of Silence', run by an American, Miss Curtis. The architect, Maclaren Ross, had lived in South America, and his buildings showed a Spanish influence, with roofs of shallow-curved red tiles. The main house was three storeys high, and the first floor opened on to a wide loggia overlooking a paved terrace, from which terraced banks led down to a large quadrangle, round three sides of which ran the cloisters. On one slope, flanked by a large tree, a Greek theatre had been made. The site is on a fir-topped hill some six miles to the north-east of Newbury, on a patch of gravel above the prevailing chalk. From the valley the hill appears insignificant, and indeed it only rises some 200 feet, to its 517 feet above sea level. Once up there, you have the impression of a commanding height, for the ground drops steeply away from the school buildings, and the view extends over the lower wooded ridges of the Kennet valley to where the sun sets behind the Newbury hills. As I wrote in my book, those who sat at work by certain windows would be distracted from Pythagoras or Magna Carta as they gazed down over the steep woods to a pond where horses drank, in a field of toy-sized cows, and would watch, mesmerized, the smoke of a train as it snaked along the valley. Oakwoods then covered much of the hillside, and red squirrels were still there while I was at school; wild daffodils and lilies of the valley are still to be found, and bilberries.

When I arrived at the school, three years after the move, the numbers had grown to 120; by the time I left they had reached about 250. This was near the limit of an ideal size for the kind of school that Olive had made, depending very much on personal contact with her. As to that contact, Ian McMaster (a school governor and parent) said after her death:

The fact that she could greet any one of her girls, after 10, 20, even 40 and more years, by name and with a smile of real recognition was not due to her wonderful memory and tireless correspondence; but because, at school, she had seen right into them with hopefulness, and this deep knowledge and the love that inspired it, had made each an undying part of the other.

Olive could assume the grand manner when she wished, and had an imposing presence, but she never felt the need to imitate the style of Victorian headmasters, which the pioneer women educationists seem to have adopted along with the male curriculum. She was naturally dignified, yet could make fun of dignity. 'Headmistresses acquire large faces', she said, 'so that their expressions can be seen at a distance.' The respect which she inspired in her pupils had nothing in it of morbid fear or of a homosexual excitement; she had, in fact, a remarkably balanced personality; she did not need the love of her pupils, as many inspiring teachers do, to fill some void in her own heart.

She had many first-rate teachers on her staff – in particular the teaching of History was generally superlative – but her generous nature (also her interest in human beings of all kinds) led her to employ a good many lame ducks as well, and it has been said that certain of Downe's teachers inculcated only the lesson of how to get on with eccentrics. Chief among the eccentrics was Maria Nickel, who had been first engaged via a scholastic agency in about 1910 to teach geography and chemistry. By all accounts, her lessons were fascinating, but she would never correct an exercise book, or allow anyone else to do it for her; she also tried her hand at cooking for the school – brilliantly but so extravagantly that only a first-class restaurant could have retained her. By the time of the move to Downe she no longer taught, but was architect, engineer and clerk of the works. Her invariable dress was a brownish serge overall, belted and reaching nearly to her ankles (generally stained with machine oil and with a packet of cigarettes tucked into the breast pocket), rubber boots and a grey felt 'Safari' hat. No one ever saw her without this hat on, and she had no room of her own indoors – as far as we knew, she slept in Miss Willis's bathroom. She was believed to be of Polish birth: certainly she spoke, in her deep musical voice, with a foreign accent, and had been suspected by the Kentish villagers during the war of being a spy. She gave complete devotion to Miss Willis and the school.

Lilian Heather, Olive's second-in-command, showed equal loyalty but was certainly not an eccentric, though her fiercely protective devotion to Olive could make her alarming at times. Once, for instance, she launched into an accusatory tirade ('Heartless, selfish child') which reduced me to helpless sobs, when she and Olive had seen me from below, kneeling on an inside window-sill in a position they considered dangerous. She was a brilliant teacher of mathematics, but unfortunately her time was so much occupied with administration that she only taught the older girls who were to pursue the subject.

One other member of the staff I should mention before I start my narrative: Miss Croft (Caw), who, as I mentioned in my first chapter, had been governess to the young Milfords. After relief work in France she had joined the staff at the old Downe, aged twenty-three: she was delightful to look at, with coppery hair. The new girls and the young became her especial care, and she provided a centre of comfort and reassurance in the sometimes bracing atmosphere (in every sense) of Downe. She taught geography and maths to the younger forms and later, more successfully, weaving; she played the organ for week-day chapel services, and supported the orchestra with her violin and viola.

The record in Mother's diary notes that she 'took Anne up to Paddington and saw her off. Pippa was there to befriend her and she did not cry.' It was an unspoken point of honour not to cry, and on this and many subsequent term-beginnings one regarded with a critical pity a girl called Chucky who regularly dripped through the first few days. Pippa, now aged sixteen, was a kind but fairly remote figure, and it was the youngest of the three Stainer sisters, Alice, who took me in hand.

This first journey passed in a daze. At Newbury we were met by the school bus, which took us along the plain and up the hill (where it groaned and always seemed about to give up and fall backwards) to Downe, and I remember that during the approach along the drive I caught sight of the strange figure of Miss Nickel in her overalls and Safari hat among the pine trees. No one else showed any surprise, I noticed.

I had been assigned to sleep at Ancren Gate, a house built as a retreat for herself by Miss Curtis, founder of the Ladies of Silence, a quarter of a mile away from the main building. Miss Croft was in charge of Ancren Gate, and I was to share a room with Alice Stainer and another junior, Effie Vaughan-Johnson, so I was being given an easy start.

Ancren Gate, in a clearing amongst the trees, backed on to Red Shute Hill where the road wound steeply down towards the village of Hermitage, and the station on the Great Central Railway was close to that. Next to Ancren Gate Olive had put up another building to serve as the Sanatorium. That first evening I somehow managed to be left behind when unpacking my things, and heard the strains of singing from the cloisters when I returned to the main house. What should they be singing, as I stood miserably at the entrance to the cloister steps, but the Cowper hymn we had sung at Fairlight? I saw no mercy in the clouds, but apologized to Miss Willis as she came out, and she did not seem at all annoyed. I don't remember anything more about that first evening, except that Caw came into our room after lights out as I was lying awake, with 'Well Anne, does it all seem very strange?'

The walk to the main house through the woods (there were oaks as well as pines), with the occasional sight of a red squirrel, was very pleasant in summer. We had chapel in the cloisters before breakfast, which was in the dining hall (now the staff room), filled with round tables large enough for a dozen people. The staff only ate with us at lunch, when each presided at the same table for the term, but our groups rotated, moving every half week. The groups contained one from each form, headed by a sixth-former, who had 'picked' her table at the beginning of term, in strict rotation down the list. Girls who were easy talkers and could chat to the staff were in demand, and I certainly did not figure among those in my early years at school. At tea we could sit where we liked.

The sixth-former helped out the dishes brought by the domestic staff, and I was surprised to see the first plate of porridge travel all the way round the table from the girl on her left to the girl on her right. I was also surprised by the convention that you never asked directly for anything you needed, but offered it to your neighbour (even if she had already got some sugar, milk or whatever), hoping that she would respond. I never discovered how this absurd convention arose, but I have heard that it obtained in other schools as well.

The encouragement to chatter resulted in a crescendo of treble voices, and when the noise became unbearable Miss Willis would utter a loud Hush; after which the talk would begin again on a lower note. Priscilla Hayter has written that the influence of Downe has left her with an incurable nervous impulse to fill every pause in the conversation with a remark, no matter how idiotic.

The food at Downe was palatable, in so far as mass-cooked food can be, and we had excellent bread made from stone-ground flour (grey bread, the foolish christened it). The only uneatable dish was 'mackintosh eggs' – baked until the whites had formed a tough rubbery glaze on top.

Thanks to my poor arithmetic, I was placed in the small bottom form, Form Two, with my room mate Effie, but not with Alice, though I joined her at Michaelmas in the Lower Third. Miss Croft was our form mistress, and taught us maths and geography, but except for arithmetic, I didn't pursue those subjects up to School Certificate level. This was not from any choice of mine – merely the exigencies of the timetable (which cost Miss Heather many weeks of each holidays), and left me very ignorant of the map of the world. I enjoyed geometry, but I should certainly have failed algebra in my School Certificate, so it was probably wise to make me learn botany instead. Unfortunately I was not interested in the subject then, and neglected opportunities which I should value now.

Our subject-periods were of forty minutes – eight of them, with two half-hour periods at the end of the day, and these seven hours included times for gym or dancing, preparation and instrument-practice each day, drawing, orchestra and sewing once a week. Saturday was a half day, but the afternoon had to be allotted to some sort of exercise, if we were not watching a match. Rehearsals for plays had to be squeezed into the short time between supper at seven and lights out at ten past nine.

I did come to feel, when I compared the organization of our days with that of my brothers at Rugby, that we had too little time when we could follow our own devices. But of course we had no studies where we could be private: the nearest approach to these was provided by the thirteen music rooms off the cloisters (once used by the Ladies of Silence for their meditations, with special wooden armchairs retained by the school) which were available on Sundays to be 'bagged' by groups of friends; and in summer we could spread our rugs together on the various lawns.

And how important one's friends were! In our early years at school we would walk with arms round each other's waists, and at all stages their support was an effective substitute for what we had lost – the unquestioning environment of home.

That accepting atmosphere was, of course, supplied to some extent by Olive Willis herself, who made frequent nightly rounds of bedrooms, and bestowed a never-mechanical maternal kiss on each child. At the end of term she gave interviews to all, known as jaws, which lasted anything between a quarter and a whole hour, with penetrating comments on work and character. Long after I had left, she wrote a response to some reminiscences I had contributed to a memorial scrap-book which shows how she viewed me in my early schooldays:

Your reminiscences are so true that they take me right back to the days when a little Johnnie-Head-in-Air used to wander about with an abstracted air, which concealed at times a very clear and forceful opinion and a *quite* clear determination to have her own way. I wanted to protect you, but I also wanted you to accept conditions and you were not very willing – or so it seemed to me… You have made the picture as I know it – except that I come out as a slightly vague fairy-godmother – but – yes, I believe I felt like that. I was always wanting to give you [she means her pupils in general] special treats – to turn your pumpkins into carriages, because youth is so short and so painful, and there is no reason why it should be *dull* as well!

Her attitude was bracing as well as affectionate, and she rather welcomed the small physical hardships incidental to the haphazard domestic organization of Downe in those first years, as well as its airy situation. These she thought helped to build character. Moreover, she tried to prevent her staff and pupils from falling into a rut by changing the form structures from time to time. Miss Nickel's arrangements for electricity and water heating were always liable to go wrong: many a prep in the winter had to be truncated 'because the lights went out', and at Ancren Gate we often had no hot water. It was a rule to have open windows at night whatever the weather, and in my first year I was not alone in being afflicted with such bad chilblains on my toes that they burst.

Those hardships, however, were still to come, and the summer term passed pleasantly enough, with sleeping-out (on our own camp-beds) in the open space surrounded by the cloisters; cricket and tennis after tea (the playing fields were a quarter-mile along the road towards Cold Ash, the hard tennis courts alongside the drive), and occasional visits to the open-air swimming baths in Newbury. I passed the test to get into the Choral Society, and also conducted our form of about ten in an internal singing competition, in which we were commended. The summer play which Miss Willis always produced in the Greek theatre was a translation of the Alcestis of Euripides, with Priscilla Hayter as Admetus. It was characteristic of Olive that she decided to cast the homesick Chucky as the little girl who movingly laments her mother's death, and she must have delivered the lines with genuine feeling, for I remember how she said them. Form exams ended the term as usual, and I never minded these: I usually came top or second in English and History, and bottom or near it in arithmetic and algebra.

Mother met me at Paddington, and after the stay in London for Lords came six weeks at Mount Grace Priory near Northallerton in Yorkshire, shared with the Phipps family, who had been lent it by their friend the owner, Sir Hugh Bell. This had been the guest house of the Carthusian monastery, the ruins of which surrounded it – and have now been partly restored and opened to visitors. It lies at the foot of heather-covered moors, and is within reach of more famous monastic ruins such as Rievaulx and Fountains, which we visited in borrowed cars. We were a large party, as besides the five Phippses and various short-term visitors, Edward and Christopher were both with us – Edward before his first term at New College, and Christopher on holiday from Amen House in the City of London, where he worked in the editorial department of the Oxford University Press. (After Christmas that year he went out to India to work in their Bombay branch.) Emma, our beloved former School Field cook who had left to get married, came back to cook for us, and we took four other maids. There was a lawn-tennis court, on which we played as a change from picnics on the moors, and indoors there was a piano for ensemble music and singing, with Mother on her violin and Ann Phipps on her clarinet. Moreover, Nicholas Phipps and I had invested in a toy theatre from Hamley's, in which we put on plays we had written ourselves. Nicholas was later to become an actor, and even as a small boy, clowning on the sands, could keep the company in fits of laughter.

The Bells lived at Rounton Grange within bicycling distance, and we paid them visits or they came to us. They had a distinguished house party, with Sir Hugh's daughter Gertrude, the famous traveller, an elderly aesthete called Sir Valentine Chirol, and Dame Elizabeth Robins, the American actress associated with the early productions of Ibsen's plays in London. (Anne Tibble, daughter of the Rounton coachman, describes the place and family in her autobiography *Greenhorn*.) One day, Colonel Bell (Sir Hugh's son) gave us a guided tour of the iron works at Middlesborough, Dorman Long, with which Bell Bros was amalgamated.

On the way home (by train of course) we stopped in York to see the Minster, and Nicholas came on to Rugby to stay for a week. At this time and for several summer holidays, he and I had a very enjoyable companionship, but I can't remember thinking much about him betweenwhiles, and it seems to have been a boy and girl relationship with virtually no sexual feeling involved. We had occasional meetings en famille at other times of year, to see a play in London, and sometimes wrote to each other. My three brothers admired Ann Phipps who (it seemed to me) favoured whichever of them was the eldest present during the holiday, but Christopher was the only one who kept up with her in later years.

The following, winter, term meant lacrosse every week-day afternoon, and an exciting new History teacher. This was Jane Martin, fresh from university, and engaged to the brother of a girl in my new form of the Lower Third, Kinta Waterfield – of whom more anon. Miss Martin was fascinating to look at – a *jolie laide* – and as she had not taught before, she tended to treat us as though we were mature students. My essays (which had to be written in a single forty-minute period) were generally approved of, but I remember once finding at the bottom of the page, in her small cultivated handwriting, 'Rotten, superficial work' – which surprised me very much, as I had not been aware of writing anything different from usual. She only taught us for one term, I think, and alas for Kinta's brother, she threw him over in favour of Kenneth Clark, and the rest of her story as one of the Beautiful People is rather a sad one.

I enjoyed lacrosse at first, but the position on the field where I was always placed, Attack Wing, with the expectation that because of my long legs I should be able to run fast, didn't really suit me, for I am no sprinter, and it was not until, in my last winter, I played in a position (First Home) where you need quickness in catching and shooting goals, that I did well and sometimes played for the first team. So I became discouraged, and very bored with the daily stint of going out to the field, playing, going back to my bedroom and 'changing down' to the skin, and dressing again in 'Private Clothes'. Gym, on the other hand, was never boring to me, and the various stunts on the horse – Quick Squat and Slow Squat, Short- and Long-Arm, handstands off the end – were exhilarating. And days when the field was too wet for games brought variety, for we were allowed to go for walks in threes, and the country round about was beautiful.

Half way through the term the new chapel was dedicated, and our icy Sunday mornings wrapped in rugs in the cloisters came to an end. The chapel is one of Miss Nickel's most successful buildings, riding out from the hillside above the cloisters. Of course the roof was not yet watertight, and drips into various buckets played an accompaniment to our services for a good while to come.

I was again sleeping at Ancren Gate, with different room-mates – one of them an older girl, Lena Westropp, one of a pair of identical twins who both distinguished themselves in later life – Lena as a member of the LCC, Celia as a scientist. I think it was in this term that the music staff decided to produce Robin Milford's children's opera, *The Shoemaker,* with a libretto by his mother based on the Beatrix Potter story. I was one of the six mice, and Alice was another: she had a solo, a lovely setting of words by Robert Bridges, 'A frosty Christmas Eve when the stars were shining'. This experience was magic, and so was the evening at the end of term when the older members of the Choral Society sang carols outside Ancren Gate, and wound away through the woods singing

Haydn's canon 'Gloria, Gloria'.

During the Christmas holidays we paid our usual visit to Bourne-mouth, not staying at 2 Richmond Gardens but in a boarding house next door, as Granny Milford was failing, and Aunt Beatrice was paralysed after a stroke. Granny died a couple of months later, aged ninety-two.

After this we stayed in London with Oscar Ashcroft, a wealthy and generous Old Rugbeian who was devoted to Mother and Father, and always treated us to a theatre visit and to various exhibitions. His house in Elm Park Gardens displayed a fine collection of oil paintings which he had inherited – now in the Birmingham Art Gallery. Oscar (born Fleischmann – he had changed his name during the War) had a very poor circulation, so that his skin was a darkish mauve in colour; for travel about London he had a Rolls Royce and a chauffeur, and we went to the theatre in style. He was a bachelor, and guardian to his actress niece Peggy and her brother Edward; when later on he made a very happy compan-ionate marriage, he and his wife Isabel offered the same hospitality to us.

This winter, my treat consisted of an outing with my former governess Miss Ohlson, who gave me supper at a Lyons Corner House (it included Pêche Melba, I remember) and stalls for *The Ghost Train* by Arnold Ridley (later a character in Dad's Army), which frightened me out of my wits.

The following Lent term was an unlucky one for me. It should have been a happy one, as Priscilla Hayter invited me to act the part of a *gamin* in a play which she and some seniors were putting on, produced by Miss Wale, the English mistress, and we had begun to rehearse it when I fell ill with infectious jaundice. Moreover, there was a hard frost lasting several weeks, which meant skating on the pond in the valley every day instead of lacrosse. But I was in the San all the time, and so missed the play and the chance of learning to skate properly. Mother came to fetch me home at the end of term to Rugby, travelling by the old Great Central Railway.

The General Strike of 1926 sent us scurrying back to school for the summer term at a few hours' notice. Miss Willis thought we might be in danger from the strikers if we went for walks in our usual threes, and we were condemned to the repellent 'crocodile'. I was still sleeping at Ancren Gate, with a new friend, Audrey Wheeler ('the other Audrey Wheeler'), whose mother, Lady Wheeler, was an old friend of Olive's, and her father was, I told my parents, 'Governor of India or something' – actually Bihar and Orissa. Audrey was excellent company (the quality which endeared her mother to Olive), but she left school I think before the sixth-form stage, and though I visited her in her Kensington home while I was living in London, she was something of a socialite, and our paths diverged.

In August we met the Phipps family for a second holiday in Brittany – a more commonplace venture, at a hotel in a small resort called Trébeurden. There was a tennis court, but no picturesque peasants or exciting cliffs: however, we made one trip which was nearly an adventure. Ann Phipps and Edward set out to paddle a large canoe, in which Nicholas and I were passengers, round the promontory between our bay and the next, where the others waited with a picnic lunch. The sea was quite calm, but when we got beyond the promontory there was a strong current against us, and the paddlers had great difficulty in making any headway. Nicholas and I sat cracking jokes on the floor of the canoe, quite oblivious of the trouble, but our parents on the shore became more and more anxious, till we finally appeared round the point. Lunch tasted very good when we got there, and French picnic food was always delectable, with Chocolat Meunier to finish with, but I didn't care for the oft-repeated pudding at the hotel of crême caramel. Guests were always given chocolate soufflé on their last evening, and that really was a treat.

For the Michaelmas term of 1926 I finally left Ancren Gate behind and slept more cosily in the main house, with a girl in my form called Margaret Freeman, who later became an artist and won prizes with embroidered quilts of her own design. She had a young cousin, new that term, who shared our room. We became worried because Hilary seemed very homesick, so we decided to ask Miss Willis for advice. At that time the theories of M. Coué were being much discussed, and Olive suggested that we should try them on Hilary: waiting till she was asleep, we should then repeat several times 'You are happy here, Hilary; you are *quite* happy here.' This we did for about a week, without noticeable results; Hilary said nothing, but she was an enigmatic child, and I have often wondered whether she was awake and laughing at us under the bedclothes.

For 26 October, Olive's birthday, the whole school always made birthday cards, and I remember that this year I wrote a poem about a sea wizard called Lord Grognor, which Margaret illustrated very vividly. Her talents did not lie in academic subjects, and as we sat next each other in form I used to help her with her Latin – for which I was reprimanded. Alice then addressed a poem to me which began:

Do, dare, dedi, datum,
Don't help Margaret with her Latum...

Some time earlier, I had joined the school Guide company, much encouraged by Olive, who became a Guide Commissioner. Margaret was already an experienced Guide, with a string of badges on her sleeve, but I never took to it, and joining was a mistake. In theory one could resign, but the attempt which Audrey and I and others made to do so was firmly blocked by Olive. So I continued with the weekly stint of boring team games and scrappy badge-gaining, until the final reward of an enjoyable three-night camp during the summer term – I think in my penultimate year.

Caw came to spend Christmas with us at Hillbrow, and during our London visit to Oscar Ashcroft we saw an Eden Philpotts comedy, *Yellow Sands*, and Henry Ainley and Sybil Thorndike in *Macbeth*, which I had been studying at school. VAB notes that I was ill with a persistent cough and had to go back late to school, and I suppose that this was the beginning of an infection which made me deaf the following term, and ended in an operation for mastoid (almost unknown now, in these days of antibiotics) which caused a hiatus in my education.

I went back from school at the end of term with a sore throat, and on the night when we arrived at Shipton Gorge in Dorset for our usual spring holiday, I developed violent earache. The week that followed was a blur of pain, punctuated by visits from the elderly Bridport doctor, who had no instrument for looking down my ear, but pulled the lobe back and peered. A night nurse who was engaged, afraid or too lazy to go downstairs in the dark to fetch some water, gave me drinks from my hot-water bottle. Father, walking on the hillside above the village, thought of all the epitaphs he had seen of children who had died of a fever, and expressed his acute anxiety in a poem, 'Shipton Gorge':

'Sick of a fever', through the long long ages
Rings the sad word,

Sick of a fever lies our little daughter:
Heal her Oh Lord.

At last Dr Grey from Weymouth was sent for, and said he must operate for mastoidectomy immediately (interpreted to me by Mother as 'a little operation that he wants to do'), and we went by taxi into Moffatt House in Weymouth for an operation under general anaesthetic that night.

Dr Grey was a charming Scot and a skilled surgeon (he told me he used to practise tying knots with one hand while listening to the wireless or at any odd moment during the day), so that he made a very neat job of the incision behind my ear. Unfortunately, though, he omitted to take a swab at the time, and the streptococcal infection continued to cause high fever and attacks of 'rigor' – violent shivering, when the nurses would bustle round me with blankets and hot-water bottles. I was told afterwards that an opened bottle of champagne was kept upside-down in a bucket of water by my bed in case of emergency. (Who ultimately drank it, I wonder?) But I did not know that I was dangerously ill, of course – only that nights and days merged into each other, and that the promise of what I heard as 'baked cutlet' for lunch turned out to be dismal baked custard, spoon-fed to me by a nurse.

Father had to go back to Rugby for the beginning of the summer term, leaving Mother in the Weymouth lodgings, and still I didn't improve, till Uncle Godfrey paid for the clever retired Rugby School doctor, Dr Simey, to come down and examine me. He brought with him (on the chance that it might be needed) a stock vaccine, with which I was inoculated, and my temperature began to subside at once. (It seems that he also prescribed quinine, Vivian's favourite remedy.) I was very weak though, and I remember the new sensation of being able to move my legs about again in bed. Luckily the hearing in the 'mastoid' ear was barely affected.

After five weeks in Moffatt House I went with Mother to her lodgings on the Esplanade in Weymouth, where she wheeled me about in a bath chair, and various friends came to visit us, including Moly, Aunt Marion and her sister Dorothy Hale White. We had a fortnight there, and then returned to Rugby for the rest of the summer term, where I did no work except some desultory Latin.

One piece of excellent news which cheered us while I was in the nursing home was that Edward (who was then touring Greece on holiday) had been awarded a First in Mods (Honour Moderations).

By August I was back to normal, and we set off with the Phippses (whose train we joined at Rugby station) for four weeks in the Lake District. Our two families occupied the whole of the Traveller's Rest Inn at Ulpha in the Duddon Valley, where they kept their own poultry, and the string of ducks that waddled about the yard diminished as our Sunday lunches went by. A good bathing place in the Duddon was just across a couple of fields, and I begged to be allowed to swim, in spite of a prohibition by Dr Grey. My parents gave way, on condition that I kept my head above water, and must *never* dive.

The inn is at the foot of a long steep hill, so our walks were chiefly along Dunnerdale. On the third day after our arrival, Father's nailed boots slipped on some stepping stones across the river; he fell and gashed his shin, and was immobilized for the rest of our stay – a bitter blow. One day we hired a car to drive him and some of the party up the hill behind the inn to Devoke Water, and this I think was the only lake I saw on that first visit.

My enemy of septicaemia was not quite vanquished yet, and erupted in the form of impetigo behind my ear when, after our return from the Lakes, we were staying at Wells with the former Rugby music master, Basil Johnson, and his wife Bessie. So I found myself back in Moffatt House, where Dr Grey operated – to drain the abscess I suppose. This meant another ten days in the Home, and I had to go back to school a fortnight late; worse still, my hair had to be cut in an Eton crop.

I had been dreading the return after missing a whole term's work, and this late arrival, with a conspicuously odd hair style, was a real trial. However, it was good to see my friends again, and our Sunday music-room group (for letter-writing and card games) had an addition in the person of Margie James – Philippa – who had started at Downe in the summer. (She was to adopt the name of Philippa in adult life, to escape confusion with a Margaret James who was a professional recorder player.)

My form had been divided in two, and all the forms were now given alphabetical names. D1 would take the School Certificate the following summer, and D2, where I was placed, the following Michaelmas. I was to start the violin (a cherished plan of Mother's, as she had derived so much pleasure from her own violin-playing), and in order to accommodate the extra 'forties' required in my timetable, Miss Heather had cut out Latin – without consulting my parents or me. Latin was always taken as a separate School Certificate subject, later than the rest, and I was expected to start it again when I had got my certificate, working with the others who had had four or five terms without me. I found this impossible when the time came, and the school said they could not provide the extra coaching that Father asked for: hence I learnt no more Latin at school, and have regretted it ever since, though my grounding has enabled me to read with a crib.

Learning the violin, however, brought me much joy. Marjorie Gunn was a teacher with great charisma, and she contrived that I should play in the orchestra from the very beginning, arranging easy parts for me as Third Violin and lending me a good violin instead of the cheapish one we had bought. Philippa was the leader of the orchestra, and we went up to the Central Hall, Westminster that winter, to take part in a competition which we won, playing the March from Holst's 'St Paul's Suite', and beating the orchestra of St Paul's School where Holst was music master. I gave up piano lessons for the time being (I had learnt from a very uninspiring teacher, aunt of Evelyn Rothwell), and merely had time allotted for practices, supervised by Margaret Nowell Smith, who had returned to Downe to help with games and musical appreciation. A term or two later, we were very smitten with her performance as Dido in Purcell's opera *Dido and Aeneas* which she and other staff put on.

The school had added netball as a winter game, and this year I was directed to play this instead of lacrosse, as it presented no risk of being bashed about the ear... After Christmas we went to Studland for a snowy seaside holiday, taking the Canadian-type toboggan which had been my Christmas present. I was surprised to find how vividly I remembered the nooks and crannies of the red rocks on the shore, into which my infant fingers had fitted.

In the Lent term, 1928, aged fifteen and a half, I was confirmed by a charismatic Bishop (of Willesden I think) whom Miss Willis regularly invited rather than Bishop Strong of Oxford, reputed to be a misogynist. Although the confirmandi went weekly to Cold Ash for classes with the Vicar, our real preparation was with Olive, and the question-and-answer sessions which we had with her remain in memory as among the most valuable parts of my schooldays. 'She made Christianity seem exciting', one pupil wrote, and because she had discovered her own faith in adolescence, taking nothing for granted, she was able to respond with sympathy to all our doubts and confusions.

The Cold Ash Vicar came once a month to celebrate Communion in our chapel: he gabbled the words in a monotonous sing-song which was anything but inspiring. Olive explained to us that his Anglo-Catholic approach meant that he viewed the service as a whole Act, which took little account of the details. The explanation did nothing to endear him to us. Olive's own reading at our services was beautiful (as was her reading of poetry in the evenings while we did our mending), and her sermons at their best were memorable, but in her anxiety for truth and clarity, speaking from notes, she sometimes wandered from the point and, especially when she was tired, went on too long. I wrote in one of my letters home that the sermon had beaten the service in length by ten minutes – whereupon my parents, failing to compare notes when they wrote back, *both* quoted George Herbert:

> Judge not the preacher: if thou mislike the sense
> God takes a text, and preaches pati-ence.

After the fiasco of the Barn, our parents had decided to look for a house somewhere in the Chilterns, to be in real country yet not too far from London, and within reach of Lawrence and Barbara Hammond, who lived near Hemel Hempstead. So during the Easter holidays we stayed at the Alford Arms, Frithesden, and bicycled about the countryside looking at houses for sale. It seemed to me that an East wind was blowing every single day of those expeditions, and as nothing we looked at seemed attractive, the only pleasure was in our cosy evenings of card games – Casino or Poker Patience. Finally a possibility offered in the shape of a field for sale at Ringshall, facing a tract of woodland owned by the National Trust and only a couple of miles from Ivinghoe Beacon. It seemed so promising that our parents decided to give up house-hunting and commission a local architect called Hopkins to draw up plans for a five-bedroomed house on the site.

That summer, Matt's long five-year stint in Assam had earned him six months of leave. He caused a sensation among my friends when he came to visit me at half-term, and for the summer holidays drove some of the family down to Aldeburgh in the Morris tourer he had bought for his time in England. We had taken lodgings on the sea front, and the Milfords were near by. The attraction of Aldeburgh for the family was its golf links and annual tennis tournament, for which Uncle Humphrey, David and Matt entered with some success. I never cared much for the shingle bathing by comparison with the rocks of Cornwall and Wales, but it was a happy time, as any time in Matt's company was bound to be. Thanks to the car, I was able to bring my newly-acquired gramophone (a Cliftophone), with my first records – Mozart G minor Symphony and Hunt Quartet (played by the Lener), and the Temple Church treble, Master Lough, singing Mendelssohn. Also Kreisler playing a morsel by Boccherini, with which I 'played along' on my violin. I exorcised my memory of *The Ghost Train* by seeing it on film. And the Phippses were staying at Orford, farther down the coast, so that we could exchange occasional visits.

Uncle Humphrey always played in the Mixed Doubles at Wimbledon in June, and had found a partner for Matt this year – a very pretty Epsom girl called Janet Walters. This turned out just as their elders had hoped: they fell in love while playing some well-matched tennis, and she accepted Matt's proposal. She was nearer in age to me than to him, but they seemed in many ways ideally suited to each other, and it was certainly a love-match. She came to stay with us at Hillbrow, and they both drove me back to Downe. Matt had to go back to India alone in October, where he would now be in the Shaw Wallace Calcutta office, and Jan would join him early in the following summer. Meanwhile intrepid VAB had learnt to drive, and she and Father bought the Morris from Matt – a great addition to the pleasures of our life.

I duly gained my School Certificate that term – not very gloriously, with passes in arithmetic and the necessary 'science' (botany), and credits (A in French) in the other subjects I took. One result that shook my belief in exam results for ever after was in the English paper, where I was marked as having failed in the Précis. How could that have been right, when it was one exercise I *knew* I was good at?

During the Christmas holidays Edward (in his last year at Oxford) had a mild attack of mumps, and the resulting quarantine meant that I was once more late in going back to school, though I didn't catch it. His college friend John Witt came to stay at Hillbrow, and we enjoyed listening to Schubert's 'Death and the Maiden' quartet (played by the Budapest) on my gramophone.

Back at school, I began the really enjoyable part of my time at Downe. The two D forms were united as the Lower Sixth, in a room where we could light a fire at week-ends and be comfortable. We made a very congenial group, and sometimes went on outings together, once taking the train from Hermitage to a station beyond Newbury and climbing one of the downs for a picnic. Rosemary Murray ('Archimedes', later the first Principal of New Hall, Cambridge) had brought the map and wished us to eat at the highest point, where there happened to be no view. (We also met after we had all left school, to have lunch together in London and see Shaw's new play *The Apple Cart.*) Some other members of the form besides Philippa and Alice now became my close friends – notably Jean Wilson, whose parents lived in Switzerland, and Miss Willis's niece Mary Wright (now Guillemard). Jean was dark-haired and rosy-cheeked, and shared my liking for History; Mary had her aunt's warm-hearted sympathy and her interest in people; as you know, we still see each other often.

Apart from group outings, we had freedom now that we were older to wander off alone in a way which would never be possible nowadays. I spent at least one bonus whole-school holiday exploring the countryside by myself, getting a lift in a rag-and-bone man's cart at one point; and one Sunday morning Alice and I collected our breakfast sausages from the kitchen and bicycled to a spot near Blewbury, where we lit a fire and cooked them – hurrying back in time for morning chapel.

At some point I began working for the Higher Certificate (the equivalent of A-Level), taking English and a subject designated History-with-French, but after a term or two I think that neither I nor my teachers were enjoying that much, and it was abandoned in favour of the divided subjects of History and French. The History period was the nineteenth century; the English books included *Richard II* and Landor's *Imaginary Conversations,* and the French, Corneille's *Horace* and Racine's *Britannicus,* memorably taught by the redoubtable Mademoiselle Agobert, a fiery and capricious character who produced excellent exam results with her pupils. With juniors, her habit of driving home the rules of agreement of the Participe Passé by accurate shots at offending pupils with the chalk, and with elders her dictation of elegant critical dicta, were all successful, though she did not encourage independent opinions. She put on Rostand's *Cyrano de Bergerac* one year, and some time after I left she took some of her pupils to act in France.

History was excellently taught by Anne Evans, an Oxford graduate who returned there later to be a tutor. A new building had been raised to house the Library (formally opened in the summer by the Duchess of Atholl) where we could work for our essays: Jean Wilson and I particularly favoured an old-fashioned account of the Industrial Revolution which we found there – I think the author was called Bright. The school ordered (and our parents paid for) Shorter Oxford texts of Milton, Shelley and Keats, which I still have. For our form play (always performed some time in the winter for Miss Heather's birthday) we put on *The Dover Road,* which I think is by A. A. Milne, and I scored a hit as the enigmatic Mr Lattimer who brings eloping couples to their senses. We gathered afterwards that Olive had been rather dismayed at our choice of this play, but she did not make us aware of this at the time. Miming shadows behind a sheet had been an earlier success.

The house in our eleven-acre field near Ringshall (700 feet above sea-level) had been growing steadily, and our parents had been over during the winter to see it. They had determined that £2000 was their limit of cost, and the first plan drawn up by Mr Hopkins had been much too expensive. He was unwilling to alter it, until they told him that he had better plan for one sitting-room only: thus convinced that they were in earnest, he produced a second plan, with sitting and dining rooms opening on to a south-facing terrace, about half-way up the sloping field. Along the side of this field was a strip of beechwood spinney, covered with bluebells in spring, and at the back was scrub woodland as far as the edge of the escarpment, where one looked north-east towards the Dunstable Downs and Whipsnade. At the bottom of our field was the road leading from the hamlet of Ringshall to Ivinghoe Beacon, and from the house (reached by a long and expensive drive bordered by flowering cherry and crab-apple trees) we looked over it to the National Trust common covered with bracken. The house had to be placed high enough to get this view, and this meant that the water piped from the neighbouring covered reservoir had to go into a tank farther down the field whence it was pumped to us (by a Petter oil-engine, the bane of Father's life). The house was wired for electricity, but it didn't come to the neighbourhood till the mid-'thirties, and we depended on Aladdin lamps for reading.

During their winter visit, Mother and Father had made the acquaintance of Nellie Pinner and her father, living in a cottage just across the field from us – a most fortunate meeting for our family. He had been under-gamekeeper to Lord Brownlow at Ashridge, and had supported his wife and family of five children on wages of twelve shillings a week – which even when supplemented by gleaning in the fields for their bread, and harvesting wild fruit in season, did not provide enough to eat. (The gleanings were thrashed by Pinner in the cottage kitchen, and taken to be ground at the local flour mill.) Nellie told me that they would sometimes gnaw turnips from the fields on their way to school to banish the pangs of hunger. She left school at the age of twelve to 'go into service' near Dunstable, and for a whole year looked across the valley to their cottage on the hillside facing the Dunstable Downs without being able to visit her home. Later she found work as a clerk in London with Hutchinson's, the publishers (after so brief a schooling!) and this, she would say, was the happiest time in her life. But when her mother died, she as the unmarried daughter (for alas her fiancé had been killed in the War) had to return home to look after her father. When Mother and Father knocked on the door of Reservoir Cottage and asked whether they might have a cup of tea, Nellie and her father welcomed them, and she promised to come and be our daily house-help when we moved into Ringshall End. (This name for the house had not yet been chosen, and old Pinner suggested Geesefield, as that was the name by which our field was known. I rather favoured this, but my parents rejected it as likely to give rise to recurrent and tedious jokes.)

But by Easter Ringshall End was not yet ready, so when we moved out of Hillbrow we stored the furniture and went to occupy Oatfield while the Hammonds were away in Greece. Christopher was with us for the move, on holiday after his three years in Calcutta. His personality seemed greatly changed, after some bad experiences in India. When he had arrived, aged just twenty-one, at the Calcutta office of the OUP, the manager was a man called Vaughan Jones who was an alcoholic, and not long after disappeared without warning, taking a substantial sum of OUP money with him. Christopher, left in charge, kept in constant touch with Ray Goffin, the manager in Bombay, who always afterwards spoke warmly of Christopher's competence and coolness in the crisis. But this experience, and perhaps other aspects of the expatriate society he found himself in, had given him a cynical and disillusioned outlook on life which was a considerable shock to our parents, and puzzling to me at that time.

When I went back to school, Christopher accompanied our parents and Jan on a holiday in Savoy, after which she went out to India for her wedding, and he to the Press headquarters at Amen House in the City, where he worked under Gerry Hopkins in the publicity department.

By midsummer, HCB and VAB were settled at Ringshall End, with a very unsatisfactory local girl, Rose, as cook, living in, and daily help from Nellie Pinner. Rose did not last long: one day she disappeared, leaving a note behind: 'This place is too lonely for a young girl who wants to see life.' I can't remember who replaced her, but before long Nellie's father died, and she came to live with us, a priceless support and member of the household for our parents' remaining years.

We then had daily help from Emmy Garrett, who lived with her sister in the bottom end cottage at Ringshall, and between them they did our laundry. Emmy's gait as she departed after her morning's work is clear in my memory: three or four steps with her short legs, and then a hurried trot for three or four more. She and Nellie were always very outspoken with each other. Here is Nellie's report of one exchange, as Emmy surveyed some linen lying on the kitchen table. E: 'Are those rough-dried?' N: 'O pray, I says, I've only just hot-ironed them.'

Old Pinner had spoken darkly about the locals when Mother and Father first met him. 'Ringshall? Oho, I could tell you a thing or two about the people of Ringshall!' But we never had cause to complain of them. It was really not the Garretts's fault that black beetles came to

Ringshall End by way of the laundry basket, and lived with us ever after behind the warm Aga stove – a startling sight all over the kitchen floor if you came downstairs in the night and switched the light on.

Edward completed his time at Oxford with a triumphant First in Greats, and spent the rest of the summer at Ringshall, helping to mow the rough field grass into lawns around the house – smooth enough ultimately for our favourite game of Golf Croquet (the rules devised I believe by Father, for croquet on a roughish lawn). Then he went out to Austria to learn German, before starting to teach at Merchant Taylors' School. We did not go away en famille that August, but I went to stay with the Stainers in Cornwall, in a house lent them by a close friend. It had a lovely position perched on a cliff at Polruan, opposite Fowey, and we had a rowing boat in which we fished for mackerel or explored the river as far as Llanteglos. Robin and Kirstie were also of the party; and Alice and I went by train to stay a night with the Fischer Williamses at their house, Lamledra, on the coast near the Dodman, which I had not visited since our long-ago holidays at Tregavarras.

During this autumn of 1929 the great exhibition of Italian art was put on at the Royal Academy, and a party from Downe went up to see it. It was a revelation for me, as up to then my knowledge had chiefly been derived from Arundel prints – I had not even seen the National Gallery collection. Kenneth Clark, who had been instrumental in organizing the exhibition, came down to talk to us beforehand, with slides: I remember one in particular, a detail of the clasped hands of the three nymphs in Botticelli's *Primavera,* on which he discoursed with aesthetic rapture.

I had made some progress on the violin, and this term I joined Alice and Philippa (clarinet and violin) who were already members of the Newbury amateur orchestra, being driven down once a week for the practices. It was conducted by Douglas Fox, the music master of Bradfield College, who had lost an arm in the 1914 war, but still performed miracles as a pianist. We had sung for him as the Gingerbread Children when he produced *Hansel and Gretel* in Newbury, accompanying it with a colleague as a piano duet. But Miss Read had vetoed our joining his Chorus in the Choral Symphony, for fear of damaging our adolescent voices. I had heard the orchestra in that performance, and now that I played in it myself, was surprised to find that one or two of the violins seemed to be total beginners. In particular there was one teenage boy (whom we called the Infant Prodigy), sitting near me at the back of the second fiddles, who appeared to play only on the open strings, and was frequently to be heard in the pauses. Douglas Fox would glare angrily in our direction, but took no action. We gave a concert that winter which included Beethoven's Overture to *Coriolan*; I forget what else.

At the end of one of the winter terms I was elected as secretary of the Philosophical Society, an honour I would rather have declined, as I felt rather out of my depth in the subject, and still more out of my depth with its founder and president, Miss Jean Smith, a fairly recent addition to the Staff. She had been secretary to Gilbert Murray, and the Oxford University Press had published a volume of her poems, on the recommendation of Murray and of Charles Williams. So far so good: but her habit of shaking with silent laughter over something which did not seem to us to be very funny, and her extremely High Church ardour, which meant that one might discover her flat on her face in the Chapel nave at any odd time of the day, made us uneasy. We were used to eccentricity from Miss Nickel, but this was rather different. However, I bought her poems on behalf of the Society (finding that she had not got a copy herself) and persuaded her to read them to us at our first meeting. We enjoyed hearing her read them – one was about 'Hermes Psychopompos' I remember – and a relationship was established, though I remember nothing about our philosophical debates. The Historical Society (presided over by Anne Evans) and the Literary Society (presided over by Mamie Poore) were both a source of pleasure. In the former, I remember that I read a paper on Erasmus, and that we visited Avebury (which then lacked the long avenue of stones since excavated); in the latter, we read Charles Williams' *A Myth of Shakespeare*, my first introduction to his work, except for my reading, in bed with suspected mumps, of some of his early poems, brought me by Olive.

At the end of the Michaelmas term, Alice and I were elected as Seniors for the Lent term, heading the list in that order. (Philippa, who was six months younger, followed us for the summer term.) This democratic process of election by the votes of the whole school was occasionally slightly rigged by Miss Willis, as I discovered later when I helped to count the votes myself, but on the whole it produced good results. The ten or a dozen Seniors occupied the Garden Room, a small sunny room on the upper floor of the building at the end of the cloisters, once occupied by the foundress of the Ladies of Silence. Their duties were not onerous (chiefly supervising rest for the younger children, giving out notices, ringing the bell for chapel, and so on) and their privilege was a greater contact with Olive – especially for coffee on Sunday afternoons in the drawing room, when we experienced the delights of her conversation and tried to elicit our favourite anecdotes.

During the Lent term I slept as Senior in charge at the so-called New House, a utility-style dormitory building erected by Miss Nickel during my time at school, and housing mostly the younger children. I read aloud to them at bedtime on Sunday evenings, choosing I remember some of Tolstoy's *Ten Tales*... Rather improbably, I won a County competition for the best essay on the League of Nations. And, towards the end of the term, Charles Williams came down to lecture to us on Blake.

Charles and Olive were old friends, having been introduced to each other by Humphrey Milford, and I am sure she must have been invited to the Amen House Masques which Charles wrote and produced. But I knew nothing about him before he came, and was unprepared for the electrifying effect of his lecture: his eloquence, the passion with which he declaimed the verse, in a Cockney accent, and the characteristic gesture that accompanied moments of special intensity, hands raised in front of him in the shape of a cup. Much that I heard in that first experience, I came to know as part of his critical writing on Blake, but there must have been some topical reason for the attack he then made on the journalistic (and general lazy) use of great poetry to emphasize trivial opinions – 'Let not Mr Baldwin lay the flattering unction to his soul that... his party is well placed to win the next election,' for example. I was struck, too, by the trembling of his hands, which of course I ascribed to nervousness. On the contrary, as I later realized, he was not in the least nervous in public appearances, but suffered all his life from neurasthenia, which, he used to say, caused his aunts to suspect him of leading a debauched life.

Did I speak to him after the lecture? I can't remember, for I was not to know that the sequel to this encounter would change my life; but I remember the fury with which I noticed a girl from one of the forms imitating his hands-uplifted gesture.

Otherwise the term fizzled out in disappointment. A case of mumps caused Miss Willis to give parents the option of bringing their daughters home early: Philippa and Alice both went, though I did not, and the joy of playing with them, for Miss Gunn, the slow movement of Bach's Concerto for Two Violins and Continuo was brought abruptly to an end. Much worse than this was that during the holidays Alice had a mastoid operation, from which she did not recover in time to return to Downe for her final term.

I became head Senior in the summer term, by virtue of the date of my birth, and slept in a corner room on the first floor of the main house, opposite to Miss Willis's study. I was to take the Higher Certificate during the term, but I remember no pressure of work: my immediate concerns were first, the summer play; second, the Berks, Bucks and Oxon music competition; and third, cricket, as I was in the First Eleven – but this was soon eclipsed by the play, *Much Ado about Nothing*. Miss Willis had cast the characters and invited a professional actress, Miss Raymond Barker, to produce it. I was cast as Verges, one of the comic Watch, but shortly after rehearsals began, Diana Hambro, cast as Beatrice, fell ill with mumps and (thanks to some prompting by Philippa, who was Benedick) I was tried for the part, and got it.

It was thrilling for us to be coached by a real professional, and for the next few weeks the play filled our thoughts – the more so because we all fell in love with Miss Raymond Barker. Even the fiasco of the first cricket match of the season (an away match, but I forget the school), did not weigh at all heavily on me, though perhaps it should have done, for our entire side made only a dozen runs (I, going in first, was out first ball), and Miss Willis made 'lack of morale' the subject of her sermon next day – an intrusion of ethical judgment into sport such as Father always derided.

All the badinage between Beatrice and Benedick seemed to come easily to Philippa and me, and I remember the swagger with which, persuaded that I was dying for love of her, she announced 'I will go get her picture.' But Beatrice's great climactic moment, when she cries *Kill Claudio!*, tested me beyond my powers. 'I know you are naturally a comic,' said Miss Raymond Barker to me, 'but for this scene you have to be in a towering rage.' And she made me sweep up and down the stone floor of the Greek theatre, as I declaimed 'Is he not approved in the height a villain… O God, that I were a man! I would eat his heart in the market-place.' This angry pacing was at least much easier to do effectively when I was clad in a beautiful long red dress rather than a djibbah: like all the hired costumes, it was superior to our usual turn-out, thanks to our professional producer, and I think the performance, on a fine day, was quite a good one. Mary (Guillemard) acted Claudio with passionate intensity; Mother and Father, who came over for the week-end (staying with Old Rugbeian friends at Chieveley) approved.

And now there were only three weeks to go for me before the Higher Certificate exam, and it was hard to settle down to work – especially when heartsick for our producer. Philippa and I confided in Olive, who was sympathetic, and answered our questions about her own youthful romantic feelings. But she did not invite Miss Raymond Barker a second time.

I did manage to work hard for the three weeks, and gained the certificate (in English, History and French) without strain. My lack of hard work in trying to improve my batting resulted in my being dropped from the First Eleven, and I captained the Second for the rest of the term. For the Berks, Bucks and Oxon Festival I think we went over to Abingdon, and we were judged by Ivor James, the cellist of the Menges Quartet. I was playing piano in a Mozart Trio with two younger and much more brilliant players, and in a violin sonata with Joyce Matthews, Philippa's companion at the first desk in the orchestra.

I don't remember where we came in the competition, though I know that kindly Ivor James praised the musical qualities of our playing.

Two more musical events were notable towards the end of term. First, a comic opera, *The Babes in the Wood*, which members of the Music Society had written and composed, was performed in the Greek theatre. This had been pushed to completion by a girl called Elizabeth Clay, who wrote a good deal of the music, and I think I only contributed some dialogue and the words of a song or two. But I enjoyed appearing over the ridge of the cloister roof (something I had always fancied doing) in the character of the Father – after which I expired, singing a mournful duet. (We repeated this performance during the summer holidays, at the home of Philippa's cousin Nancy James, Upwood Park, near Oxford.)

The crowning musical event was the visit of Myra Hess (a close friend of Marjorie Gunn and her sister Sazzie) to play the Bach D minor Piano Concerto with the orchestra. The weather was beautiful, and instead of having to huddle into the gym where we usually played, we were grouped round the piano in the middle of the cloister quadrangle. After the concerto, she played for us the piece for which she became famous: her arrangement of the Bach Chorale 'Herz und Mund und Tot und Leben' ('Jesu joy of man's desiring'), later hackneyed as a recording in crematoria chapels, but breathtaking when new-minted by her.

I could at that time have wished my schooldays to go on for ever. Though warned by Father that I should not dwell on a sequence of last-everythings and so 'wallow in the mire of self-pity', I found it painful to say good-bye to so many people I was fond of, and a community where I finally felt valued and at ease; moreover I had no clear idea of what I wanted to do or be. I certainly had no idea of becoming a poet, nor had I read much contemporary poetry, though I had responded to *Ash Wednesday* (then a new book) when Olive read it aloud to us one summer evening as we sat on the grassy banks near the chapel.

At my final 'jaw' Olive opined that I should probably marry, but not for some years, for the young men 'do like 'em sweet'. She did not repeat the criticism she had made in an earlier jaw, though it was still valid, that I was apt to be too much guided by my emotions – 'and the fact that these are generally good does not abolish the danger'.

Saying a pupil's good-bye to Olive, sad though it might be, was a prelude to a new relationship with her, and the first chapter of this was to begin at Aisholt in a few days' time. Her niece Mary (who was to stay on for one more term, her first as a Senior) had invited me and two other friends (Jean Wilson and Diana Hambro) to spend a week in one of the cottages which Olive owned there, and I was to go back with Mary to her home in Blackheath, before setting off for Somerset next day. This week was to change my life, and it must begin a new chapter.

CHAPTER III

AISHOLT AND ITALY August 1930

Aisholt is a village of farms and cottages lying on either side of a valley at the foot of a combe on the eastern face of the Quantock hills, ten miles from Bridgewater, and two or three from Nether Stowey, where Coleridge was living at the time when *The Ancient Mariner* was written. Olive Willis had loved the Quantocks since living near Taunton as a girl, and had acquired a cottage at Aisholt, either during or before the First World War. She came to add other cottages and farms almost (it seemed) like the growth of the British Empire, 'in a fit of absence of mind' – in fact to prevent unsuitable development. Holcombe, her original cottage, was some way up the valley close to the stream which ran down from the ridge (and became a rivulet after storms): the placing of small bedroom windows under the thatched roof made the cottage look, as Mary said, as if it was winking. As one walked up the path to the front door one met a spicy smell of wild garlic, and there was a spring of delicious water in the garden. I like to appropriate to this cottage the lines that Walter de la Mare wrote in the visitors' book belonging to Sir Henry Newbolt, who owned a cottage farther down the stream:

> Happy art thou to lie in that still room
> Under the thick-thatched eaves in Aisholt combe,
> Where sings the nightingale, where blooms the broom

The cottage we had been lent was designated as Miss Heather's, one of a row of three or four – the others occupied by farm workers. Thence one looked across the valley to the church high on the opposite side, where most of the houses clustered, and in that group was another belonging to Olive, where, as we soon learnt, Charles Williams was staying with his wife Michal and eight-year-old son – also Michael, but with an e. (Michal had been given her name by Charles, after Saul's daughter who mocked David when he danced before the Ark: the analogy was Michal's protest at Charles's chanting verse aloud in the street.)

We settled into our cottage, which had a Calor gas stove but no lighting except candles, very contentedly. Another amenity was a large rosemary bush by the front doorsteps, on which I liked to rub my fingers after washing up. Mary was the only one who was a competent cook, but as the weather was fine all week, we had most of our meals out of doors. Diana, only mentioned hitherto as suffering from mumps, came of a rather wealthier 'county' background than Mary, Jean or I did: she had an ebullient personality and a powerful brain (she went on to read moral philosophy at Cambridge), but at this stage at any rate she was no more sophisticated than we were – and was equally excited by the marvels of the place.

On our first morning we were eager to reach the moors, and walked up the lane which led along the hillside to Will's Neck, the highest point of the ridge, where there is a wonderful view away to the distant Malvern hills on one side, and the hills of Exmoor on the other. 'And ever Exmoor lay beautiful and hopelessly far, With unknown turrets and the named points.' Here a partridge flew ahead of us, simulating a broken wing to lure us from its nest; we picnicked in the heather and ate ripe bilberries. After picking some more for Olive, we descended by way of a path through the combe which would take us past her cottage, and left them there for her. As we walked on home we met Charles Williams in the lane: he moved politely aside but gave no greeting – a fact which afterwards distressed him, but why should he have recognized any of us?

By the next day he had learnt who we were, and was not much surprised when one after the other we jumped from a wall into the upper lane at his feet, as he and his family were returning from watching dowsers at Will's Neck. Some years afterwards, Charles wrote to me that he always confused this descent of ours with Keats' leaping over a stile on his first visit to the Lakes: 'Now tell me that he didn't and you didn't: it's no use, the meeting is fixed like that in my mind.'

We were all to meet for tea with Olive (and Lilian Heather) at a hut she owned, high up on the valley-side opposite the church. I sat there that afternoon on the wooden steps outside the hut, looking out over the 'green fields and happy groves', while Charles read aloud from the proofs of his *Heroes and Kings* (poems which included some from his first Arthurian cycle), and a whole new world opened out.

We were rash enough to invite Charles and Michal to supper the next day, primitive though our conditions were, for it was impossible to be shy with them. If his eloquence and erudition induced in us something of what he correctly named servile fear (as opposed to a proper awe), he had, as T. S. Eliot has remarked, the kind of personal humility that puts all others at their ease, and Michal herself was welcoming and not at all highbrow. It was as well that they were undemanding, for we discovered that the ham we had intended for supper was maggotty, and Mary had to improvise omelettes. We had fresh peas, though, and bilberry pie and cream. Another evening we all supped with Olive, and Charles read aloud his verse play, *The Chaste Wanton*; we met at church on Sunday; we walked along the valley in the dark, delighted that Charles picked out the place (known to us but not to him) where ghostly tremors from a Danish battle had been felt. And on our last evening we were invited to supper with Charles and Michal (young Michael being in bed, as children conveniently were in those days) and heard more Arthurian poems and, best of all, a poem written for us on the myths associated with our names: '*A Song of the Myths*, for Anne, Diana, Jean and Mary, made at their request.' (It was published in his *Three Plays* in 1931. I knew by then how powerful a word *myth* was for him: at first, equating 'myth' with 'legend', I had felt a shock of surprise at hearing him say: 'Effective as the myths of the New Testament are…')

Charles walked back with us to our cottage on this last evening: we said goodbye to him outside, opened the door and walked into a blackness which matched my feelings of blankness and loss.

There are life-changing episodes in our existence which are bound up with particular places. This week and Aisholt are connected and illuminated in such a way for me, so that every scene, every conversation, stands out in its physical setting. Wordsworth is of course the poet who has immortalized this experience, and although he is writing of the Lakes, the Quantock hills were also part of his vision.

> And O ye fountains, meadows, hills and groves,
> Forbode not any severing of our loves!
> Yet in my heart of hearts I feel your might:
> I only have relinquished one delight
> To live beneath your more habitual sway

It seems curious to me, as I explore my memory of the year 1930, that the great economic upheaval of that summer affected me and my family so little. My father of course was keenly interested in politics and, always a member of the Liberal party, had canvassed for the Liberals in Rugby. Now that we lived not far from the Hammonds, and Uncle Lawrence still wrote leaders for the *Manchester Guardian*, we had up-to-date political news, and he rang up Ringshall End when the National Government was formed and Britain left the Gold Standard. I answered the telephone, and he must have been surprised at my lack of excitement. I had not then formed the habit of reading a daily paper, and party politics seemed very remote from my interests. Financially speaking, the American crash did not affect our family, and the stay in Italy which we had long looked forward to was made all the easier by the strong position of the pound in relation to the lira.

We were to leave England in early October, but first I had planned one more expedition with school friends, and before that came a letter from Charles Williams enclosing a manuscript copy of *A Song of the Myths*. In my excitement it didn't occur to me to wonder at the labour it must have cost him to write out the quite lengthy poem five times – one for each of us, and one for Olive Willis...

In 1930, the Youth Hostel movement was just getting under way in England, and I had planned with Alice Stainer and Diana Hambro to use the hostels for a short walking tour along the South Downs during August. The only one we could find at the western end where we wanted to start was some miles from Petersfield station, where we arrived on a rainy afternoon, so we looked about for bed and breakfast, and finding none, appealed to the stationmaster, who offered to put us up for the night. After supper, we learnt that he played the violin, and Alice offered to accompany him, doing her best with the tattered jazz pieces he set before her. The next night we did sample the rather bleak hostel, of which we were the only occupants, and then had a ten-mile walk, mostly on the soft turf of the South Downs Way, till we descended at the village of Cocking. Here the innkeeper, a middle-aged woman very much the worse for drink (though in our inexperience we did not realize this at first), offered us a room with a triple-sized bed, and kept bursting in on our supper with admonitions not to look at her. 'If any of you pretty young ladies look at Old Mother, she will turn you out of the house.' In the dark house we found her rather alarming, and were glad to retreat to the large bed upstairs, where we discussed the meaning of life until sleep overcame us. Next morning she seemed quite normal, and told us of her early widowhood, and the temptations, in her situation, of the bottle.

Next day we walked on to Amberley, a welcoming place where a fine Sunday morning tempted us to loiter about there and return by rail next day, instead of walking on to Steyning as we had planned.

My parents' love-affair with Italy had begun during their early married life with two holiday trips, given them by the bachelor Rugby housemaster, Mr Michell, for whom HCB was house tutor. We planned to spend nearly three months in Florence, with Alice and Mother's recently widowed sister Ella David as our companions; Philippa was to join us for a stay in Rome, when Alice returned home at Christmas. Father had written for full-board terms to the Pensione Norchi, which was on the Lung' Arno della Zecca (= Mint), just where the road turns to go up to Settignano, so that the screech of tram-brakes punctuated our hours indoors. There we had two large and one single bed-sitting-rooms from which we looked across the road and river to the hillside of the Piazzale Michelangelo. We arrived late at night and tired after our 24-hour train journey, but woke with rapture to hear the church bells from across the river, and drawing back the curtains, to see the bells swinging clear from the open belfry, unlike the bells on an English Sunday morning.

The Norchi was an inexpensive family pensione, and I think we were the only English people during our stay. We had breakfast in our bedrooms, with lunch and dinner at our own table in the dining room: I think these were for residents only, for the fare was simple and rather monotonous – I swore I would never eat plain spaghetti with grated cheese again after this winter, though I enjoyed the other regular dish of polenta, and dessert was always delicious, even though Alice and I had not yet acquired my parents' passion for green figs. For tea-making in our sitting-room we had brought a little stove heated by slabs of *meta*, and we used to buy various delicious biscuits – *Diti d'Apostoli* and the like. Roast chestnuts from the hills of Vallombrosa could be bought at almost every street corner.

The weather continued as warm as a temperate English summer until mid-November; after that we found the indoor heating very inadequate, even though our standards at home were considered spartan by Americans. We had brought hot-water-bottles: when later on mine leaked, it became the subject of recurrent jokes from Maria, our cameriera: 'Lei ha fatto pipi.' Alice and I were on good enough terms with Maria, but our favourite was Nello, the waiter who brought us our piccola colazione of coffee and rolls, and would enter the room with a lyrical description of the weather: 'Che bella giornata per andare lontano lontano nel paese!' Nello was the first of the many charming, friendly Italian servants who have sweetened my times in Italy – and are still to be found when one moves aside from the package-holiday track.

I did keep a diary intermittently during our stay in Italy, but on reading it in later years I was so dismayed by its adolescent gushing that I destroyed it. I wish I had it now, to check my impression that we set off for San Miniato on that first morning, to exult in its superb view over the whole of Florence to Fiesole and the surrounding hills. Perhaps we only went as far as the Piazzale Michelangelo, where the view is nearly as good, but certainly San Miniato is in my mind as one of the first and indelible impressions of Florence: its beautiful green and white marble façade; its nave and raised choir with marble pillars also green and white, and luminous alabaster panel at the east end; and the exquisite Rossellini relief carving of the Madonna and Child in a side chapel – my first introduction to the genre.

I can also recapture the excited anticipation with which I first climbed the stairs to the Uffizi Gallery, knowing that I was going to see again the masterpieces I had seen in London, and making for the Botticellis first of all. Father was I think unusual in his generation in prizing Piero della Francesca above all other Italian painters: the Uffizi has the wonderful Montefeltro portraits and Triumph, and when I had seen other of his paintings I came to feel the same (with Bellini a close second). Bernard Berenson of course had already written influentially of Piero, but most of the guide books we had with us still held up Raphael's Madonnas for supreme admiration.

Our great good fortune in those days in Italy was, first, that all the galleries and museums were free (courtesy of Mussolini's wish to attract foreign tourists), so that there was no temptation to extend a visit to the

64

Anne aged 2 (*above*), 5 or 6 (*above right*), and 9 (*right*).

(*Left*) Dan Bradby in uniform. He died leading his company of the Rifle Brigade at the battle of Arras in 1917.

(*Below*) Matt Bradby in naval uniform, August 1917.

Family group: back row, John Milford, Edward, Christopher and Anne;
front row, HCB and VAB (Kit and Violet Bradby).

(*Above*) Anne aged 7 or 8.

(*Opposite*) Anne, left, as Beatrice in *Much Ado About Nothing* in the 'Greek Theatre' at Downe House, summer 1929.

(*Above*) Anne, right, and Audrey Wheeler performing *As You Like It* at School Field, Rugby. Anne as Autolychus in *A Winter's Tale*, School Field, Rugby.

Left to right: head of Patty Chitty, Matt holding Nicholas Phipps, Edward holding Jenifer (or ?Judy) Fisher-Williams, Christopher holding Anne, Christopher Chitty holding Prue Fisher-Williams.

Edward, Violet and Anne at Hillbrow, Rugby, in 1926 or 1927. Violet, Anne and Kit on the steps of School Field.

(*Above*) Violet, Kit and Olive Willis at Lerici.

(*Right*) Mary Wright (later Guillemard) at Ringshall, 1932.

Kit, Christopher, Jan, Violet and Edward at Ringshall.

Anne and Alice Stainer (later Pennant) at Fowey, Cornwall.

point of surfeit; second, that our stay was so long in comparison with the usual holiday. A short tram ride took us to the central area which held so many marvels apart from the Uffizi – think of it, all within a square half mile: the Piazza Signoria, which still displayed the original rather than a copy of Michelangelo's *David*, and Cellini's *Perseus* in the Loggia dei Lanzi; more Michelangelo in the Bargello, with the *Davids* of Donatello and Verrocchio; the Duomo with Uccello's *Condottiere* and, very dimly, Michelangelo's unfinished *Pieta*; Giotto's polychromatic Campanile, so startling to us at first sight (indeed Edward, when later we showed it to him, asked whether he was supposed to admire it); the Baptistry, with Ghiberti's and Andrea Pisano's bronze doors, not then cleaned; Michelangelo's Medici tombs in San Lorenzo; Benozzo Gozzoli's Magi Procession in the Riccardi Palace, as bright as if it had just been painted; the Singing Boys of Donatello and Della Robbia in the Duomo museum...

On our first exploration we walked to the centre via Santa Croce rather than taking the tram: the Giotto frescoes, much restored, were rather a disappointment; I imagine that later work improved them, before the floods of 1966 damaged them again. A short way up the hill, a day or two later, took us to the Convent of San Marco, to see the frescoes and altarpieces by Fra Angelico; these were the paintings that appealed to Edward above all others, when he came to stay at Christmas. On the other side of the Arno is the Carmine chapel with the Masaccio/Masolino frescoes (now splendidly restored) and the ornate Pitti palace, not a favourite place, but it contains the Giorgione *Concert*, now said to be by Titian, and wonderful portraits by him and by Raphael.

I have named only the works that appealed to me most on this first visit, and even so I have left out Santa Maria Novella, with the Brunelleschi Crucifix, the Ghirlandaio frescoes, and those of Uccello in the cloisters. It was on later visits that I was struck by the bold self-confidence of the new railway-station façade, built so close to the fifteenth-century Santa Maria Novella.

Our sight-seeing always started fairly promptly in the morning, because most of the churches and museums closed at noon for siesta. After lunch (generally at the pensione) we would set out again to walk or shop, or take the tram up to Settignano, or further, to Fiesole, with its

Roman amphitheatre, relief-carvings by Mino da Fiesole in the church, and the best vantage point from which to watch the sunset behind Florence. Once we walked up behind Fiesole into the ravine where the Serchio, a tributary of the Arno, flows; our strolls inside the town were sometimes to the Boboli Gardens or, once, to the Cascine Gardens where Shelley is said to have seen the autumn leaves as 'pestilence-stricken multitudes': an uninteresting park, we thought. After tea or in the evening Father would read aloud, Italian history, or art criticism – or Browning's *The Ring and the Book*. And Alice and I did pursue some rather low-powered Italian language studies with a young woman called Giovanna Calastri: sometimes we struggled with conversation on walks with her, or read the inevitable *I Promessi Sposi* (novel by Manzoni), in which Mother joined us. I had learnt some Italian at school – one lesson a week for two terms – and I now began to read Dante with Wicksteed's homely parallel translation; Alice had not learnt it at school, but we could both understand enough for conversations with Maria, on trains and so on. I regret not having acquired the fluency that staying in a family would have given. Father, who knew the language well for reading purposes, was tongue-tied when he tried to speak; Mother, who actually knew rather less, employed her vocabulary with great panache, though occasionally falling into traps as when, conducting a railway-platform conversation about Protestant beliefs, she assured our fellow-passenger that we believed in Jesus 'ma non nelle Pape' ('we do not believe in breasts'). You may wonder at our lack of contact with young people. We must have had one introduction, for I remember one tea-party where the seniors were in one room and the juniors in another, but it was a very starched affair and did not lead to more contacts. We also went (unwillingly except for Mother and Aunt Ella) to an English expatriate tea-party, where I tried to talk to a deaf lady whose hearing aid consisted of a disc held against her teeth, so that she could not listen and eat at the same time. There was quite a large English colony, with a church which we attended on Sundays. (It was not till Assisi and Verona, I think, that we attended whole Roman Catholic services, apart from hearing fragments of a Mass or intercession.)

Sometimes we went on longer expeditions, taking the train a few stations away: to climb Monte Morello; to visit Pistoia and Prato, where there were frescoes by Filippo Lippi, or the Certosa monastery where we must have bought green Chartreuse (perhaps that was reached by bus), or Impruneta, a village in the hills west of Florence: there we were lucky enough to coincide with a Festa and a fine Church procession (with *baldacchino*, and Brothers of the Misericordia in their cowls). I also saw there for the first time the sale of little song-birds strung on a pole: on walks in the hills we had already lamented as we heard the singing of caged finches as decoy-birds.

By catching an early train we were able to get to Pisa for the day, with its dazzling Campo Santo so compactly placed, and time to ascend the Leaning Tower. To Siena we went for a whole week-end, and our train journey took us through the mountains so much fought over by Guelphs and Ghibellines. From our lodgings we could see the black-and-white tower of the cathedral, and a short walk took us to the centre – the Campo where the famous race is run, and the Mangia tower (named after a celebrated bell-ringer), behind which there was a workshop where they were beating copper vessels. I bought a large and a small copper jug there: the small one I gave to Charles and Michal Williams; in the large one, which now holds Jane's beech leaves, I packed my pyjamas on our subsequent travels. My memory of our stay is overlaid by our visit of a few years ago, but some of the same works of art are supreme in both recollections: the Pisano pulpit and the mosaic pavement in the cathedral; its Piccolomini Library with Pinturicchio's delightful frescoes of the life of Aeneas Silvius, the second Piccolomini pope, and its museum, with the Duccio Madonna. We spent one day on a visit to San Gimignano with its thirteen competing towers, and there I was anxious to see the Ghirlandaio fresco in the cathedral, of Santa Fina lying on her board, because Olive Willis had sent me a postcard of it when I was lying ill with mastoid.

Back in Florence, where we now felt very much at home, we resumed our pleasant routine, and visited some of the less famous sights – a convent with paintings by Orcagna, for instance. We went to orchestral concerts by the resident symphony orchestra, conducted by Vittorio Gui: classical programmes, but Mussolini had decreed that each concert must contain at least one modern work. I think I applaud this measure, but alas, I do not remember enjoying any of the works so included.

The strutting Fascists, of course, were ever visible: we loathed the regime, but were obliged to the benefits it brought us as tourists. English friends, too, who were not concerned in politics, continued their lives as usual. We were invited to lunch at the Villa Medici by Percy Lubbock, while Kitty Calderon (widow of Father's close friend George Calderon) was staying with him and the invalid Lady Sybil, who spent most of her time lying in a darkened room. Percy Lubbock would memorize quantities of poetry and prose to say to her with no need for a light. I regret to say that I remember nothing of the villa interior: I only remember the dried-up lawn, which Percy told us had to be re-seeded every spring.

I mentioned Kinta Waterfield in the previous chapter as our school-fellow at Downe. Her parents were old friends of Olive: he a landscape painter and architect, she a superior journalist – correspondent in Italy of the *Observer*. They had bought and renovated a castle at Aulla in the Carrara mountains (Lina Waterfield wrote of it in her autobiographical *Castle in Italy*), and she had later inherited from her aunt Janet Ross a Renaissance mansion in Settignano, Poggio Gherardo, which was the setting for Boccaccio's *Decameron*. Unfortunately the Waterfield parents were away that winter, so that we never saw inside Poggio Gherardo, but Kinta was staying with friends, and came once to take Alice and me for a drive up to the chestnut woods of Vallombrosa.

Kinta has written *A Tuscan Childhood* about her upbringing in the castle at Aulla which was a revelation to those of us who were her contemporaries at Downe, where she seemed to have little to offer beyond her striking good looks. Evidently the gulf between her existence in Italy, where the peasant children were her companions, and her school environment, was too great for her to be able to bridge it verbally, and we never unlocked the deep knowledge of Italian peasant life which is shown in her autobiography. She was sent to Downe very young, before she had even learnt to read English properly, so was always at a disadvantage academically, and she left before reaching the sixth form, under a cloud because of some petty thieving – those who knew about it were sworn to secrecy. I shared a room with her one term, and felt ashamed when I read her book (written with the help of her son) that I had never penetrated to the reserves of her childhood knowledge. I did

68

however make some amends for my obtuseness after I had read it, and before her death a year or so ago. Alice had got to know her rather better – or anyhow had shown more sympathy – and was invited to go to Aulla for a couple of nights – a visit from which she returned with much relief, as Kinta seemed terrified of her father.

Alice and I had a hired piano in our room, on which we practised and played duets; another pleasure we shared was by turns to choose and read to each other a poem out of my *Oxford Book of English Verse*, the last thing before going to sleep. Now as Christmas approached we had to say good-bye, as she and Aunt Ella were to travel back to England together, their places being taken by Philippa and Dorothy Read (inspiring Downe House teacher of singing and piano). Aunt Ella, who was a good many years older than Mother, must often have found our activities tiring, but I don't remember that she ever complained. I viewed her with my youthful intolerance of Milford aunts and uncles (Uncle Humphrey always excepted), but I think I did recognize the courage with which she put her sorrow aside and enjoyed the months in Florence.

We had booked rooms for Christopher and Edward too – Christopher on holiday from Amen House, and Edward after his first term teaching at Merchant Taylors' School, then still at its London site. At dinner on Christmas Eve the Norchi family produced a Christmas tree for their guests (it seems to me that we were the only ones), with cards and a statuette of Canova's *Three Graces*, dubbed by Christopher the Three Disgraces. After dinner, knowing that Miss Read was a piano teacher, they asked her to perform on their parlour piano, which rather flustered her, as she had no piece in her head; and then a Norchi niece played endless sentimental waltzes, until we enquired whether perhaps she might not be tired? No, they assured us, 'non e mai stanca' – and at last we escaped upstairs, to sing some carols from the just-published *Oxford Carol Book* which Dorothy Read had brought with her.

She had also brought a few madrigals, and our best effort in parts was Weelkes' four-part setting of the Collect 'Let thy merciful ears, O Lord', Philippa taking the soprano, I the alto, Edward the tenor and Christopher the bass. One day when we were in the Spanish Chapel at Santa Maria Novella, with no other tourists around, DR suggested that we should try singing it in the resonant chapel. By now we had it by heart, and the result sounded so fine that DR was enraptured, and often reverted to it as having been one of her best musical experiences.

Kinta invited my brothers, Philippa and me to a party at the Berensons' house 'I Tatti', which she and her brother John were occupying for the holidays. We were supposed to go in fancy dress, and after snacks we played 'Murder', which I found very tantalizing, as the lights were sure to go out just as I had focused on some special masterpiece in the corridor. But a truly damp party was given on New Year's Eve by Mother's distant cousins the Dursts, who lived in the Casa Guidi, once the home of Robert and Elizabeth Browning. Games were intended but not planned, and we found ourselves obliged both to suggest and organize them.

A day or two later, we all set off for Rome, peering excitedly through the carriage windows as we passed Lake Trasimene in the darkness, and imagined the battle there between the Romans and Hannibal's army. Our arrival, however, was farcical. In those days of plentiful porters, they had established a tariff of about 5 lire for every package they could lay their hands on, however tiny – hence our exit from a carriage was generally a battle to keep hold of as many parcels as we could. The pensione we were bound for, the Primavera, was within walking distance of the station, and their factotum was waiting for us with a trolley. But Father refused to pay the exorbitant sum demanded by the railway porter, who pursued us, expostulating, as we followed the trolley (my copper jug hanging from the handles), while Father kept putting his hand in his pocket and drawing it out again, empty, until finally he gave in. And then what a disappointment awaited us! The Primavera had been recommended by some Rugby master, and proved to be a complete Englishman's Home from Home, both the clientele and the cooking. I remember that the wallpaper of a gaudy all-over pattern covered even the doors in the bedrooms, so that you felt imprisoned; and in one of them we sat for a council of protest, while Father tried to counter our disgust by quoting *Paradise Lost*: 'The mind is its own place, and of itself Can make a heaven of hell, a hell of heaven.' But No, we said, we can *not* stay in this dreary place for our two precious Roman months, and the next day we set out to look for somewhere better. And there our luck was in. At the top of the Spanish Steps in the Piazza Trinita dei Monti on the

Pincian Hill we found the Pensione Pfister, kept by two Swiss sisters, who could give us two double rooms on the first floor, one of which opened on to a roof garden with a wonderful view over roof-tops to the Pantheon and the more distant Michelangelo dome of St Peter's. The sisters could also take the rest of our party for the next few days.

Father had the unpleasant task of extricating us from the Primavera, which he did with some compensatory payment. We could not have chosen a better place to stay than the Pfister, for apart from the charm and the centrality of its position, the meals were far more varied and to our liking than those at the Norchi, and each day began well with delicious Swiss cherry jam for breakfast. We had the park on the Pincian Hill and the gardens of the Villa Borghese close at hand, and were within easy walking distance of the Pantheon and the Piazza del Popolo, with Pinturicchio frescoes in the church there. On the Spanish Steps, not crowded then as now, were the first spring flowers for sale – especially violets from Lake Nemi – and at its foot was an English bookshop where I bought (and devoured) the early poems of Robert Graves. And there, as well as the sad house where Keats died, was a puppet theatre where we saw the amazing armoured conflicts of 'Podrecca's Piccoli'.

The Forum and the Vatican were to be reached by a bus, frequent but filled to bursting (just as nowadays), and on our first journey we did not realize that on entering you had to start pushing your way to the front immediately, in order to get off where you wanted. Once we got the hang of it, we found the bus service excellent and cheap. The traffic even then seemed very noisy, partly because the Fascists had decreed that horns should be sounded at every intersection: Italians were happy to obey this even on empty roads late at night.

In those days the door which gave access to the Vatican from St Peter's Square was not unlocked for tourists, and one had to walk on weary feet all round the building to the back, drenched (it seemed every time we went) by water-spouts from the roof. The Sistine chapel was quite uncrowded, and no one prevented me from reclining on the bench to survey the ceiling. In the galleries I remember particularly, besides the Raphael *Stanze*, the Melozzo da Forlì *Angels,* and the sinister portrait of the Borgia pope and others.

In St Peter's, Michelangelo's *Pieta* (carved when he was twenty-five) is close to the entrance, and by contrast with its stark simplicity, the stupefying ornateness of the huge building was what struck me most. 'Stupefying' was also the word I applied (following Father's opinion) to the clouds of incense smoke we saw covering some cardinals in the Choir. My description of this visit in a letter to Charles Williams called forth a protest from him: 'Your Cardinals may be trying to be safe, but what in the end do we all desire but safety in the truth? The Mother and Mistress of all Churches is not what she might be, but then, as Chesterton wrote –

> If she on earthly props must lean
> Of earthly fame and ancient arts,
> Put up with Raphael and Racine,
> Make shift with Dante and Descartes,
> Not wholly will she hide her grief,
> But touch the wound and murmur sadly
> "These lesser things are theirs to love
> Who lose the love of Mr Bradley."'

I took the protest to heart, but I was not really convinced: it was not until I had experienced Assisi, and Good Friday at Verona, that I learnt to appreciate the liturgies of Roman Catholicism.

Walks in the Forum and on the Capitoline were enlivened by Father's knowledge of Roman history and his translations of Latin inscriptions – also, on the Palatine, by his delight in the brave flowering of the Iris stylosa during the coldest days of winter. The weather, in fact, was soon warm enough for us to eat picnic lunches in the sun and out of the wind, and I remember sitting out of doors in various nooks, reading Shakespeare from the tiny three-volume edition which had Dan's name on the flyleaf.

There were concerts with famous conductors in the Augusteo (the hall made from the mausoleum of Augustus), and Philippa and I queued and stood to hear Adolf Busch play and Klemperer conduct. She was taking weekly violin lessons from a well-known teacher named Corti, and I sometimes accompanied her in the basement of our pensione where there was a piano. We all went to a staged performance of Berlioz' *Faust*, a most unusual chance, and the music was then unknown at least to Philippa and me. There were elaborate flying arrangements for Margaret's soul, I recall. Thinking of those times, and of the solace that music always was to us in times of *angst*, I wrote in a poem for her:

JUBILATION

Flames upon your forehead still
And warms me, as when we emerged from school,
With bursting hearts, inquisitive eyes,
Perplexed at evil, dazzled with joys,
To travel wrapped in our own concerns
And see great cities on our own terms;
Our growing-pains compressed within
The marvellous walls of a violin.

We made several expeditions to the Alban Hills south of Rome by slow tram, used by the country folk and therefore with many stops on the way. Our first was to a village called Rocco di Papa, whence we planned to walk over the slopes of Monte Cavo to Albano and return from there. As we set off from the tram terminus we were surrounded and pursued by about thirty ragamuffins demanding soldi, and we did not shake them off till we had gone half a mile or more. Until I lived in London, beggars were an unfamiliar sight to me, and the poverty we saw in Italy troubled my conscience, but Father, an active member of the Charity Organization Society, would never give to a beggar in the street.

Our way led through fields of dark violets which scented the air, and we had splendid views over the Campagna towards the sea and down to Lake Nemi, bright green like a tarn among the surrounding volcanic tufa mountains.

Another day, a visit to Frascati produced the most delicious wine I tasted in Italy; and best of all were Hadrian's Villa, and Tivoli beyond it. The villa, laid out like a small town by the Emperor to recall by monuments in stone and water the scenes of his travels, was fascinating even then, though much of what I saw on a later visit in 1976 had not yet been excavated. At Tivoli the Villa d'Este, so glowingly described by Georgina Masson in her book on Italian gardens, must have been closed, for I remember only that we picnicked on a hillside above a deep ravine, where we heard the sound of pipe music. Philippa wandered off and encountered the shepherd who was playing, and was given (or bought?)

one of his wooden pipes.

Ostia Antica at the mouth of the Tiber could be reached by train, and we spent a whole day there, picnicking among fragmentary ruins among the cypresses (not the endless brick buildings that Vivian and Colin found in 1976), and dabbling in the underground canals, making gentle ripples which caused the water-snails to grate against the walls. The one expedition, hoped for by Father, which we failed to make, was to Monte Soracte, mentioned by Horace, seen far away to the east of Rome.

My parents' old friend Bessie Johnson had asked them to visit the landscape painter Carlandi who had been her teacher, and to choose one of his paintings as a present from her. We enjoyed our visit to his studio, but found it slightly embarrassing that we all preferred his earlier paintings to the recent work which he showed us. Edward now has the one we chose, of birch trees beside the Tiber.

We were no luckier in our choice of an Italian teacher than we had been in Florence: this time she was middle-aged, and her idea of a reading-book was a bound volume of an Italian version of the *Boys' Own Paper*. We did not persevere with her for long, and apart from the newspaper I think Dante was the only Italian I read while in Rome. We were much aware of the Fascists, of course, faced with Mussolini's grandiose Vittorio Emmanuele monument whenever we went to the Piazza Venezia, and one day some of our party saw the arrival there, among cheering crowds, of the aeronaut Balbo from a much-hyped Atlantic flight. He later fell into disgrace, and was I think imprisoned for a time.

When in early March it was time to say good-bye to Rome, I took a long walk to visit for the last time some of my favourite works and places. I started with the *Pieta* in St Peter's, and returned across the Tiber by the Castel Sant' Angelo, ending in the Piazza del Popolo with the *Nativity* by Pinturicchio, where a goat is leaping over a precipice in fright at the song of an angel, high in the sky. You may notice that I have said nothing here about mosaics, which so impressed me on my later visit. Certainly I have left out many things which did excite me, such as the coloured marble inlays by the Cosmati brothers in many churches (at San Clemente in particular, where it is fascinating to see Christianity superimposed upon the worship of Mithras); Michelangelo's *Moses*; and the Greek *stelae* in the museum at the Baths of Diocletian. Moreover mosaics, in the dark churches before spot-lighting was installed, were not nearly so striking as now. But it is a fact that I did not really appreciate them at that stage. As to the Baroque architecture which Rome is so rich in, it repelled me at that time, and I still have to make an effort to enjoy it.

So we left Rome for Assisi, which I was to revisit quite soon, but I did not see Rome again for forty-six years. When the train drew in at Assisi, our baggage had to be hurled after us from the carriage windows to get it out before the train started off again – a timing which continues to this day, as I have learnt from other travellers. Then a taxi took us up the hill to the Hotel Subasio (not at all grand in those days), where Sabatier had stayed when he was writing his *Life of St Francis*. From our bedrooms we looked across the plain to Perugia, whose lights we could see twinkling at night. And at the end of our first-floor corridor was a little room, with a large table and an end window looking down on to the piazza and its encircling cloister, which leads to the great church and monastery of San Francesco, riding out from the hillside. It is built of the rose-coloured stone from Monte Subasio, some fragments of which we have on our chimneypiece. No one else came to this little room, and we used it as our sitting-room.

Each day we could walk across the piazza to the church and study the frescoes, or sit to hear the monks at their orisons. In the dark lower church we peered at the *Life of St Martin* by Simone Martini, a Cimabue Madonna and other works by Lorenzetti and Giotto's pupils; in the upper church, bathed in light, is Giotto's *Life of St Francis*.

We walked down to the little hillside church of San Damiano, or up to the castle above the town, which Mother sketched from the road at the back. One day, we climbed to the top of Monte Subasio, passing St Francis's Hermitage on the way, and where we halted to look back from above it, Mother recognized the blue Anemone hepatica, with its liver-shaped leaves, in flower. Just below the snow-line were sheets of purple crocus, and an eagle (which Philippa said she mistook for a turkey) flew up as we approached. Father enjoyed a sorbet of snow with his orange, and we had egg sandwiches made by folding an omelette into the bread – a speciality of our French Maître d'Hôtel at the Subasio.

We went to Perugia for the day by bus, and were thrilled to discover Piero della Francesca's *Annunciation*, not signalled by our Baedeker and so not anticipated, leaning up against the wall in the picture gallery. Otherwise, I remember the great fountain with sculpture by Nicola and Giovanni Pisano, and the view back to Assisi on its mountain. One night, on the Feast of Sant' Antonio, the plain between the two towns sparkled with small bonfires.

Towards the end of our three weeks at Assisi, Philippa's mother Angela James came to stay for a couple of days before taking Philippa home. They were to visit the minute State of San Marino on their way, and we went with them by car as far as Spello, at the other end of the Subasio ridge, where there are still more Pinturicchio frescoes, of the *Annunciation* and *Nativity*.

Our final destination was Verona, vivid to me already in imagination as the place where Dante spent his exile and learnt 'Si come sa di sale Lo pane altrui' etc. ('How bitter the bread and how hard the ascent and descent of the stairs in another's house'). We spent Holy Week and Easter there, nine days in all, and the Good Friday ceremony of 'creeping to the Cross' in the Cathedral impressed me very much: some of my Protestant prejudice had already vanished in Assisi. The picture gallery in Verona is especially delightful, in a castle built by Can Grande II alongside a bridge over the river Adige: one sees the pictures (which include my favourite Bellini *Madonna and Child*) as though in their natural setting. In the church of Santa Anastasia there is a delightful St George and the Dragon by Pisanello; and best of all is the twelfth-century church of San Zeno, with its carved Lion Porch and Mantegna's triptych of the Madonna and Saints, bordered by fruit and flowers. Napoleon stole this triptych, and the predella panels are still in the Louvre and at Tours.

We sat in the beautiful terraced Giardini Giusti, and explored the Roman amphitheatre; and we went for the day to Mantua in its drab surroundings, where the ducal palace of the Gonzagas contains the wonderful Mantegna Camera Picta, showing members of the household, painted when he belonged to their court in the sixteenth century. Tantalizingly, we had to join a guided tour which lingered over all sorts of things we didn't want to see, and gave us only about ten minutes with the Mantegna. Nevertheless, it was a memorable day.

So ended our Grand Tour.

With the summer at home ahead of me, I still had no clear idea of what I wanted to do. Charles Williams (henceforth referred to as CW) sympathized, for as a young man he had felt the same, and classing himself as a 'second-rate sensitive mind not at unity with itself' (Tennyson's description) he wrote: 'There do seem to be an awful lot of us about the world!' Journalism seemed a possibility, and King's College London offered a two-year course leading to a diploma, which included some lectures designed for the degrees in English and History, as well as criticism of literature and art. Father went up with me to see Professor G. B. Harrison, the Shakespeare scholar, who accepted me to start in the autumn, though thinking that I should really be taking an English degree. (At London University this involved a whole year taking the Intermediate exam, of general studies, so it did not attract me, and in any case my lack of Latin ruled it out.)

Uncle Lawrence Hammond suggested that in the meantime I should go to Germany to learn the language, which would have been valuable, but I had no inclination to learn German at that time, and decided to stay at home and equip myself with typing and shorthand. I mastered the theory of both from books, and went down to Berkhamsted for three or four typing speed lessons from a lady who used a gramophone to tap out the rhythm (a regularity which I soon lost). I also went to London once a week for violin lessons from Marjorie Gunn at her house in Abbey Road near Lords, after which I played second fiddle in Haydn Quartets with Nancy Hawksley (later Dick Milford's wife) and other of her pupils, to my great enjoyment. Edward taught me to drive our Morris Oxford: no more than two or three outings were needed, for it was so easy on the quiet roads of those days, the only tricky part being to double de-clutch without scrunching the gears, before the invention of the fluid flywheel. My licence, acquired without a test and valid to this day, entitled me to drive all kinds of motor vehicles, including a tractor.

It was blissful (apart from the *angst* of adolescence) to spend a whole summer at Ringshall, exploring the beechwoods and chalk downs. I got to know the summer flora of our countryside, although I affected in those days to think it pedantic to know their names: the little yellow cistus and purple field gentian on the short turf of the downs, toadflax and ladies' bedstraw, and rest-harrow in the scrub woodland behind our house. In those woods I could occasionally see a grey-mottled nightjar flying, though never close enough to see the bristles round its mouth with which it traps insects. We regularly heard its 'jarring' at night, but never any nightingale – at 700 feet we were too high for that. In spring our rarity among flowers grew on one steep chalk slope: the purple Anemone pulsatilla with its long eyelashes.

The ecstasy of our black mongrel sheepdog Pooh added to the pleasure of those walks. (He had been named by the Lockharts at Sedbergh who had acquired and house-trained him for us while we were in Italy.) As I sat reading or thinking one day on a spur of the hillside he must have run off hunting, for a pair of green woodpeckers displayed their courting dance a few feet away from me, circling each other and wagging their heads from side to side.

When it was hot we would drive down to Tring Reservoir, five miles across the plain for a bathe. Our croquet lawn at the side of the house had been mown by short rushes with the hand machine, and gave us many delightful games of 'golf croquet'. And I think that by this time the tennis court behind the kitchen garden had been mown and marked out. You had to keep a sharp eye on the ball for eccentric bounces, and we never invited outsiders to play on it, but we had great fun with family tennis, especially when Uncle Humphrey came to stay. Mother still played in family doubles – excellent at the net, and capable of dramatic shots by throwing her racket at the ball. Father served under-arm as in 'real' tennis, with deadly accuracy. Some of our neighbours who invited us to tennis parties had equipment hardly of Wimbledon standard: at one, I noticed Father surreptitiously pacing the court to find out why so many of his shots were going out; sure enough, it was a couple of feet short; and at another, our hostess said: 'I can at least vouch for the balls – they're pre-war'! At Potten End, home of the Cohen family, Father and I were playing against our host and his daughter Ruth, later head of a Cambridge college. Old Mr Cohen regularly pronounced our serves 'out', and Ruth as regularly contradicted him with 'Nonsense Father, that was well inside the line.'

Although by the map Ringshall End was actually in the parish of Ivinghoe, down in the plain below Ivinghoe Beacon, Little Gaddesden was our local church, and Father and Mother were soon active in its affairs – the Church School among them, where Father became a governor. We made friends with the Barkways at the Vicarage – parents and two grown-up sons. Because the adult students at Ashridge House attended Little Gaddesden church, the Church authorities always chose an intellectual as its vicar, and Canon Barkway was a very interesting preacher. Mrs Barkway was an invalid, and could not play much part in the village; the elder son Oswald was bound for the ministry, and was described by his father as dangerously parsonical already; the other son, Michael, was my age, and healthily critical of his father. He went on to join the BBC under Sir John Reith.

When we arrived at Ringshall, a battle was going on between the Diocese and the owner, called Cuthbertson, of the land on which the church was built. He wished to put up a marble tombstone in the cemetery, whereas the Diocese had decreed (for aesthetic and economic reasons) that all outside monuments must be of stone. Poor pacific Canon Barkway was caught in the middle of the row, and in a face-to-face encounter Cuthbertson had threatened to knock him down; further, Cuthbertson fenced the space round the church gates so that cars, which had to drive a quarter of a mile along the field-road to reach the church, had no room to turn round when they got there. After mattins one Sunday, Christopher, Edward and I pulled up this fence, as others had done before us, and the village policeman, on watch behind a hedge, came out and took our names.

In the end it was discovered that Cuthbertson had infringed a right of way for coffins to enter the churchyard, so the fence had to be removed, but he proceeded to put up a marble tombstone just outside the cemetery, on his own land. He also put up several notices: 'Beware of the Bull', though no bull was ever seen to graze there.

Towards the end of the summer, Alice Stainer invited me and a group of her Downe House friends to stay for some days at High Kingsbury, her sister Lib's and David Milford's house in Marlborough, while they were away. I remember that Margaret Freeman was one of the party, with an ominous account of Nazi influence in Austria, where she had been pursuing her training as an artist. (That was the last time she and I saw each other, though we have corresponded lately: she tells me that she has my poems by her bedside, and she sent me a photograph of a most beautiful-looking quilt, designed and made by her, for which she won a national prize.)

In September came the annual Three Choirs Festival, held that year in Gloucester, at which Robin's oratorio *A Prophet in the Land* had been chosen for performance, and my parents, Edward and I were able to be there with the Milford and Stainer contingent. The Oxford University Press had published the *Prophet* beforehand, and Edward and I had tried a good deal of the delightful music, including the 'Pipe Tunes' which I attempted on a bamboo pipe I had made. (The one piece still played from the work is the prelude on the tune 'St Columba', which is included in a collection of organ pieces for wedding voluntaries.)

Just before driving over to Gloucester, I received from CW a copy of his new novel, *The Place of the Lion*, which Victor Gollancz had published in his cheap 'Mundanus' series, hoping for a wide sale. Its theme, brilliantly worked out, is the loosing upon the world of elemental beasts, Plato's *archetypes*: it is still my favourite among CW's novels.

We had decided that it would be best for me to live in the King's College Hostel near Hyde Park, at any rate for the first year of my diploma course. I had been interviewed by the lady Warden, and told that I should be sharing a room with one other student. I found the Warden rather prim and conventional, but I have always been grateful to her for her choice of a room-mate for me – Joyce George.

CHAPTER IV

King's College Hostel for women students was in Queensborough Terrace, a mid-nineteenth-century development for the well-to-do, near Queens Gate (now Queensway) station on the Central line, with Hyde Park just across the main road. Many of our neighbours were still well-heeled, and could be seen in their furs taking their Pekinese dogs out to relieve themselves after dark. The lady Warden, whose name I have forgotten, was much concerned with discipline, and the notice-board in the hall seemed to me to be over-full of prohibitions. You had to obtain permission from her and give reasons if you wanted to be out after 10 pm; there was a rota for sitting at her table at mealtimes, and I remember one notice deprecating something about the way we were arranging this, 'as though it were an onerous duty to sit on High'. After a year of freedom from all rules, I found the atmosphere irksome; but what chiefly depressed me was the attitude of the other students there who were studying English literature: they seemed to treat the poetry as merely a task to be got through on the way to qualifying as a teacher, never as a source of inspiration or pleasure.

I took an instant liking to Joyce George, as she did to me, though she told me afterwards that the reproduction of one of Melozzo da Forlì's Angels which I hung in my corner of the room made her fear our tastes might not agree. (She had a reproduction of a Dutch interior or something of the kind.) Joyce was about to study medicine, having passed her First MB at school, and was engaged to a Norwich bank clerk. Her daily reports during the year we spent together, on the progress she was making in her dissection of a human body, were fascinating (her subject had evidently had arthritis, I recall), and she brought back a piece of skin for her father, who managed a tannery in Norwich, so that he could test its response to the tanning process. How could either of us have thought what horrors such an experiment would later imply? Joyce was tall and fair, with a strong face: her engagement to a bank clerk seemed to her anything but glamorous, but Douglas was also a talented artist (he ultimately gave up banking for sculpture), and their marriage after their long, long engagement was a very happy one.

On the first day of term, I merely had to register and attend a service in St Clement Danes, the island church opposite the College gates. It was exciting to make my own way about London, and I soon put on the nonchalant air of a habitué as I changed trains or waited for a bus. The sermon in St Clement Danes was preached by Billy Temple, who had lately become Archbishop of York. He was a familiar name to me from Rugby, though I had never seen him: I was surprised by his boyish-looking face and impressed by his directness and sincerity, telling us of the great opportunity we were offered. I had lunch in the very cheap College cafeteria (I think I managed to spend only 6d), and then, waiting in the queue to register, I saw Audrey Wheeler from Downe appear, looking a brightly-feathered fowl among our drab flock, and (no doubt urged on by her godmother Olive Willis) intending to take the Journalism Diploma. (I too had some bright feathers, though never so smart as Audrey, for Olive had given me a piece of hand-woven green tweed for a dress, and I had a becoming small black hat with a feather.) In fact Audrey only stayed for a few weeks, but it was agreeable to have her there at the start.

Our preliminary lecture, the next day, was given by Jack Isaacs, author of (among other books) *Shakespeare as Man of the Theatre.* I remember part of the lecture vividly, and I was totally won over to his point of view. Now, he said, was our opportunity to study poetry with the passion it deserved; 'later on, your emotions will begin to creak'. He spoke of contemporary poets he knew – Edgell Rickword, Edith Sitwell – or had known – Isaac Rosenberg, whom he had met all too briefly before his death in the war, when Isaacs was an officer and Rosenberg a private. 'He was afraid of my uniform, and I was afraid of his poetry.' Later in the term Isaacs lectured on Milton, with much emphasis on the music of Milton's verse – something that he was well qualified to illustrate, for he had a beautiful speaking voice and was one of the best readers of poetry I have ever heard. I still hear certain lines of Shakespeare, Drayton, Donne as spoken by him. He recommended that we should read *Paradise Lost* through at a sitting, as he had been obliged to do (having put off reading it) just before his Finals. Jack Isaacs was portly and very Jewish-looking, with heavy-lidded eyes that surveyed you, blinking, critically. He would then have been in his early 'thirties I suppose; a few years later he married the College librarian and they had two daughters.

I soon realized that among the Journalism students – about twenty-five in number – were two very congenial girls from South Africa, Grace Harvey and Kay Harrison: their families were friends, and Kay's parents had come to London to chaperone them, living in, as far as I remember, a boarding house in Highgate. I became very close to Grace, whose excitement over our discoveries in English literature was as great as my own, though I teased her sometimes over her romantic tastes. The three of us sat together at lectures, and groaned with disapproval when the male students (especially the medics) began to stamp their feet whenever a lecturer made the faintest reference to sex.

Professor G. B. Harrison lectured on the Elizabethans. He was urbane and lucid, but one rarely felt that his interest was fully engaged by what he was saying, and when in later years I had occasion to examine some texts he had edited, I found him rather a lazy editor. By comparison with H. V. Routh, however, he was vitality itself: Dr Routh merely delivered word for word the substance of a book he had published on, I think, the modern drama.

Our essential books for the study of aesthetics were Aristotle's *Poetics* (of course), Lessing's *Laokoön* and Longinus's *On the Sublime and Beautiful.* Jack Isaacs talked to us about contemporary art and about the cinema: he had helped to move the camera about for Pabst at the filming of *Kameradschaft*, and had heard Eisenstein talk about *montage*. He knew actors and actresses – admired Edith Evans but pronounced her not as intelligent as she thought she was; criticized the mannerisms of John Gielgud in recording 'To be or not to be', and quoted a German producer as saying that no actor under forty should attempt Lear (as Gielgud was then doing, still in his twenties: I saw him and thought him wonderful); urged us to see the Habima Players and the Compagnie des Quinze. He sent us off to the Tate Gallery to bring back postcards of what interested us, and to say why; also to choose contemporary poems and read them aloud. He said that if some contemporary writing repelled us, we might have to overcome our own prejudices: he had had to do this in his youth with D. H. Lawrence; we might have to make a similar leap with, say, E. M. Forster. He also warned us in our reading of novels not to be 'hypnotized by the story' so that our critical faculties went to sleep. Once, only once, he not only set us an essay but also corrected it. I've forgotten the subject, but I remember a marginal note in mine: 'You make some very good points. Try to weld your material into a less jerky argument' – advice which I have been trying to follow till this day.

(I think Jack Isaacs was not entirely approved of by his academic colleagues. While I was working for Eliot, with whom he was friendly, a letter came from him asking for a testimonial towards a professorship in London: he didn't get the job, and went out to Jerusalem. When he was again in England looking for work, F. P. Wilson spoke of him rather disparagingly to me. But he did in the end get a professorship, at Queen Mary College.)

The purely journalistic part of our curriculum was farcical. We were lectured to once a week by a sub-editor on *The Times*, known to Lawrence Hammond as 'old Hawke', and my account of his instruction amused Uncle Lawrence mightily. I chiefly remember that as reporters we must never offer an opinion on what we wrote about. Apprentice jobs in the long vacation could be arranged, but only a few of us tried them, most having other plans.

We attended undergraduate lectures in Constitutional History given by Prof. A. H. Driver, and in European History by Prof. Earnshaw. The latter I found exceedingly interesting, especially as the history I had learnt at school had been exclusively English and colonial, but the other subject was very dry, and I ploughed through Stubbs without any profit. Speaking of 'Wessex' and other supposed kingdoms of pre-Norman England, Prof. Driver would say: 'Journalism students can believe in these; others must treat them with scepticism.'

There were student societies, of course. I heard W. J. Turner read his own poetry and speak rather querulously about contemporary taste. Wal Hannington, a Communist, came to give a lecture open to all: he had hardly begun when some men in the audience made a rush for the platform, and he had to be hustled out by some of the porters who had evidently been prepared for trouble. In the main hall, Rupert Doone (who later founded the Group Theatre) came with a partner and performed a medieval dance play. And Uncle Lawrence gave a lecture, in which he urged the need to raise the school leaving-age from fourteen – as in fact it remained until well after the war.

Theatres, concerts and galleries offered thrilling opportunities, and could be considered as part of the curriculum. One could get cheap seats for the theatre pit or gallery by booking a chair in the morning queue, returning to claim it half an hour before the show. At the Old Vic in my first year I saw (as I have said) John Gielgud as Lear, with Ralph Richardson as Kent. I remember Gielgud's first entrance as Lear, with stupendous music – surely it was Berlioz' Funeral March from *Hamlet*? though I did not know it at the time. In *Julius Caesar* Robert Speaight was memorable as Cassius, and Marius Goring was Brutus's very young attendant, who later had his chance as understudy to play the part of Romeo in a production I was lucky enough to see. Later, when Tyrone Guthrie was director for more than one Old Vic season, Charles Laughton was an eccentric but strangely compelling Prospero, and his wife Elsa Lanchester ideally cast as a (literally) hovering Ariel.

Mary was living at home in Blackheath while she worked at Latin for her Oxford Entrance, and we did various things together. During the summer we had had lunch with Charles Williams in the wine vaults on Ludgate Hill and returned to his little room at Amen House with its view of the Old Bailey, which he shared with Frederick Page – deep in a manuscript and somehow managing to block out the torrent of talk coming from Charles. We were invited to tea at Charles' and Michal's flat in Parkhill Road, Hampstead, and in return gave them supper at a Chinese restaurant. Now in the autumn Charles was giving, at the London Day Training College in Southampton Row, a series of evening lectures which were later published as *The English Poetic Mind*. Mary and I attended these, and afterwards signed up for his weekly Extension Lectures on early Christian thought, given at Tooting Broadway. The long trek by Tube meant that we missed supper, but what did that matter, when we were learning about the *Consolations* of Boethius and his definition of Eternity ('the full and perfect simultaneous enjoyment of interminable life')? However, Mary's mother insisted on making us sandwiches to eat in the Tube.

One other regular evening journey for me was to help at the Time and Talents Settlement in Bermondsey run by two Old Downe girls, Gwynneth Richards and Kit Stewart, to which Alice also came. Here she and I tried to amuse a group of children of primary school age, getting up little plays and teaching them country dances; also playing the harmonium for the hymns at their separated services – Alice for the Roman Catholics and I for the Protestants. I continued this Settlement work for several years – joined by Philippa when Alice had to give up – and it had its rewarding moments (especially when the children enjoyed fireworks on the roof of the Settlement), but I stopped going with some relief when I began work at Fabers in 1935.

The Freshers at Queensborough Terrace were expected to put on an entertainment in their first term, and Joyce George and I were both involved – she taking the chief part in a one-act comedy, and I organizing some 'shadow plays' (remembering the successful ones our form had put on at Downe). I chose two poems to be illustrated by miming behind a sheet: one by Robert Graves about the ghost of 'old Becker crawling in the night From his grave at the stair's foot', and the other the Ballad of Young Lochinvar. I recited the poems at the side during the action, and Jack Isaacs, a guest for the evening, was interested, and asked me to dance. Did I write poetry, he enquired, and if so would I like to show him some?

This I plucked up courage to do, handing him the typescripts after one of his Milton lectures, and afterwards going to his study. He sat behind a large desk on which, I saw to my surprise, he operated a novel filing system. When the top was covered with papers, he spread a large sheet of brown paper over it and started again. He was then on his third layer, but had not lost my poems. He treated them seriously (more than they deserved, callow as they were), and gave me good advice: that when I had an idea for a poem, I should bury it in my mind for a while 'and see whether it will come up ripe'. (He might well have quoted Shelley to Keats: 'Load every rift of your subject with ore.')

On the last night of term, I fell ill with mumps, and Mother came up by car to fetch me home to Ringshall. I had evidently caught it in Bermondsey, where they had an epidemic. I was quite ill, but this was nothing to Alice's bad luck for she caught diptheria, supposedly from the same source.

Alice was studying at the Royal College of Music with Frederick Thurston, the well-known clarinettist, for her A.R.C.M., and also took piano lessons. We both played during this winter in Marjorie Gunn's amateur orchestra, where Evelyn Rothwell and Natalie Caine, both pupils of Leon Goossens, were the oboes (after that, Alice joined the Boyd Neel Orchestra which was just starting). But when Miss Gunn needed for another pupil the violin she had lent me, I gave up playing. It would have been costly to buy another equally good, and although I missed the occasional ensemble with Edward and Mother, I was too dissatisfied with the tone I was able to achieve, to enjoy playing alone.

I think it was early in the spring vacation that I went to stay with Joyce George's family in Norwich. Her father was delightful, with a quirky sense of humour, and obviously very proud of her. Joyce showed me the sights – the Norman Cathedral and the Maddermarket Theatre, and Lady Julian's hermitage. One day we went to Yarmouth, the deserted esplanade a poetry of desolation on a wintry day. Later, in real spring weather, I went for a week to a cottage at Polzeath in North Cornwall, on a 'reading party' with Edward and his fiancée Elizabeth Wright (sister of Edward's New College friend Humphrey), her brother Philip and their friend Betty Fagg. The cliffs were glorious, and it was so hot one day as we walked along them, that we cast off our clothes and plunged into the sea off the rocks. I sat out reading Thomas Aquinas and dreaming; Philip, who had Greats in mind I think, was reading Spinoza.

Elizabeth was a most charming person and I became very fond of her. But she put Edward through a great deal of misery later on (and for his sake his family also) by her indecision over their projected marriage. Her feelings were complicated by the fact that she was so fond of us all, and already seemed like one of the family. First she broke off the engagement; then it was on again, and they had actually received several wedding presents when she finally lost heart. Edward was devastated, but with his indomitable courage decided to start a new job, giving up teaching for a while: he was appointed secretary of the English committee of International Student Service, and came to live in Bloomsbury near their office in Endsleigh Street, as I shall later explain.

The summer that year of 1932 in London seemed very hot: Joyce and I sat out under the trees in Hyde Park one week-end, and on another she came down with me to Ringshall End. But I was soon to leave her at the hostel, for I had given in my notice for the autumn, whereas she intended to stay on. Matt and Jan came home from Calcutta for his six months' leave, and we had a family holiday at Olive Willis's cottage at Aisholt. There I had to learn to accommodate my enchanted memory to a family setting, and I found it hard. But Charles wrote to me, quoting Wordsworth's *Intimations* (the lines which I cited earlier): 'But O ye fountains, meadows, hills and groves, Forebode not any severing of our loves.' And there were good days. I remember one in particular when we had picnicked on the moors, and Father and I decided to walk right to the seaward end of the ridge – another eight miles or so – while the rest returned home. We had covered about half the distance on our way back when we saw far off the shape of Pooh, our mongrel sheepdog, racing towards us; he had seen the others safely home and then set off to gather us up.

For the autumn term I went as a paying guest to handsome Alice Dodds, née Moore, an old acquaintance from my childhood when we had stayed at the old Downe during the 1914 war. She had recently lost her husband (a singer whom she accompanied at his recitals) and she now shared a house in Earl's Court with another ex-Downe House mistress, Winnie Morgan Brown, a most amusing talker, whose face resembled a parrot. They were very good company, but my stay with them was short, for Alice was being courted by another musician, Bernard Robinson (famous for the 'music camps' he ran in the summer holidays), and after Christmas they decided to marry. I then moved to Bloomsbury, to a boarding house in Torrington Square which gave me breakfast with two other lodgers and supper by myself. Work proceeded on its leisurely way, and I was now producing a weekly essay for G. B. Harrison, on subjects I chose myself: he commented on them kindly, but with his usual half-bantering air.

While Uncle Humphrey was staying with us at Ringshall during the Easter holidays, he received news from Amen House that Charles Williams had been rushed to University College Hospital with a dangerous abdominal crisis – 'intus-susception', as I later learnt. For some days he was in danger, and it was 'adhesions' from this operation, I believe, which ultimately caused his death; but now he recovered, and he had another twelve years of life, and the writing of some of his finest books, before him.

Uncle Humphrey had observed my distress, but said nothing, and it was not until I was crossing London shortly afterwards (on the way to stay with a friend) that I managed to enquire at the hospital and learn that CW was 'comfortable' – a word which means one thing to the nursing profession and another to the patient. I left for him a reproduction of Blake's picture, *David delivered out of many waters*. After he was at home and convalescing in Hampstead, he and Michal invited me to tea, and I learnt something of what he (and she) had been through.

For the summer term I found a more congenial lodging than the Torrington Square boarding house, on the top floor of a women's club in Marsham Street, behind Westminster Abbey, where I could boil a kettle and make my own breakfast and supper. The gasworks were prominent in the view, but there were also lovely skyscapes in the evening, and it was good to be near the Abbey, the river and the Tate Gallery. (As I was kneeling in the Abbey to say my prayers one day, among the usual crowd of tourists, a verger enquired whether I was ill!) The little room did become stiflingly hot as the summer progressed, and I used to sit out on the Embankment to work in the evenings.

Our Finals started on a Monday in early July, with rather an agitating prelude for me. I travelled up from Berkhamsted on the Sunday afternoon – got out of the underground at Charing Cross... and realized as the train drew away that I had left my handbag on the seat. It contained my money (£5, which I recovered with the bag from the depot some days later), my fountain pen, and worst of all the front door key to the Club in Marsham Street, which I knew was normally closed at least till midnight on a Sunday. I knew the telephone number of Grace and Kay's boarding house, but I knew they would be out for the afternoon, so the best plan seemed to be to walk to the Tate, where I stayed till it closed at six. Then I walked to Marsham Street – impregnable as I expected – and persuaded the local café owner to let me telephone to Grace and Kay. The reassuring voice of Kay's father the other end promised to come down by car directly and to shelter me for the night.

So, with a borrowed pen, I set off with the two girls next morning for the institution somewhere in South Kensington where we sat our exams. Kay and I got our diplomas, though we had no detail of how we had done in any of our papers. Grace, alas, had failed in History, which had not interested her at all. But it was not too disastrous for her, as she had cousins in England with whom she lived until, after private coaching from Professor Driver, she took the History papers again and passed.

As soon as the exam was over, I went with Philippa to Scotland for a holiday we had planned together, taking turns at the wheel in her family's Austin Seven. We intended to camp for part of the time, so I had bought a tent just big enough for two to crouch or lie in (it cost me 8s 6d), and we each had a mattress and sleeping bag. Our first camp site was on a farm near Pitlochry, and we had settled down contentedly for the night after a sunset supper, when the tent walls began to sag alarmingly as the guy ropes were alternately loosened and tightened. This, we realized, was the work of an unprepossessing youth who was also camping on the farm, whose overtures we had politely discouraged earlier. 'All he wants is for us to rush out in a rage,' we whispered to each other, 'so if we keep quiet he will get tired and go away.' But he did not, and after about half an hour of his antics, accompanied by the ringing of a handbell, my patience snapped and putting my head out I let fly such a stream of invective that he slunk away. I had a good night after this, but poor Philippa's inflatable mattress slowly subsided, and she woke early, on the ground and very cold.

Unluckily Philippa had caught a chill and had to stay in bed for the couple of days we had planned to spend in Edinburgh. We found a reasonable hotel, and for our main meals picnicked in our room, from food which I surreptitiously brought in paper bags. I explored the Cathedral and National Gallery (where Gauguin's Breton peasants stand out in my memory), and walked up to Arthur's Seat, where I sat admiring the view over the city until a friendly youth from Newcastle (his accent so strong that I could hardly understand him, and he found me almost equally unintelligible) escorted me down, saying that it was not a place where respectable girls lingered by themselves.

Our next objective was to stay with Philippa's friend James Peebles (a cricket Blue) at his father's manse near the Moray Firth. We stopped a night at Kingussie on the way and went to a fair (the last time I ever consented to ride on a merry-go-round), and then had Sunday at the manse. When I looked out of my bedroom window before breakfast, I saw the minister standing motionless in his garden, and I later commented on his early rising. 'Yes,' he said, looking as I thought rather fierce, 'I have to get up airly to indulge ma favourite hobby.' 'O? And what is that?' 'Doing NOTHING!' Hospitable Mrs Peebles showed us the Scottish way of making porridge, on a small stove kept near the breakfast table: water in a saucepan is kept constantly on the boil, and the oatmeal is scattered on to it, a spoonful at a time. I think they then ate it with salt, not sugar. The morning service was my first experience of a Presbyterian liturgy with its rambling extempore prayers: the circulation of the collection plate on a long wand seemed the most solemn part of the service.

James took us to call on a famous old Scottish folk-fiddler whom Philippa was anxious to hear. His playing had an electrifying rhythm and a harsh sound, achieved by a nearly-slackened bowstring. When Philippa had played for him a little (first tightening up the bow) he said wistfully: 'I would give all ma reels and strathspeys if I could play like that.'

Next we were to cross to the island of Skye in the Hebrides by ferry from the Kyle of Lochalsh: 'By the lone shieling of the misty island... And we in dreams behold the Hebrides' I thought, as we pitched our tent in rain by a loch on the way there. We woke to sunshine, and crossed, and camped near the Cuillins, planning a mountain walk next day. But a plague of midges drove us to the car, and we went north towards Portree, whence we intended to go on next day to call on The MacLeod of MacLeod at Dunvegan Castle, to whom Philippa had an introduction. (I say *we* intended, but I was very reluctant.) On the cliffs overlooking Raasay Sound we were not troubled by midges, and sat in the evening sunshine eating melon after our sandwiches, feeling at peace with the world. But something worse than midges struck in the night. Philippa woke first, and called out that she was covered with black, itching spots. Evidently a flock of sheep had been grazing at the place where we had pitched our tent, and had left their ticks behind. The pests had gone first to Philippa, and I counted only about twenty of them under the skin of my arms and legs.

Clearly we could not call at Dunvegan Castle in this state: we must get rid of the ticks and then start for home; but first we needed cash, for our money had run out. I had written to ask Father to send money to the Poste Restante at Portree: the envelope awaited us, but alas it contained not notes but a cheque, and the bank refused to cash it for us. I forget how we persuaded them to do so, after ringing up Lloyds Bank at Berkhamsted, but we did, and then rather shamefacedly booked into a boarding house where we could have a piping hot bath that evening, and dig the ticks out of each other by pressing on either side of the spot.

We drove south by the western route, and having had enough of camping, stopped at one or two hotels. Philippa's plan at these was to arrive too late for a costly dinner, and to ask for cocoa and biscuits to see us through till breakfast. In April of this year of 1933 the Loch Ness Monster had first been reported, but I don't remember that we looked for it. The Vale of Glencoe looked very eerie under a lowering sky.

After we had parted, Philippa wrote: 'I never remember a holiday which I have alternately hated and loved so much.' And that, I think, summed up our two or three weeks very well.

I had a different sort of holiday in September in Eskdale with my parents and Alice. We took the miniature railway from Broughton in Furness to Boot (it was then, of course, a regular means of transport) and lodged at a farm called Penny Hill. The Dugdales were pleasant people, but on our first evening we were disappointed to have white machine-sliced bread for supper: the Co-op had already corrupted the Lakes. Father, Alice and I climbed Scafell from there, and on less strenuous picnics he read aloud *The Prelude*.

After a week Alice left us, and while Mother took the luggage round by train, Father and I walked over the passes via Goat Tarn to Coniston. From our lodgings there we looked across the lake to the Old Man, his side horribly gashed and disfigured by quarrying. During the week we spent there we could easily visit the Wordsworthian holy places, and I had my first visit to his school at Hawkshead and his cottage at Grasmere.

Charles Williams (with Uncle Humphrey's approval) had promised me some editorial work from the Oxford Press, and as Christopher was leaving Rugby House and looking for a flat, we decided to set up house together. He would still be working in the City, but no longer with the Press, as he had accepted a promising offer from George Bell and Sons, publishers of educational and general books, to start up a fiction list for them: they gave him a contract for five years in which to make this profitable. He now found for us a very pleasant maisonette on the top two floors of 15 Taviton Street, which leads northward from Gordon

Square towards the Euston Road. The houses were part of a builder's development in the early years of the nineteenth century, and ours had some interesting small stained-glass window-panels and mosaic paving designed and added by Lewis Day, a follower of William Morris, who had lived there at some period till his death in 1909. We rented our part for £120 a year from the Public Dental Service Association, who occupied their offices during the day, but we had the house to ourselves at night, except for a caretaker called Button and his wife, who lived in the basement. Not only was the street very quiet, and surrounded by the tree-bowered squares of Bloomsbury, but it was only five minutes walk away from Euston (reached by a short cut through the garden of Friends' House), whence we travelled to Berkhamsted at week-ends. A quarter of an hour's walk took me to the British Museum, where I intended to work in the Library.

The flat was unfurnished, and much of what we now had was provided by our parents, who had I think kept some pieces in store for later use by their children – notably a fine walnut bureau. We had this in our sitting-room, which looked on to the street, as did the kitchen-bathroom, where a wooden lid covered the bath when not in use. Of course we had no refrigerator, but we sometimes hung a meat-safe on a hook outside the window for coolness. The dining room, in which I installed a Broadwood upright piano, looked west on to the back gardens of our street and the parallel Malet Street, and stairs led up from our tiny hall to the front and back bedrooms, which had pent-house roofs. A parapet at the back stretched all along the row, and I walked along this from our neighbour's house once or twice to climb through my bedroom window when I had locked myself out. The lavatory was on a half-landing below the flat.

Mother helped us to plan our arrangements, and with her usual flair discovered a local 'bodger' who would put up shelves, and a charlady, Lotty Plunkett, widowed mother of three, who would come in on weekdays to clean and leave supper for us to heat up. It was just as well that she could cook, as my Girl Guide badge had not taken me beyond the one-off apple dumplings. (I remember ringing up Mary Guillemard for step-by-step instructions on making a spinach soufflé.) Lotty Plunkett stayed with us and then with Vivian and me until the war broke up our ménage, and her only misdemeanour was to put a broom-handle through the paint of Lynton Lamb's *Taxis behind Euston Station*, a joint purchase by Christopher and me. (Lamb over-painted the mark, but it is still visible.) Lotty worked hard for her 17s 6d a week, and I think with shame that she was not paid during our fortnight's summer holiday (nor did she ever suggest it); but I was certainly an easy-going mistress, and perhaps made up for my shortcomings by much time spent listening to her stories of ailments – her own and other people's: curiously enough, I don't remember any tales of her children.

As I was usually at the Museum when Lotty left, she would leave written messages for us – e.g. 'I cannot shut the kitchen window: perhaps Mr C can do it as he is taller than I am', or (sounding like a cookery book) 'Have thoroughly covered the onions with brown sauce and left in oven'. At Christmas when I asked what she would like for a present, the invariable answer was: 'Unless I had another little piece of stuff for a dress...'

Christopher attended to the wine supplies, which were called on only when we entertained one of his authors to dinner. One of these was an American called Paul Engle, who had come to England to live the simple life at a cottage with no modern conveniences. This he was convinced would be beneficial to authorship, and he brushed aside my questions about the time he would have left for writing. I was later amused to find that the experiment had only lasted six months. Another visitor was Antonia White, author of *Frost in May,* a witty account of her convent education. (I think she must have already published this, and Christopher was trying to get another book out of her.) Later on we had Dorothy Pilley, wife of the critic I. A. Richards, who had written a book on mountain-climbing which Christopher published. I liked her book, but because I could refer to some good passages in conversation, I perhaps made her think I was more of an admirer than I truly was.

Of course Christopher and I entertained our own friends. I had a second bed in my room where various of my ex-school friends stayed, and later on Christopher had a brief affair with a lively and glamorous woman called Sheila Borrett. I was careful to keep out of the way when she was staying.

At Ringshall, however, we had a joke about the girl friends whom Christopher would invite for the day and then, finding them rather tedious, would leave Mother and me to amuse them. When Bip Pares came on the scene (having I think done some illustrations he commissioned), she had her own house in Frognal, and did not spend nights at Taviton Street.

The painter Lynton Lamb and his wife Biddy were friends with whom we regularly exchanged hospitality: they lived not far off in Camden Town. Lamb was a very literate painter, as his writings on art show; he dressed elegantly, with a bow tie, and he and Biddy (who was also an artist) lived in not at all a bohemian style. He employed his whimsical sense of humour in stories of his fellow painters. Lamb was retained by the OUP to design book jackets and to illustrate some of the World's Classics, and Christopher had got to know him at Amen House. Now he had begun to paint in oils, and was a member of the 'Euston Road' school, to which Coldstream also belonged. Christopher and I were excited by the paintings which we saw on visits to his home, especially one depicting the taxis ranked at night in Ampthill Square behind Euston Station, their sombre colours lightened by the street-lamps and by the white nose of the animal belonging to the one horse-drawn cab. We bought the picture jointly for £15, and when I married I kept it, paying Christopher his half of the price.

The work which took me daily to the British Museum (a short, pleasant walk across Gordon and Russell Squares with their trees nodding, and full of blossom in springtime) was to select poems for the proposed *Oxford Book of Modern Verse* from a list of poets drawn up by Lascelles Abercrombie. He had been commissioned by Oxford to edit the book, but was now too ill with diabetes to finish what he had begun. So for the whole of one winter I scanned the pages of poets good, bad and indifferent, and selected what I thought best – I had of course no right of veto. One day Jack Isaacs discovered me doing this, as I sat at one of the desks that radiated out from the central space where the catalogues were kept, under the dome of the Reading Room, and expressed his amazement at the responsibility I had been given. 'Though better you than many people', he said. He exclaimed at some of the names on the list I showed him: *Pinto!* he repeated with expressive scorn. But he need not have worried, for in the end Abercrombie had to resign from the job, and the Press decided to appoint W. B. Yeats instead. The resulting choice of poets was equally wayward, though very different.

My next job for the Oxford Press was more rewarding: it was to edit a World's Classics selection of Shakespeare criticism, to follow the volume edited by Nichol Smith which had ended with Carlyle, and bring the selection up to the present day. I soon realized that it would be unsatisfactory to try to cover in one book the nineteenth-century aesthetic, which approached Shakespeare as though his characters were real people who could be extracted from their context, and that of the present day, where context is all-important. So I asked to be allowed to cover only the post-war period, 1919–1935, starting with J. M. Robertson on Hamlet, and ending with an essay by George Rylands, the only contributor born in this century. It is I think a well-balanced selection, the result of intensive reading (most of which I have now forgotten) over about a year, and with the advice of Charles Williams to monitor my opinions. (To monitor but not to overwhelm: now that I re-read my Introduction, its strongest debt seems to me to be owed to Coleridge.) I earned an outright £25 for the book, which was what Charles himself had been paid for something similar: it was published in 1936 and reprinted the following year, and several times since; it is still in print, now with my married name.

I continued to hear a weekly lecture from CW, but now I heard it not at Tooting but at the City Literary Institute off Holborn: I was the class secretary and recorded the numbers attending, occasionally being optimistic by one or two. Afterwards I would walk with him to the Tube station, or to the offices of Chesterton's paper *G.K.'s Weekly* to pick up books he was to review. I studied his poetry with a view to getting a selection published, and what was more important, I became his audience with a licence to criticize, for the new versions of his Arthurian poems, later published under the title *Taliessin Through Logres*. About once a week after he left Amen House at 5.30 we would go to a café, and he would read the latest poem, or expound a theory about, say, the connexions between Logres and Britain, or the symbolism of Merlin, who represents Time in the cycle. And sometimes we lunched together in the City.

CW had been commissioned by Victor Gollancz to compile an

anthology to be called the *New Book of English Verse*, which was to contain nothing that had been included in the Oxford Book or the Golden Treasury, and I trawled through the British Museum collections of fourteenth- and fifteenth-century poetry for unfamiliar poems. These I would read in the Manuscript Room, and it was exciting work, to be handling the originals of these masterpieces.

> From alle women my love is lent
> And lyte on Alisoun...

I think my liking for the name dates from that experience. Charles's introduction to the book, which was published in 1935, discusses at length the nature of Cant when found in poetry, and one of the projects which he suggested I should work on (but which I found too difficult to plan) was to compile a Dictionary of Cant in literature.

Once or twice I sat in on meetings of the small committee at Amen House which was helping to compile the *Oxford Dictionary of Quotations*, under the guidance of Alice Mary Smyth (later Hadfield). Alice Mary was red-headed, with striking good looks and many male admirers: these included Gerry Hopkins (translator of Mauriac and great-nephew of the poet) and so added a new thread to the complicated pattern of Amen House love affairs, which I don't propose to go into here. (Alice Mary became an ardent disciple of CW and his teaching, and the account which she gives of the Amen House relationships in her biography of him is full and accurate.) The drama had begun in the late nineteen-twenties before she joined the Press, and most of the characters appear in the two Amen House Masques, written and produced by CW and acted in the Library there. The central figure in the story was Phyllis Jones the librarian, 'Celia' of hundreds of unpublished poems by him (now deposited in the Bodleian), and Gerry Hopkins wrote his own account in a novel called *Nor Fish nor Flesh* which startled the participants very much when it was published. All this I came to understand as I grew close to Charles, and when in August 1934 Phyllis (placed between two distinguished lovers neither of whom felt able to divorce their wives) decided to break with Amen House and marry a man of her own age, CW turned to me as a confidante in his misery. So for the next three years he filled my thoughts even more obsessively than before.

My love is of a birth as rare As 'tis for object strange and high,
It was begotten by Despair Upon Impossibility.

Of course I quoted Marvell's lines to myself, but the poem continues:

Magnanimous Despair alone Could show me so divine a
    thing…

which is also true, and especially in relation to such a man as Charles
Williams.

The work I did at the Museum, interesting as it was, brought in no
money, and apart from a little reviewing for the *Yorkshire Post* which
Christopher and I did, under a pseudonym which I forget (Bonamy was
the first name), I was not earning anything. I made one or two attempts
to get into publishing, and did some reporting on MSS offered to Bell
and copy-editing for Christopher: one bizarre manuscript I remember
was by a scientist who was about to set up house in the Galapagos Islands
with his wife, where they would be the only inhabitants. Fearing that he
would be a martyr to toothache, he had all his teeth pulled out, and was
fitted with a set of iron ones, to be of use in pulling up saplings for
fencing! Bell's did not publish the book, and I do not know what became
of it.

Some time during our first year together, Christopher went on a long
visit to America to scout for authors. He made a very good impression
on the publishing world there, as I learnt later on from Frank Morley,
and made offers for various promising books, but he was fighting a losing
battle against established fiction publishers, and literary agents such as A.
P. Watt who favoured them. So (to anticipate), at the end of the
stipulated five years, he had not managed to establish a profitable fiction
list for George Bell, and they did not renew his contract. Luckily he then
found a job with Macmillan.

I was not at all lonely in the flat while Christopher was away, as I had
plenty of friends with whom to go to concerts or the theatre; and of
course I spent most week-ends at Ringshall End. I have already mentioned Canon Barkway, the Little Gaddesden Rector, who gave such
excellent sermons and became such a friend to Father – and confidant
and adviser to me. His son Michael worked for the BBC, and I

occasionally went out with him. Philippa had introduced me to Mervyn Horder and James Robertson (later conductor at Sadler's Wells), who shared a studio near the Foundling Hospital, and I used to go round to sing madrigals with them. This led to my joining a small choir conducted by Arnold Goldsbrough; and later I sang with an amateur madrigal group directed by Cuthbert Bates, founder-conductor of the Tudor Singers. I had considerable respect for Arnold Goldsbrough, not so much for Cuthbert Bates, whose comments were apt to be extra-musical: 'Sing that phrase as though you were dropping a stone into a pool.' Philippa came to stay, and we went to hear Busch and Serkin again at the Wigmore Hall, or the Busch String Players playing the Brandenburg Concertos at the Queen's Hall – most loved of concert halls, which alas was bombed in the war. There I heard Schnabel play Beethoven sonatas, and Beecham conducting the Verdi Requiem: in the Dies Irae he would draw back his left arm and hurl as it were a ball from the shoulder, straight from boundary to wicket.

With Christopher I went to the London Palladium (Flanagan and Allen, Naughton and Gold, Duggie Wakefield), and to see the Marx Brothers, whose films were then new to London.

My godfather Kenneth Swan and his wife invited us to dinner parties at their lovely house in Holland Park, where Kenneth successfully kept bees on the roof. At one of these I met Donald Hyde, the American scholar who was doing research on some Samuel Johnson papers which had lately turned up in an Irish attic. He invited me to go out to dinner, and turned up to collect me at Taviton Street in a dinner jacket, so that I hastily had to change, and the evening got off to a bad start: but I enjoyed my first taste of oysters. Christopher and I met the novelist Margaret Kennedy and her barrister husband David Davies at the Hammonds', and they invited us to their parties in London where literary games were played. Christopher accepted these invitations, but I was sure I should be a fish out of water, and managed to avoid them.

In the summer of 1934 we had a family holiday with the Milfords at Rock, in the part of North Cornwall immortalized by John Betjeman and famous for the little church of St Enodoc half-buried in sand. After this I went with Mother and Father to Paris for a week, staying at the Hotel du Fleurus near the Luxemburg Gardens. We spent much time in the Louvre; visited Versailles, and enjoyed the special pudding made of cream cheese in a restaurant near the Madeleine which Father remembered from earlier visits. This was just after Phyllis Jones had departed for Java, and I received a letter from CW every day, which intrigued our concierge at the hotel when I went downstairs early to secure them. One of the poems in C's *Taliessin Through Logres* was headed (in the copy he gave me) 'In memory of the seven letters' – those that I wrote him in return.

On Candlemas Day in the following year Mary and George Wilkinson (much later Guillemard) were married. He had been a fellow student at Oxford, and when they became engaged she decided to leave the university and earn money by teaching at a Rudolf Steiner school – for George's training as a barrister meant a long wait till they could set up house together. Their wedding was in the splendid church of St Bartholomew in the City, and yellow was chosen for the bridesmaids' dresses, to harmonize with the walls. I was one, with Mary's sister Erica, Jean Wilson and a friend from St Hilda's. The best man was Peter Burra, a delightful friend of George since Oxford days, and author of excellent short books on Wordsworth and on Van Gogh. I shall write more of him later.

Mary and George settled into a flat in St George's Square, Pimlico, and when summer came, we planned to go to Salzburg for the Mozart Festival and then to tour Youth Hostels, joined by Alice and her future husband, David Pennant, whom she had met in Scotland two years earlier. David was handsome, and excellent company; his tastes in pictures agreed with ours, and if he preferred Wagner to Mozart and Beethoven, he raised no objection to standing for hours in the queue for *Fidelio*. A terse postcard from his eldest brother in response to his own excited bulletins amused us; it read: 'Aren't you confusing Baroque and Romanesque?' David was already a convinced Tory, but political disagreements hardly arose, because we were all united in our hatred of the Nazi regime which was then established in Germany, though not yet in Austria.

A sign of the times was the ersatz coffee we got in Salzburg, said to be made of acorns. But the opera was all we had hoped. The conductor was Bruno Walter, and Lotte Lehmann was Fidelio. As auditors our conditions were a test of endurance: after queuing all afternoon in the street we found that directly the doors were opened, there was a mad rush for the guichet, regardless of the queue order; then, having somehow secured tickets, we stood all evening in a hot and crowded gallery. But no backache could lessen the effect of the Prisoners' Chorus, their cry of 'Freiheit' especially poignant because we knew what a grip tyranny was establishing in Europe.

In the mountains near Salzburg the wayfarer's greeting was still 'Grüss Gott', but when we crossed into Bavaria we had to endure 'Heil Hitler'. We spent one night in Berchtesgaden, trying to sleep on a communal floor with thirty or forty others; Alice and I bought Bavarian costumes – green hat, waistcoat and skirt, with a white puff-sleeved blouse. Mine did duty for many summers till it went into the dressing-up chest. Here too I bought a descant recorder. In the mountains we found a Youth Hostel to ourselves, next to a friendly inn where there was Wiener Schnitzel and zither-playing. Alice was the only one of the party who had learned German at school; Mary and I had taken half a dozen lessons from a friend of Olive Willis, and I had recourse to my memory of Schumann and Schubert songs to increase my small vocabulary.

We had stopped at Munich for the Pinakothek on the way out, and broke our journey at Cologne on the way back; also in Brussels to see a special exhibition of Van Gogh – a revelation. David and Alice had travelled a day earlier, and had discovered that it was on, telegraphing to us that we must see it. David wrote to me afterwards: 'Odd how much marvel can be crammed into 24 hours.' Indeed it proved to be a trial trip for their life's partnership, but three more years were to pass before their marriage.

Later in the summer I went with Mother and Father to stay at Zennor in North Cornwall, a place that Lawrence and Barbara Hammond were fond of, and their friends the Arnold Fosters invited us once or twice to their house, The Eagle's Nest, on a crag with a spectacular view. Mrs Arnold Foster (Ka), celebrated for her tortured relationship with Rupert Brooke years before, had a very warm and welcoming personality; Arnold Foster himself was astringent and rather alarming, but I remember his melting a little when Mother spoke of the Monets in the Orangerie, Paris.

I was correcting some proofs of CW's *New Book of English Verse* while we were there, and commenting on his first drafts of the play about Cranmer which had been commissioned for the Canterbury Festival of the following summer. I urged him to forsake iambic pentameter in favour of the irregular metre of his latest Taliessin poems (which was the result in part of his editing of Gerard Manley Hopkins a few years earlier): from this time on his dramatic verse was free from the deadening effect of pseudo-Shakespearian blank verse.

I walked on my own to the prehistoric circle at the highest point on the moors, a lonely place whence you can see the sea on both sides of the peninsula. The result of this walk was the poem called 'The Rudiment is Single', about a man who mistakes the sea for the land, and drowns 'in earth, sea, fire or water'. These were the years when the poems I wrote first began to have any durable quality. They showed, of course, the strong influence of Auden, for together with Sir Thomas Wyatt he was (as I wrote in an essay called 'A Question of Speech') the poet who helped me to find my own voice. Apart from that, no poet of my generation could escape the influence of Eliot. The influence of CW on my outlook and experience was of course total, but I was not tempted to copy his idiom which, in so far as it did not derive from his early reading, was inseparable from his visionary subject-matter.

I had now come to a point where I realized I had to make an effort to become less dependent on him. I still wanted to get into publishing, and as the only chances that offered were to go in as a secretary, and although I had been advised that this would be a mistake, as being a dead end, I determined to qualify. I had already taught myself touch-typing, and had learnt the theory of Pitman's method of shorthand from a manual; now I signed on at the Pitman college in Southampton Row for dictation practice. I had to pass a test on the theory first; I remember my pleasure on being complimented by the examiner, though I really disliked the system, which meant pronouncing 'gentleman' 'gen'leman', and all *a* sounds in North country fashion. Then ensued a kind of parlour game, when you spent a week taking dictation at a speed of 60 words a minute, and proceeded by weekly leaps of ten a minute to the reporter's speed of 140 upward. I reached 120, and then heard from Erica Wright, who was the Chairman's secretary in Faber & Faber, that Richard de la Mare, head of production, was looking for a second secretary to help an overburdened Jane Cowling.

I was thrilled at the prospect, for was not Faber the foremost publisher of modern poetry, and was not T. S. Eliot a Director? I had already hung about near the entrance to their office at the north-west corner of Russell Square, hoping to see Eliot emerge at 5.30, and had been rewarded with a sight of him. (On another occasion I had heard him read his poetry in a drawing room full of ladies, where he seemed rather out of place.) So I applied for the job, and was interviewed by Richard de la Mare, son of Walter. I learnt afterwards that Walter's own secretary, older and much more experienced, was also applying, but obviously she would have wanted more than the £2 15s a week which I was happy to accept. So I was successful, having assured Dick de la Mare that my 120 words a minute would be quite adequate for any speed at which he was likely to dictate – and so it proved.

I was to start after Christmas, and Father was pleased, for although he had never pressed me to support myself (he had settled some shares on me, besides making me an allowance for clothes), I think he had worried at the lack of obvious goals in my life. Lotty Plunkett remarked that I was sure to do well, 'for you have been used to being with the books'.

1936

The Faber production department was housed on the ground floor of 24 Russell Square, and the secretaries' room looked out at the back on to a strip of garden where grew a beautiful black poplar, which with its reddish catkins in spring added to the pleasure of life. The original room had been divided in two, and beyond the parting wall worked the two junior editors, Pringle and Powell. Alan Pringle was quiet and judicious, an excellent editor, Selwyn Powell ebullient, and concerned with estimates and lay-outs. Adjoining us was a creaky lift, whence once, so Jane Cowling told me, the sound of banging had caused her to run out calling 'Oy, stop that', only to see a cageful of gaiters and the pin-stripes of T. S. Eliot, stuck on their way up. And next to that door was Richard de la Mare's large room, looking out on to Russell Square, and apparently lined with Faber books – until you discovered that most were only binders' dummies. Across the entrance hall was the telephone box, brooded over by Miss Swan, who had been with the firm since it started as Faber & Gwyer in the 1920s. I only use the word 'brooded' because of

Miss Swan's bird-name; she was invariably cheerful, with a sympathetic telephone personality.

I shared our room with Jane Cowling and Mr Stewart's secretary, Miss Room: O dear, I have forgotten her Christian name. Mr Stewart was the Director in charge of contracts and agreements, so that Miss Room's deft fingers twinkled away all day, producing twenty or thirty letters, as she would point out to Jane and me, with our handful each. Jane was, I suppose, about thirty, with a pale complexion, flaxen hair and a merry smile. She had had rather a sad life, for her father had deserted the family when she was still a child, and she and her several brothers and sisters were always hard up. I think she had taken some training in arts and crafts; anyhow she knew several artists, and was much more knowledgeable than I was about book production. The art critic Adrian Stokes was one of her friends, and occasionally looked in on us: he was an old Rugbeian who seemed to have good memories of my parents. Jane was clearly in love with him, but I do not know how serious their affair had been. She had a flat in Holly Lodge, the attractive estate in Highgate, where she gave me supper: we became great friends, for we laughed at the same things, and enjoyed the gossip of the firm. During the time we worked together, her delinquent father turned up in hospital, dying, and Jane had the harrowing experience of going to see him to say good-bye. His greeting, as she reported to me, was 'You've still got your same grin.' The poor pay we earned at Faber's was more serious for her than it was for me, and eventually she left to take up an offer from her friend Bill Curry, the headmaster of Dartington Hall, to be a House Mother there.

Jane and I worked together very harmoniously, dividing our time between Dick de la Mare's letters and proof-reading. I thoroughly enjoyed the life of the office and its camaraderie; the sense of belonging to a firm which was part of a fine tradition; and of doing my job satisfactorily. The books I proof-read were generally interesting, and so, often, were the manuscripts sent down from the Book Committee for me to report on. I should explain that the five Directors of the firm met weekly for lunch and the whole of Wednesday afternoon to consider plans and read reports on manuscripts which had been submitted – those, that is, which seemed worth considering; a preliminary weeding-out of the hopeless ones had already taken place (a job which I later shared with Alan Pringle). There was another meeting for some of the Board with the Sales Manager on Monday afternoons. Richard de la Mare was influential in all their decisions, and he had made Faber books the envy of the trade for their design and workmanship. He was a pioneer in many aspects of production, employing first-rate artists such as Barnett Freedman for his book-jackets, and choosing a format for books of poetry (demy instead of the smaller crown octavo) which greatly improved their sales. He had many friends among writers as well as artists, and counted Eric Gill among his advisers – Gill had designed the striking Faber letter-heading.

Although Dick let me see that he approved of my work, and after my marriage he was on the friendliest of terms with Vivian and me, I never felt entirely at my ease with him. He was certainly a shy man, but I think Jane Cowling was probably more confident than I in her dealings with him. However, I knew very well how to imitate his style, and after I moved from the production department he would always send for me to 'write a nice letter' for him to sign when turning down a book! After Dick had moved from Bloomsbury to Hertfordshire, he would sometimes say to one or other of us: 'You must come down and see us at Much Hadham', but Tigger (Selwyn Powell) was the only one to disconcert him by accepting this invitation on the spot.

On my first morning, I was instructed to go and see the Chairman, Geoffrey Faber. He was an Old Rugbeian, and told me that he had enjoyed being a member of *Eranos*, the essay society which Father ran, and remembered his attractive house, 46 Church Street. He expressed surprise that we had not pulled this string when I applied for a job (in fact it had not occurred to us to do so), and seemed pleased to see me, saying to his fellow-director Frank Morley that Dick was the best hirer in the business.

Our hours were flexible, being nominally from ten until six, with an hour for lunch, and Saturday mornings till one o'clock, but as there was rarely time to read and report on MSS during office hours, I often took work home, and stayed later than six. As I lived so close by, and Lotty Plunkett shopped for our evening meal, there was no sense of pressure on me. There were plenty of cheap places for lunch near at hand, a favourite being 'The Book' in Museum Street, where you found an assortment of cheeses and a glass of good table wine. I think it was there that I lunched one day with Moshe Oved, proprietor of the Cameo Corner jewel shop in one of the side streets, with whom I had made friends. He was as usual carrying something from his stock in his pocket, for it was his theory that jewels needed to be cherished and looked at. It had just been raining and the gutter was muddy, which enhanced Moshe's gesture as he took this large diamond out of his pocket and threw it in the gutter, calling on me to observe how it flashed out. Better still from my point of view was that he made me a present of a set of Dutch silver buttons for my tweed coat and skirt, on which he thought the buttons were inferior.

This was the year of the great Chinese Exhibition at Burlington House, to which Richard de la Mare went almost daily, leaving us to our proof-reading, and the writing of routine letters. Eric Gill offered suggestions on the lay-out of these, on the handsome office paper, and wished us to put a colon instead of a comma after the name of the person addressed. But this was not adopted by Dick: perhaps he thought it would look rather mannered. Among the enjoyable proofs I read were those of Walter de la Mare's *Ding Dong Bell*, which led to an exchange of letters in which I quoted to him our favourite epitaph found by Mother in Stokesay churchyard ('Autumn came, and Thomas had Nuts and apples for the lad...'), and he in return gave me one from Zennor which I already knew – 'Tis glorious misery to be born a man, etc. (It is, I found later, no artless local poem, but from a book of Quarles's *Emblems*.) A couple of years later, when the firm planned a selection of de la Mare's poems in their Sesame series, he suggested that I should make the choice. (I also made the selection from Eliot for the series.)

One set of proofs I should have liked to read was that of Eliot's *Collected Poems 1909–1935*, which came out in April 1936. But these had been entrusted to an outside reader, so I merely dealt with this reader's queries, and was delighted when one of them gave me a pretext to visit the top floor, where Eliot inhabited a small room at the back. (Editions of his poems are a byword for errors, probably because proof-readers treat them too reverently, and he himself was disinclined to look at past work.) On the door was a brass plate with the name 'Thomas Stearns' (his maternal grandfather), and a notice which must have been supplied by the American Director Frank Morley: 'Achtung! Bissiger Hund'. (Morley must also have been responsible for the marzipan necktie lying on the desk, which surprised Vivian on a later occasion.)

Once inside the room, I was too much concerned with its occupant to notice anything else on this first visit. The question concerned a word in 'Lune de Miel', where Eliot had written 'le Cène', and the reader had queried the gender. 'Well, that depends upon Italian', Eliot said; whereat I assured him that as the Italian was *cena*, it must be feminine. I was puzzled by his doubt, but it occurred to me afterwards that perhaps he was thinking of the masculine *cenacolo*, as the phrase refers to the Last Supper.

Another exciting book published during my first year with Faber was David Jones's *In Parenthesis*, about his experiences as an infantryman in the First World War: I still possess my bound proof copy. I don't remember that Jones came to the office, but one poet who did was David Gascoyne – 'that gloomy boy', was Eliot's phrase for him. We were publishing a pamphlet of his in connexion with the Surrealist Exhibition, and I remember querying what he meant by 'white as alburnum' – a word which signifies 'the sap-wood in exogenous trees'. I supposed he meant 'laburnum', but then that was not white but yellow: could he have been thinking of white acacia? My query, as we stood in the waiting-room next Miss Swan's box, seemed to puzzle him, and I think we left the word as it stood.

In June of that year, Charles Williams's *Cranmer of Canterbury* was produced in the Chapter House of the Cathedral as part of the annual festival, with Robert Speaight as Cranmer, following his success as Thomas à Becket the previous year. I went down to Canterbury for the last night, sat next to Charles for the performance, and went with him to the early service in the Cathedral next morning, where Martin Browne was one of the communicants. Martin the producer and Laurence Irving the designer had diametrically opposed views, Martin having a symbolic approach and Irving a strongly naturalistic one: Charles had had trouble, when appealed to, in keeping the balance between them. But the play was very well received, and it is sad that it has never been revived – except once by Martin at the Union Theological seminary in New York.

Charles followed *Cranmer* in the autumn with *Seed of Adam,* produced in Chelmsford by Phyllis Potter, who had told him that unless he wrote her a Christmas play she would have to produce *Eagerheart* again. It is my favourite among his short plays, and in this as in *Cranmer* he finally left behind the pseudo-Shakespearian metric which weakened earlier work, and found a flexible, sometimes colloquial, speech which matched his genius.

Office holidays were then a fortnight a year, with three days at Christmas and Easter. This summer Matt and Jan were home on leave, with Dan aged three and Diana aged six months, and we all went to Rock in Cornwall with the Stainers and Milfords. There was golf for some, madrigals for others, and much bathing and rock-scrambling for all. I took some riding lessons on the sands, and for the first time enjoyed being on horseback. My poem 'In the Sea' describes my state of mind – or heartsickness – in solitary wave-watching on the headland called 'The Rumps'. I found it particularly delightful to have a small nephew at Ringshall, and my poem 'Against Anger' recalls Dan in the swing in our spinney.

In the autumn came the first of the Sunday Times Book Fairs, where all the publishers took stalls, and members of the Faber production department went down to man the display – agreeable if tiring. And at the end of the year, 1936, Eliot's secretary Bridget O'Donovan left, and I was asked to take her place – which of course I accepted with joy.

Bridget wrote some years ago a letter to the *Times Literary Supplement* which implied that when Eliot was away there was virtually nothing to do in this job. I certainly did not find it so, but it is true that besides seeing the quarterly *Criterion* through the press and correcting its proofs (which Bridget will also have done) I now did some copy-editing of manuscripts, and with Alan Pringle I went through the scripts offered to the firm (apart from those commissioned), and returned to the senders those that were obviously hopeless, with a polite note. Much copy-editing was required for the books which we took on at this time written by refugees from Nazi Germany, with their unidiomatic English.

Eliot worked at home in the mornings and arrived in Russell Square after lunch, except on Book Committee days – of which more later. He would ring down for me, Miss Bradby, when he had looked at the post which I had opened and put on his desk. I worked on the middle floor of No.24, where were also the Sales Manager and his secretary; Frank Morley with the younger director, also American, Morley Kennerley; and the Chairman Geoffrey Faber. I shared a large room overlooking Russell Square with his secretary (Erica Wright at this time) and Tod Evans, Frank Morley's devoted secretary, who went to America with his family when he departed just before the onset of the war. Morley was such a slow dictator that Tod would sit for nearly a whole afternoon with her pencil poised over her pad, and then have a scramble to get the letters ready to catch the post.

Eliot's small room had a large desk with upright chair, a comfortable arm-chair, a bookcase with a clutter of books and files on the floor beside it, and a typewriter on a stand at which he stood to type his reports and some of his letters; on the mantelpiece were many snapshots of his family and friends, added to from time to time. The window looked straight down Woburn Square, and 'Lines to a Persian Cat' always make me think of Eliot gazing out, wearily at work in the afternoon:

> Why will the summer day delay,
> *When* will time flow away?

In what follows I quote from an article I wrote in 1983 for *The Poetry Review*. I sat in the armchair to take dictation, while Eliot often stood. He was measured but fluent: as with his normal speech, the sentences were perfectly formed, not punctuated with 'ers'. Sometimes his extempore criticism in a letter was so interesting that I found it hard to remember that my business was to take it down, not to think about it. Once in criticizing a story by A. L. Rowse he said that the essential message was too-obviously thrust at the reader, when it should be left for him to absorb unconsciously through the narrative – as objects are seen more vividly at the margins of the eye 'where the rods and cones are less worn, just as one can count more of the Pleiades on a clear night when one is not looking directly at them'.

It was no wonder that I was oppressed by the tedium for him of the matters I had to set before him, and must sometimes have made things worse by my tentative approach. 'What must I bear?' I remember his saying, not with a smile, after some preface of mine. Charles Williams used to make a distinction between a proper awe and the servile fear which dreads to make a fool of itself. My attitude to Eliot, at any rate in early days, partook of both.

He would challenge the fear, sometimes to make me defend myself, sometimes because it provoked his instinct for teasing. He certainly took pleasure in 'one-upmanship'; on the other hand he liked people to defend themselves vigorously, and once said as much to me. When, after weeks of vetting the mostly rubbishy poetry sent in to *The Criterion*, I felt I must show him something, and put a couple of MSS on his desk with his letters, these were held out to me later with a blank look and the monosyllable *Why?* To which I think I found no better answer than that I didn't understand them, so thought they might be good.

Eliot was the most considerate of employers where his secretary's welfare was concerned, and he had, with all his sophistication, a delightful simplicity in some practical matters. I remember his warm approbation – 'That was very smart of you' – when I had merely thought to enclose a stamped addressed envelope for him to use with something I had sent on to him.

When Eliot came to write *The Cocktail Party*, he gave Reilly's secretary the name of Miss Barraway, and barring away was certainly one of my chief functions. Not only was there a continuous stream of hangers-on and impecunious poets (these were often admitted), but there was also the pathetic figure of his estranged wife Vivienne, 'a restless shivering shadow' as *The Family Reunion* put it, who would sometimes hover in the waiting-room till he came past the window on his way to the entrance. I had to interview her once, and was given a paper to hand on to him. I showed it to Geoffrey Faber, hoping that he would deal with it, but he said 'No. People think that there should be a ring-fence drawn round Mr Eliot, but that can't be.' 'But if someone is mad...' I objected. 'She's not mad; that's the trouble', he replied.

But when I gave Eliot the paper, which concerned a parcel of books, he said miserably, 'That is quite, quite mad.'

It was understood that telephone calls went first to his secretary, and when he did answer an outside call, his voice had a curiously strangled sound. He was very conscientious in giving his full attention to any work he thought promising, but 'Sometimes I feel I loathe poetry' he once said to me, after too heavy a load of manuscripts. I admired the integrity he preserved in giving his opinions: he never resorted to the facile praise or cowardly half-truths which most of us utter, wishing to leave a favourable impression of ourselves. He did employ a skilful ambiguity sometimes, and occasionally indulged in veiled mockery, behind his *persona* of the judicious public man.

One of the young writers whom Eliot encouraged to write for *The Criterion* was Peter Burra, whom I had met when he was best man to George Wilkinson. He was writing something about Wordsworth's brother-in-law, and he had submitted an article on the writer Forrest Reid for *The Criterion*; we met for lunch and enjoyed each other's company. Not long afterwards (it was April 1937) I was dismayed to receive at Fabers an official letter enclosing one addressed to me from Peter, cheerily ending 'Viva los marineros ingleses', which had been 'found in Mr Burra's pocket after his death in the light aircraft in which he crashed recently'.

The ending referred to the Spanish Civil War which was in everyone's mind at the time, and Peter knew I must have been delighted by the exploits of Potato Jones, a skipper who had run the blockade imposed by England and her allies, and thus enabled food to reach the Government side. It seems that Peter had had a premonition of such an end to his life, for in 1933 he had written down a dream in which he died in an aircraft crash; and he had spoken of such an end as a good way to die. But to his friends it seemed an appalling waste of such a vital person. I was 'only at a friendship's entrance' as I wrote in a poem for him, but I did grieve for him.

In that same spring of 1937 a new magazine, *Night and Day* , was launched, which was to be of great, though indirect, importance to the lives of Vivian and me. The paper was modelled on the American *New Yorker*, and Selwyn Powell (Tigger) landed the job of arts editor for it. As a result, his job in the Production Department of Faber's was vacant, and David Bland, son of a Bristol vicar, was appointed. No doubt Richard de la Mare was impressed not only by David's personality but also by the fact that he and his partner Vivian Ridler, with whom he operated a private press in the basement of Mr Bland's vicarage, had had one of their books chosen by the First Editions Club as among the Fifty Best Books of the Year. In the same month, March, that David left home for London, his partner also left Bristol to work as a manager under John Johnson at the University Press, Oxford.

The sequel for Tigger was a sad one, for a libel action against *Night and Day*, as a result of a film review by Graham Greene, put paid to the paper after only a few issues had appeared.

In May, all the employees of Faber's were given a week's holiday to celebrate the coronation of George VI. How many publishers did the same, and whether this was a nation-wide movement, I have no idea, and Vivian remembers nothing about it. I can only say that it was a delightful fact, and I spent the week in the Quantock hills at a farm called Pepper Hill, together with Mother, Father and Philippa. The weather was lovely, and we had a happy week, though Father had strained his heart and could not walk as far as usual. Philippa and I found a riding stable and went out a couple of times on the moors with a group – Philippa, much more expert than the rest of us, was sometimes allowed to gallop ahead.

My main holiday was planned as a trip to Italy with Jane Cowling, but first came my twenty-fifth birthday, 30 July, when after an ordinary office weekday I went down to Jane's room to consult her about something. David Bland appeared in the doorway with a friend whom he introduced as 'Vivian Ridler from Oxford, where he works at the University Press.' On this I remarked that Humphrey Milford, the London publisher, was my uncle. David's attractive-looking friend appeared to take this as a piece of name-dropping, for he said – as I thought rather dismissively – 'O we're quite separate at Oxford.' I was wrong about the tone, it seems, for Vivian says he decided then and there that I was the girl for him.

That was, I think, a Friday, and early the next week, as I was eating sandwiches in the Russell Square garden, to which we had the key, I opened the gate for David and the same friend, who was spending a few days' holiday with him. A day or two later , when I met David on the landing outside our room at lunch time, he said that he and Vivian wanted to look something up in the British Museum catalogue and would like my help. So we agreed to lunch together, and descended the stairs to the hall, where Vivian was leaning over Miss Swan's box as he talked to her. David muttered something to the effect that 'She's coming out to lunch with us', and off we went to the Reading Room. We then went on to lunch at The Book, and that was that as far as I was concerned. But Vivian went back to Oxford and debated whether there would be any future in writing to me, or whether it would only lead to disappointment. Luckily he did write and propose a visit to a Prom at the Queen's Hall, to hear a Mozart Piano Concerto and the Jupiter Symphony. I was impressed by the handwriting on the envelope.

We met at the Hall, Vivian having caught the 5.15 from Oxford (docked of 15 minutes' pay for leaving early), and returned to 15 Taviton Street for something to eat before he left to get the last train from Paddington. I became aware as we were saying good-bye in the hall that he had very positively fallen in love; what struck me as delightful was that when I pointed out the mosaic paving and told him about Lewis Day his interest was vivid and not distracted by his feelings.

Much as I had enjoyed Vivian's company, I still felt gloomily that I should never be sufficiently heart-free to fall in love again, and I felt remorseful on his behalf: 'Love made him weep his pints like you and me' as Auden puts it.

I went off to Italy for three weeks with Jane Cowling, travelling third class on wooden seats for only £3 return, courtesy of Mussolini's wish to encourage tourists. We stayed at San Vigilio on the Lago di Garda in a fascinating guest-house kept by an Englishman: it was on a promontory, and we sat for meals looking down at water so clear that we could watch the trout swimming about. Unluckily Jane was ill for part of the time, and couldn't go with me on the day expedition we had planned by bus to Vicenza, changing at Verona. I saw the Palladian Theatre with its trompe d'oeil perspective, and climbed the magnificent flight of steps to the Rotonda just outside the town. I also took a day-long mountain walk on my own, those being times when one could go off alone without a thought.

The three rather clotted poems I wrote while away show that Vivian (who wrote me several letters) was much in my thoughts, and soon after we got back he came up to supper and my feelings began to change. A couple of weeks later I drove over from Ringshall to Aylesbury on a Sunday afternoon to meet him, and as I drew up by the roadside and saw him standing by his cherished Sunbeam tourer I realized that I was properly in love. He was wearing his blue tweed jacket, a much better garment to come courting in than the shabby old mac he had worn in London.

After that afternoon we announced our engagement, and Vivian came to Ringshall for the week-end. Mother and Father took to him at once – Father pronounced him a young man with 'lots of *go*' – and so did the Hammonds, Uncle Lawrence enquiring, with his usual courteous curiosity, about Vivian's views on the state of public opinion in Germany (Vivian and David had recently visited Paul Koch in Frankfurt). I spent a week-end staying at the Lamb and Flag in Oxford, and on another we drove from there to Bristol, where his mother and Mildred gave me a warm welcome. And of course I introduced Vivian to Charles Williams, meeting for a drink in the City after work one day. I know the meeting was a success, and that Vivian produced some piece of recondite information which intrigued Charles, but I can't remember the topic. We probably also spoke of Charles' novel *Descent into Hell*, which Faber published that autumn. It had been rejected by Victor Gollancz, who had launched him as a novelist, and he had then offered it to Faber. I was on tenterhooks to see what Eliot's report would say: he typed it himself and gave it to me to pass on to the Chairman. To my relief, he recommended publication, though he did not think the story achieved the momentum 'that kept one turning the pages of *War in Heaven*'. So Faber published the novel in September 1937, around the time of Charles's 51st birthday (and in the year when he died, they were the publishers of his last novel *All Hallows Eve*).

I was now living alone at 15 Taviton Street, as Christopher had moved in with Bip Pares at her house in Frognal. In January 1938 they married and went out to India for their honeymoon, accompanying the Everest expedition some way – perhaps as far as the base camp. I had hoped that Vivian's Bristol friend Thea Brown might come to share with me, but she wrote to cancel the plan when her horse became infested with lice and needed constant attention. Luckily I found a very pleasant house-mate instead, known to us as The Duckling's Daughter, her father an old colleague of HCB.

It seemed likely that when we married I should have to leave Faber and go to live in Oxford. But John Johnson put a stop to that idea, for when

Charles Batey (the Assistant Printer) informed him that Vivian was planning to ally himself with Humphrey Milford's niece, he sent for Vivian and gave him three months' notice, alleging as the reason that he was a selfish young man who put his outside interests before those of the Press. Nothing was said, of course, about his engagement, but Uncle Humphrey when I told him was convinced that this was the reason for the dismissal – and of course he was right, though at first we could not believe it. To Vivian himself it was a considerable blow, as Johnson had lured him from his promising job at E. S. & A. Robinson in Bristol by extravagant compliments and prospects, and in spite of what he had discovered about working under Johnson (which seems to me to have been like life in a monastery without the consolations of religion), he still had a great admiration for the man.

Before the three months' notice was up, Vivian received an offer from someone who wanted to set up a private press in London. This was Theodore Besterman, who had applied to Johnson for advice, and had received a glowing testimonial to Vivian – an ideal man for the job (proof, if any were needed, that Uncle Humphrey had been right about the reason behind the dismissal). Uncle Humphrey had met Besterman, who had unsuccessfully tried to persuade him to publish his *World Bibliography of Bibliographies*, and was somewhat suspicious of him, thinking his literary background unpromising: it included a Life of Madame Blavatsky and an interest in the occult. But the idea of managing a printing press attracted Vivian, especially as Besterman was amenable to his wish to use it for commercial work as well as limited editions. The financial backing was provided by Besterman's wealthy American wife.

So Vivian left Oxford after Christmas, and moved into 15 Taviton Street with The Duckling's Daughter and me, sleeping in a truckle bed in the dining room. He set to work to buy equipment for Besterman's press, choosing type and machinery – a Wharfedale and later a Heidelberg as well. Besterman engaged an expert binder called Coton, the source of much amusement for Vivian and many sayings, some of them unprintable, others idiosyncratic, as 'having a bit of a struggle' for sexual intercourse. Premises were found next door to de la Rue's factory, in Bunhill Row off the City Road. The building looked out over the tree-lined cemetery where Blake and Bunyan are buried, and Vivian used to eat his sandwich lunches there. For general work, The Bunhill Press was an obvious choice of name; for limited editions, Besterman chose Guyon House, the name of his rather grand house in Hampstead. (Here he employed two menservants, who expressed an objection to opening the door to Vivian when he was carrying a parcel of proofs.) Besides Coton, the only other employee was an office boy; for typesetting they used an outside firm, and Besterman himself or his wife typed necessary letters and looked after the accounts.

The press opened for business in the spring, and Vivian was kept very busy between scouting for commissions, designing the lay-outs, operating the presses and packing the parcels of finished work. The whole enterprise, and the plans we made for our wedding intended for July, were much overshadowed by the international situation. Two years previously, Hitler had occupied the Rhineland, and Britain and France had not moved; now in March 1938 he marched into Austria. With hindsight, it seems strange that we could continue our lives as though the future might be normal, and indeed many of us suffered from a kind of schizophrenia, voiced by Stephen Spender when he wrote 'Who live under the shadow of a war, what can I do that matters?' We thought that Germany might cripple us by a lightning strike from the air, so that the mere sound of aeroplanes in the sky had something threatening about it.

> Lord, our night is cursed with wings,
> Scolding conscience cries of war,

I wrote in a poem of that spring, and on a lovely Eastertide holiday which Vivian and I made to Kingswear on the Dartmouth estuary, the contrast between our happiness in the beautiful coastal country and the forebodings conjured up by the sound of aeroplanes above us, or their manoeuvres which we watched from the cliff, was poignant...

We spent some time looking for a flat which would be cheaper than 15 Taviton Street, but the contrast with our pleasant maisonette was so great that we decided to manage somehow as we were. Christopher took his furniture away, and the Dental Servants agreed to redecorate the sitting room while we were on our honeymoon. Lumsden Barkway, who had left Little Gaddesden to be a canon of St Albans, was to marry us, sharing the service with Ted Wager, our present rector. Ted was a former Mirfield Father, who had rebelled against his monastic, celibate ministry to become an extremely broad churchman and a disciple of Freud's teachings, which he used for pastoral counselling. He had made a very happy marriage, but too late for the family of children which his wife Nellie would have loved. He and Father much valued each other's company (though Father was never converted to psycho-analysis, which he thought had done nothing but harm to his sister Mick), and were in the habit of taking a weekly walk together, ending in tea in the kitchen at Ringshall End on Nellie's day out. Nellie always left a fine fruit cake for them to eat, and one afternoon that summer they found it especially nice. The sequel was that Nellie ran into the drawing room next morning, saying in dismay: 'Mr Bradby has eaten the wedding cake!' She had left the top tier of the cake she was preparing in a tin in a remote cupboard, where Father had somehow discovered it, and had cut two generous slices.

I was fond of Ted Wager, and came to admire him increasingly, but I found his soothingly therapeutic approach sometimes irritating – as the letter which Ben read out at our Golden Wedding party shows.

My wedding dress of ice-blue silk was made by two sisters, London dressmakers recommended by Bip. She and Christopher were still abroad, but Jan was home for the summer with Dan and Diana, and Dan acted as my page. Mildred and Vivian's mother came up from Bristol and stayed with the Hammonds; Vivian I think was banished according to convention to the Janeses at Ringshall for the night before the wedding. He had of course designed and printed the wedding service, and Edward led a group of our friends in singing my favourite Bach Chorale ('Schmücke dich O liebe Seele') as anthem. Father and I entered singing 'Praise the Lord, ye heavens adore him' to Haydn's 'Emperor' tune – the only bride she had seen, Jenifer Hart said, who sang as she walked up the nave, but how could I resist, with that tune?

Jenifer's mother, Lady Fischer Williams, had been asked to take photographs for us, instead of our having set groups, and she captured delightful snapshots in the garden at the reception, including an amusing one of Uncles Humphrey and Lawrence dreamily conversing, Uncle Lawrence apparently having the garden shears in his pocket. The Cake was sheltered by a marquee (although the weather stayed fine), and Nellie was photographed with us beside it. Lynton Lamb said that the icing represented the last example of baroque architecture.

The reception time seemed all too short, with such a gathering of friends. We caught a train from Berkhamsted to spend the night at 15 Taviton Street before setting off for the Lake of Annecy in the French Alps the next morning. Rather to my surprise as well as pleasure, Vivian lifted me over the threshold as we arrived, a married couple.

CHAPTER V

We were to spend our honeymoon at the Hotel de l'Abbaye at Talloires on the Lake of Annecy, which Father remembered from the Bradby European tour of 1883 as a blissful place. We had time between trains in Paris to see a French film (we think it was Jean Gabin in *La Bête Humaine*) and sat propped against each other in our third-class seats through the night to Annecy in the French Alps, where we took the steamer to our little landing-place at Talloires. The hotel was still just as Father had described it (though later it became notorious as a refuge commandeered by Fernando Marcos when he fled from the Philippines). It was a romantic place with wonderful views of the lake, and our main meals were taken under vine-covered trellises stretching to the water's edge. Breakfast was set in the abbey cloisters: chocolate for Vivian and coffee for me, with the usual croissants. The waiters were friendly, and we were happy to take their advice for the wine we chose at dinner. Most days we took a rowing-boat out on the lake, which was so pleasant that we only once took the steamer to go farther off, to Duingt on the opposite shore. Walks along the lake were tiresomely restricted by the properties claiming the shore-line, but there were paths into the foothills, where the hay was being harvested. Here we discovered that our temperaments (amicably) differed, as Vivian lacks the super-ego which drives me to yearn to reach the summit of any contingent hill.

We planned to spend two or three nights on the way home with Edward, who was now managing the ISS office in Geneva. We inadvertently took in a marvellous sunset view of rosy Mont Blanc en route, having failed to change trains, but managed to telephone a message through to prevent Edward from meeting us. Next day we took a funicular to view the town and lake, and saw the League of Nations building with all its expensive wood panelling – temple of what already seemed a forlorn hope.

(Bertha Woodall, who also worked for ISS, was another of Edward's visitors during his time in Geneva, and he began a courtship which ended in their engagement in the autumn of the following year. By then he was ready to return to schoolmastering, and had been offered the headmastership of a large public school in Ceylon, the Royal College, Colombo.)

In Paris again, after another night in the train and a morning at the Louvre, a half-bottle of wine at lunch sent Vivian into uncontrollable laughter, rhyming *nuit* with *parapluie*, and it was with difficulty that I steered him out of the restaurant and on to a bench in the park to sleep.

Our newly-painted flat welcomed us, though the wallpaper was not quite the green I had wanted, and we celebrated by supper in Charlotte Street.

While we were away, though I did not know it at the time, Vivienne Eliot had been taken up by the police, wandering the streets at 2 am, and her brother was obliged to have her committed to a mental home. TSE himself was away on holiday and did not sign the order, though he was told of the decision. The gossip-mongers have blamed him for her confinement, but it was in fact unavoidable, and lasted till her death some ten years later.

We had hardly settled into the routines of work again, when the hovering threat of war approached actuality, as Hitler prepared to invade the Sudetenland. Neville Chamberlain flew to Munich, and returned waving his piece of paper, supposed to represent 'peace in our time'. The wave of relief which we felt was countered almost at once by doubts about the reliability of Hitler's promise – quickly followed by shame at our abandonment of our Czech allies. I took one practical step as a result of the scare, in signing up for evening lectures on First Aid, and passed my St John's Ambulance test some time during the following spring.

During the anxious days when war seemed imminent, Eliot made plans to bring the *Criterion* to an end, and afterwards realized that he had lost his enthusiasm for keeping it going, so that the issue of that autumn was a farewell number. At the same time, Geoffrey Faber's secretary (successor to Erica Wright) left to get married, and it was decided that I should take over her job, in addition to the now-lightened work in Eliot's department. Although this meant a bigger load of letter-typing and filing, it also meant that I sat in on the weekly Book Committee, which was interesting.

I observed the various idiosyncracies of the Directors. Richard de la Mare was the most tenacious in pressing for a book or project he had at heart; he was also the quickest in calculating the number of copies we should have to sell, to make a profit at a given price. Frank Morley (one of a well-known American family) was worldly-wise, but also given to flights of fancy, and I remember one amusing instance, when we were considering the offer for publication of the love poems of Marie Stopes, the pioneer in birth control. Morley brought her typescript to the meeting with dramatic solemnity, saying that here we must think of a sale in thousands, given the right presentation and a binding of purple velvet. The other Directors looked slightly doubtful, but passed the script to the Sales Manager, Mr Crawley. He immediately saw that the poems were so completely wrong for the Faber imprint that we could not possibly succeed with them.

Eliot (who was, so Mr Crawley assured me, as good a man of business as any of them) affected detachment from the proceedings except where he was especially concerned, and did *The Times* crossword puzzle during the afternoon. When given a cup of tea by me he would carefully remove the spoon, to avoid slopping it in the saucer. One day he reported on an interview with Geoffrey Grigson, who was offering an anthology taken from the magazine *New Verse* which he had founded and edited. When Geoffrey Faber enquired what terms had been proposed, Eliot pretended that 'Two shy men' had been too fastidious to raise the subject of money. When his own book, *Practical Cats*, was submitted to the firm, he put with the typescript a set of imaginary reports on the poems, parodying the styles of different members of the Book Committee. Mine was scathing, and peppered with parentheses.

Some time during the winter of 1938–39, a street-rest was being installed outside No. 24, which gave me an idea for a joke. I commissioned Vivian to print a mock letter-heading, on which I typed a letter purporting to come from the Town Clerk's Office, and addressed to the Chairman. It proposed that there should be placed on the new street-rest 'a statuary group of the Directors of your Firm – preferably cast in concrete'. I intended to put this letter in front of Geoffrey Faber, although it was the kind of letter which would normally have gone first to Mr Stewart, and I counted on the Chairman's annoyance at this wrong procedure, when he looked at the letter-heading, to ensure that he would not tumble to the joke at once. And so it proved. He began to read the letter out, annoyed because it ought to have gone to Mr Stewart, and had reached the 'concrete' before he was enlightened.

Geoffrey Faber was as a rule on the look-out for practical jokes, being much assailed by the teasing of Frank Morley – hence the comical confusion that enveloped a serious letter that he received from someone in Richmond signing himself F. C. G. Larkworthy. The coincidence that poor Mr Larkworthy's initials were the reverse of his own led the Chairman to reply in a suitably larky style, and on getting a puzzled and injured reply, to continue in the same vein, sent to Richmond by express post, and perhaps yet another joking letter, before he understood and wrote an abject apology.

For lunch in the boardroom the Directors had a roast joint and apple pie, provided by the caretaker and his wife, Mr and Mrs Lister. Lister had been butler to the Fabers at their house in Frognal, and used to regale me (when I stayed late at the office) with stories of his experience there and at the Front in the First World War. When the Eliots came to dinner, he said, Vivienne would humiliate her husband in various ways, typically by breaking the string of her beads so that he had to crawl over the floor looking for them. Lister was critical of his employers: 'I think you Miss might have more sense in running this place than what they do.' Now, he and his wife had twins, and occupied the top floor of No. 24.

While the Directors and Alan Pringle ate their Wednesday lunches in Frank Morley's room (which also served as the boardroom), one of them would bring me mine on a tray. One day Eliot did this, first enquiring whether I preferred a slice from a leg of lamb 'or the nub end'. 'A slice, please,' I said (having actually no preference), whereat he said severely, 'That's very bad taste.'

I had plucked up courage some time before this to show him some of my poems – not with any suggestion of publication. His reply, which included some comments from Frank Morley, was to turn down the corners of some pages where the poems seemed to him 'to soar, if not, yet, to sing', and he handed the script back with the words 'I should go on.' This, knowing as I did his scrupulous honesty in comment, I found very encouraging, and I had even better encouragement from the Oxford Press (thanks to Uncle Humphrey and CW) when they brought out my first collection in May 1939, printed by Vivian at the Bunhill Press. The typography was exciting: it was set in Plantin with the poem-titles in Bodoni Bold, and for the magenta jacket and hard cover Vivian chose a bold wooden letter, printed in reverse. I was exceedingly lucky (compared with young poets publishing their first book at the present day) in getting a review (by Hugh Macdonald) in the *Times Literary Supplement* within a month of publication: it was quite favourable, and so was one from a critic I respected, Hugh Gordon Porteus.

Our commissariat at Taviton Street continued as before, and at weekends we enjoyed Nellie's cooking, but we also occasionally stayed in town to visit picture galleries, when David Bland would join us. And we were invited out as a newly-married couple, by Kenneth and Millie Swan to Holland Park, by John and Lucie Christie to the headmaster's house at Westminster, and by Geoffrey and Enid Faber to Frognal, where our fellow guests were Louis MacNeice (a Faber poet) and Eliot's close friend John Hayward, who till then had been only a frequently-heard voice on the telephone to me at Faber's.

John was by then confined to a wheel-chair, and partly paralysed in his arms also, through the muscular dystrophy which had been gaining on him since his undergraduate days of the 1920s. The paralysis also affected his mouth and facial muscles, so that to be seen for the first time by someone whom he had grown to like via the telephone, was somewhat traumatic for him. But we were soon on easy terms, and friends for life. Some months later Vivian and I spent an evening with him (Simon Nowell-Smith was invited too) at the flat in Bina Gardens which he rented from Eric Gregory, one of the directors of the printing firm of Lund, Humphries. It was Eric Gregory who printed the twenty-five copies of *Noctes Binanianae*, jeux d'esprit exchanged between Eliot, Faber, Morley and John himself, for which I had made the typescript, working in after-hours at the office; on the evening of our visit John presented me with my own copy, inscribed by Eliot and himself to 'the pious and accomplished young Lady, excellent in the sister Arts of Poesy and Printing'. As to Poesy, John was always in those years an interested and encouraging critic, and I never knowingly suffered from his malicious tongue – as Simon did on this occasion. But as Vivian said, to be a friend of John one had to resign oneself to whatever he might say behind one's back: as with Alexander Pope, a crippled body could well turn wit sour.

Another writer whose friendship I owed to my work at Faber's was

Lawrence Durrell. He had been recommended to Eliot by Henry Miller, and the firm had published a pot-boiler novel of his under a pseudonym. Now we were considering his avant-garde prose work, 'The Black Book', and his poetry, which both Alan Pringle and I recommended for publication. In return Larry suggested that I show him some of my work, which he pronounced 'the real egg', and it was through him that I had poems published in various coterie magazines before my book came out. He was living in England for a year or so with his wife Nancy, a painter, and invited Vivian and me to dinner at the flat in Camden Hill which they had been lent by a rich American, Hugo Guyler. George Barker came in after dinner, talking rather complacently, I thought, about being a Communist. We invited the Durrells back, and another time we all went to see the Marx Brothers at the Hampstead Everyman cinema; and Larry would drop in on me in Taviton Street when he had a new poem to read. One of these, 'The Sonnet of Hamlet', he dedicated 'To Anne Ridler and the lady in the picture, Ophelia'.

Larry was wonderful company and a life-enhancing friend. You might think, from passages in his later novels, that some part of his psyche was twisted: that was never apparent to me. We disagreed, of course, about religion, and he had a propensity to fall for some very boring sages – as they seemed to me. In those early days his pope was a psychologist, Graham Howe; later on it was a writer called Motte, who was vocal on the influence of pre-natal experiences. I was grateful, though, for Larry's recommendation of the writings of Groddeck, whose *Book of the It* anticipated Freud and taught me a lot.

It was at about this time, too, that I first met Enrica Garnier, who was to become such a dear friend. She was unofficially engaged to Norman Nicholson, and came with him when he kept an appointment to see TSE.

I think we had exchanged letters already, and I went down to see her as she sat in the waiting room while Nic had his longed-for interview: our friendship began that day, and I anxiously followed the course of her long relationship (at a distance except for summer holidays) with Nic, ending at last for her in disappointment.

The Bunhill Press flourished in its commercial dealings, and the Guyon House Press achieved a *succès d'estime* with its editions of Magna

Carta and *This Man*, illustrated by Elizabeth Rivers. In July Vivian and I took a fortnight's holiday in Cornwall, staying at a farm in Zennor. It rained a good deal, but luckily we had brought some solid reading matter: Vivian read Uncle Lawrence's newly-published life of Gladstone, and I St Augustine's *City of God*. (This begins to sound like Rebecca West's home life with her husband, as described in her autobiography.) On good days we enjoyed the cliffs and the moorland stone circle (where I'd written a poem on my earlier visit), and took a bus to Land's End; we made friends with the farmer's young daughter Eva, and Vivian gave her his stamp collection.

All through the summer we thought of the approaching war, and Eliot's finest play, *The Family Reunion,* was put on (directed by Martin Browne) in a very unpropitious climate. The part of Harry, pivot of the play, was acted by Michael Redgrave, whose portrayal emphasized the more disagreeably priggish elements in the character, and it was a great pity that Eliot had refused to offer the part to John Gielgud, on the ground that he was not a religious believer. The critics were baffled or patronizing, and it was not till long after the war that the play had a truly successful production, by Michael Elliott – one that Eliot did not live to see. The Eumenides (Furies) who pursue Harry, unseen by the other characters, were then treated in an unashamedly sensational way, appearing as vast white figures among the audience, and preceded by an electronic vibration. Martin Browne, who did live to see this production, entirely approved, but told me that he could not have attempted such a treatment in 1939.

Some time during the summer Eliot wrote to his namesake in the manor at East Coker and paid his first visit to the Somerset village whence his ancestors had emigrated to New England – the visit from which sprang the second of his 'Four Quartets'.

Family memories were stirred for me when Philippa and I went in late August on a short tour in Wiltshire and Sussex, starting with East Knoyle, Mother's birthplace. I was born too late to have enjoyed holidays in the Rectory with our grandparents, as my eldest brothers did, but when I stayed in the village as a child the Milford memory was still very much alive among the villagers, and even when I went with Philippa the name was still magic for one or two. We drove on to Heyshott, near

Midhurst in Sussex, where my parents and Uncle Humphrey were in lodgings, and Vivian was to join us at the week-end. The week I spent there stands out in memory in brilliant colours, focused on the figure of Philippa, singing and playing her accordion in the sunshine outside our lodgings, as we sat round to listen. (HSM, though, was not his usual vigorous self, and a few weeks later an Oxford consultant, Farquhar Buzzard, diagnosed pernicious anaemia, only just in time for the treatment to save his life.) Just as Vivian joined us, the long-dreaded blow fell: Hitler mobilized his army to invade Poland and war was inevitable. Uncle Humphrey was fetched away by the Oxford Press car, and Philippa left us. We stayed over the week-end, and I wrote the little poem ('Now Philippa is gone...') which expressed my sense of an ending to shared gaiety: it does not attempt to touch on the tragedy that war meant.

The following Sunday (3 September) Vivian, David Bland and I were in St Pancras Church round the corner from Taviton Street, taking part in mattins and listening to a sermon from the incumbent, Bishop Crotty, when a verger handed up a message to him in the pulpit. Visibly shaken, he announced that we were now at war with Germany; an air-raid warning was sounding; and we were to adjourn to the air-raid shelter next the church. We felt that he should at least have said a short prayer or heartened us for the ordeal in some way: as it happened, the immediate result of his words was rather comic. A man who had been sitting a couple of rows in front of us stood up, clapped on a gas mask and dashed off down the nave. The rest of us filed out calmly, and Vivian, David and I hurried to 15 Taviton Street, where, according to the instructions previously circulated, we filled the bath with water. This was one of the more sensible precautions that householders were advised to take, as was the provision of a stirrup pump, which we had obeyed. But one of the dottier instructions, as I remember it, was that one should actually get *into* the bath, in the event of a threatened mustard gas attack.

The Dental Servants had constructed a shelter in the garden, but the All Clear sounded before we thought of going into it. During the previous days, children in England's big cities had been despatched to the country, and the Ringshall End household had agreed to take five from London. David's flatmate Basil Page, who was a doctor, was called up, and David came to share our flat for the time being, as he and Vivian would both continue their jobs while waiting to be called up (both electing for the RAF). Besterman had told Vivian that he would only be able to pay him when there was work to be done, at an hourly rate of 3s, so it was helpful that the PDSA agreed to reduce our rent to £100 p.a. In the meantime Vivian and David signed on for the Auxiliary Fire Service, locally stationed at Maple's in the Tottenham Court Road. At Faber's I was directed to circulate the procedure to be followed after an air-raid warning: Morley Kennerley, the youngest Director (an American) would ring a bell, and we would all go down to the basement.

That first alarm turned out to have been caused by a stray unidentified English plane, and after the Germans and Russians had divided up Poland we English settled down for the winter to the 'phoney war'. Many of the homesick evacuees returned to the towns, including, by degrees, the five who had been quartered on Ringshall End – but not before they had left a legacy of head-nits behind them.

Edward and Bertha were to be married on 11 October, less than a month after she had finally agreed to marry and accompany him to Colombo, and their passage was booked for the 21st. We were invited by her parents to a celebratory lunch at the Savoy, and to stay at their spacious home, Yotes Court near Mereworth in Kent for the wedding. Vivian and I arrived by train the night before, and were shown into the drawing room where Mother was sitting with Mr and Mrs Woodall. I was surprised to see that her hair, normally worn with a bun at the back, had been elegantly bobbed, and when I went over to kiss her she whispered 'nits!'. The 11th was a crisp and sunny autumn day, and the woodland groves of Yotes and the Palladian-style church at Mereworth (where we had early communion and the wedding at midday) looked very beautiful, and 'far above noise and danger'. Edward and Bertha drove off to a week's honeymoon at Olive Willis's Aisholt cottage, before setting sail for Ceylon.

Christopher was with us at the wedding, and temporarily unemployed until he could take up a commission in the Royal Army Service Corps. (We did not know until later that he had lost his job at Macmillans – a great blow.) Matt of course had been recalled to the Navy, and was to be stationed at Colombo: so it fell out that he and Jan and their children were there when Edward and Bertha arrived.

VAB had always kept a diary of the family holidays, and from the beginning of the war she made it a weekly record – a fascinating mixture of domestic and military news: e.g. 'Aug 9th, 50th week. Picked first pound of blackberries on Aug 3rd. Germans dropped leaflets with Hitler's last speech.'

I rely on this for details in the years that immediately follow, and I see that as soon as the evacuees had left Ringshall End, we continued to spend most week-ends there, often accompanied by David, and that he and I were both allowed to sing in the Festival Chorus for a performance of the *Messiah* in the Dean's Hall in Berkhamsted in April 1940, conducted by Reginald Jaques, with Eric Greene and Keith Falkner among the soloists.

The Oxford University Press had been evacuated to Oxford, and Uncle Humphrey and Aunt Marion had settled into a quite pleasant house in Hilltop Road – she being, as he wrote 'as always the Queen Trump on emergent occasions'. Early in the spring of 1940, however, when she had not been well but was recovering, she took an overdose of her sleeping tablets (quite possibly by mistake), and never recovered consciousness, though Robin, David and Pippa all came to be at her bedside. She was buried near her parents at Oborne, close to Sherborne: Mother and I were driven down to the funeral from Oxford with Uncle Humphrey, Robin and Pippa in the Press car – a sad day.

Uncle Humphrey moved to a smaller house off the Cowley Road (christened 'the Bijou Residence' from the agent's description), and there Vivian and I visited him for a week-end, and saw Pamela Brown and John Gielgud at The Playhouse (my very first visit) in *The Rivals,* also (but perhaps this was a later visit) a production by Neville Coghill of a Shakespeare play in, I think, Exeter College garden, where a distracting fountain plashed the entire time, as we both remember.

The plan of having David Bland to share our flat was delightful for Vivian and me, but perhaps not such a good idea for him. I had not realized, he being tongue-tied where the expression of emotion was concerned, that he had been in love with me even at the time when he brought Vivian to Faber's – 'Just like a bad novel', he wryly said when I first realized the situation. 'Never introduce your Dona to a pal' was CW's comment when I confided in him. Still, we had some very happy times together, culminating in a May holiday at Aisholt, when some of David's family came over from Bristol for the day. (His brother John was already a pilot in the RAF, and was soon to be killed in the Battle of Britain.) Then, breaking over the sunshine of Aisholt, came the news of the German invasion of France, soon to be followed by the collapse of the Allied forces and the retreat from Dunkirk.

Mrs Haste stood waving at the gate as the taxi carried us away, and the doom of parting, so long dreaded, seemed actual at last.*

Back in London, we tried to carry on our life as usual while awaiting the call-up notices. Robin briefly came to stay, after a disastrous attempt to join up in the Army: having spent one night with his fellow-recruits he broke down, and came to us before joining Kirstie and Barnaby in a cottage at Downe (they had let their house on Red Shute Hill for the duration of the war): here he resumed his teaching. Before May was over, I found that (as we had hoped) I was pregnant, and decided to warn Faber's to look for my successor, as I did not intend to stay alone in the flat after Vivian had to leave. I felt extremely sick, and did not enjoy our nocturnal descents to the shelter in the garden – always for false alarms.

Faber's in fact appointed two people to succeed me; a young man, Barry Sullivan, as the Chairman's secretary, and one of the current secretaries for Eliot. They promised to keep me supplied with editorial work, and so in mid-July I went to live permanently at Ringshall End, with Vivian, and often David, coming down on Saturdays as before. I was sad at leaving the firm, although Jane Cowling, my closest friend among the secretaries, had already left to become a house-mother at Dartington Hall, where the headmaster, Bill Curry, was a friend. As I've already said, I enjoyed the comradeship of the office; I was fond of Geoffrey Faber and Frank Morley, and what I felt for TSE I have described elsewhere. But my thoughts were bent towards the new life of our child. And down at Ringshall I found plenty to do, with work from Faber, helping out at the local farm, and, when Nellie went away for her annual three-week holiday, sharing the cooking with Mother. She was

* Poor Mrs Haste, always the mainstay of life at Aisholt. Her son Fred proved inadequate to manage the farm in wartime, and Olive was obliged by the authorities to replace him, which meant that she had to sell it. Mrs Haste took to the bottle, we were told, and I think she died not long after.

not at all well at that time, for it had been discovered, through a blood test taken when we knew that Uncle Humphrey had pernicious anaemia, that she too suffered from the condition. She had been having weekly liver injections, but evidently needed them more frequently, and soon improved when the dose was increased. (She could not abide liver to eat, and before injections became possible would, she said, have died rather than consume the necessary threequarters of a pound each day.)

The weather all summer was beautiful, and my poem 'Ringshall Summer' expresses something of the conflict of our feelings in the brilliant sunshine, as we listened to the distant gunfire of battles in France, and heard the daily news of retreats. The air-raids on London did not begin until 7 September, but even in our remote spot we were occasionally woken by sporadic bombs, probably aimed at a radar station in the valley, when we would get up and come down to the hall for a short while. Some of the villagers (VAB recorded) did not go to bed, and had not undressed for days. In the daytime some of us took turns to man a telephone to relay air-raid warnings, but I never had to sound an alarm.

On a night in mid-September, when Vivian and David were both at Taviton Street, a land-mine was dropped in the parallel street. They had just returned from fire-service duty and were half-way up the stairs when the explosion shook the whole house and the landing tiles lifted in front of them. As Vivian described it afterwards, they clutched each other in bewilderment, first about to run down to the basement, then realizing that they must go up to see what had happened to the roof. There the skylight had been shattered and a small fire had started, which they were able to put out with our stirrup pump, thus saving the whole building.

They spent the rest of the night in the basement, and were woken early next morning by air-raid wardens, who told them to vacate the house because there was a time-bomb in the street. On going outside they saw that the whole of Taviton Street was covered with debris – floor-boards, water-tanks, tiles, chimney-pots. They both came down to Ringshall and commuted from there, but David was called up before the end of the month, and went to start his training as an RAF pilot at Pensacola in Florida. We ended our lease of the flat, and stored our furniture in a disused stable in Little Gaddesden, kindly lent to us by the Grays. Lotty Plunkett found factory work, and though I tried to get her to come to us when we returned to London after the war, she wrote that the factory had spoiled her for domestic service, though 'the time I spent with you was some of the happiest in my life'.

In December Vivian was sworn in by the RAF, but continued to go up daily to the Bunhill Press while waiting to be called up. So it happened that we were able to have Christmas together, and Uncle Humphrey came for a week to share our early Communion in the dark Little Gaddesden church (only one hooded candle on the altar), chicken instead of turkey, marmalade made from orange-peel and apple-pulp.

Many fires were started by the raids on London, and we could see the lurid glow in the night-sky (described in my poem 'London's burning'). Worst of all was the night in the first week in January 1941, when the water supply to the City was used up and the fires there raged unchecked. Vivian went up to work next morning as usual: entering Bunhill Row he saw a mass of the magenta jackets of my *Poems* in the gutter, and so realized that the Bunhill Press had been hit. Everything was lost, as happened also to the bank-note printers, de la Rue, next door, who had just installed new machinery.

Vivian was in fact due to join the RAF in ten days' time, so we knew he would not be at home to see our baby's birth. A sore throat and fever slightly delayed him, but on 23 January, in miserable weather, he departed for Padgate in Cheshire to begin his training as a wireless operator.

Less than a fortnight later, on the snowy night of 4 February, Jane was born.

As I have expressed my feelings about this great event in poetry, as for the births and infancy of our other children, I shall only attempt a factual record here. She was born with lots of dark hair, and an average weight for a girl of 7lb. 4oz. (When earlier I had mentioned 8lb. to Vivian as a likely weight he had exclaimed 'Heavens, that's as heavy as a rifle!') We had engaged a monthly nurse, Miss Tookey, who was highly recommended by Rhoda Miller's relations and very efficient, though inclined to be censorious. Jane was an eager feeder at the breast, and gulped in a lot of wind, with consequent colic, for which I was held responsible. So many of Nurse Tookey's prescriptions seemed self-contradictory that I composed some doggerel, 'Maxims for Nursing Mothers':

O drink for the sake of your health, dear,
Refrain for the sake of the child;
And whatever the midwife adwises,
Perform it, and answer her mild.

O stand on your head in the bed, dear,
But not on your feet on the floor;
And remember that bearing a babe, dear,
Is as easy as shutting the door.

Vivian had to wait a whole month and four days before seeing his first child, and it seemed interminable to both of us. He got over from Padgate just for one day, before going to Cranwell to continue his training, and was allowed by Nurse Tookey to bath Jane, earning approval for his confident handling. He hitch-hiked again for Jane's christening at Little Gaddesden on Low Sunday, 20 April. Her godmothers (Philippa Kingsbury and Alice Pennant) could not be there, but her godfathers, Charles Williams and Robin Milford, both managed to get over for the day, Charles being brought from Oxford by Anne Spalding's brother John, who as a doctor had petrol. Christopher and Pippa also managed to come, and Pippa sang part of the christening piece Robin had composed and played for us on the piano – our Broadway baby grand. Jane behaved seraphically, merely clutching at Ted Wager's beard as he splashed water over her.

VAB's diary for that week has these juxtapositions: 'Jane put on over 6oz. and is now 9lb. 4^{1}/$_{2}$oz. Germans pushing BEF troops back in Greece… Greek Govt and King went to Crete.' (So did Larry Durrell with his wife Nancy and baby Penelope, shortly to be driven out again, to Alexandria.) Soon afterwards Vivian finished his course at Cranwell, and had a week's leave before being posted to the RAF camp at Kirkwall, in Orkney, on the watch for enemy aircraft coming to attack the naval base. Here he slept in a Nissen hut, eighteen to a hut, until I joined him the following spring.

Those spring and early summer months of Jane's babyhood were in one way very happy ones, and briefly blissful when Vivian was on leave and could share the fascination of watching and caring for her. But the month of May also brought personal tragedy with the death of Robin and

Kirstie's precious only child, six-year-old Barnaby, run over by a baker's van on the quiet Cold Ash road at Downe, as he was returning on his small bicycle from fetching some music from Robin's hut in the pinewoods. Apparently the van driver, coming round a bend, did not even see the little figure (though wearing a bright red coat) so close to the ground.

After the funeral at Downe, Robin came to us for several weeks. At first it seemed as though he was less utterly shattered by the loss than Kirstie, as he was able to take comfort from the thought that Barnaby was now safe from all the suffering he was bound to have faced on earth: 'Fuor sei dell'erte vie, fuor sei dell'arte.' ('Yet O,' as he wrote to me, 'who will jolly me along life's ghastly track now that he is gone?') He enjoyed hard physical work, continuing to dig a new patch of ground that I had started so that we could grow sugar beet to supplement our sugar ration. Robin always presented the paradox of someone who looked at life with the utmost pessimism, yet possessed the keenest aptitude for enjoyment – not only of music, but of human company, wine and games, talk and discussion of religion. 'You're depressed but you're not depress*ing*', as I once heard Kirstie say to him.

Kirstie too came to stay briefly, before they resumed their lives at Downe. But later in the summer Robin attempted suicide by poison, though leaving a note which ensured that Kirstie could find him before it was too late. In hospital he made another attempt, after which Uncle Humphrey and Kirstie reluctantly gave permission for him to be given the dreaded electro-convulsive treatment. This did have, temporarily, a good effect, and he was able to go home and to work again.

He began to write a 'Mass for children's voices' in memory of Barnaby, and I helped him to plan the words for it. For Faber I selected and edited poems for *A Little Book of Modern Verse*. I was also reading and making notes for a book on English metrics which Eliot had encouraged me to write. The only tangible fruit of this was an essay, 'Ambiguity in English Verse rhythms', published in *A Measure of English Poetry* fifty years later, though there was profit for my own poetry as well. I was also trying to teach myself Greek, starting with the excellent primer produced by the Dragon School classics master, L. A. Wilding, and continuing with Father's help. After Jane was settled in bed, I got out my Loeb editions with parallel translations, and we read together for an hour or so before supper: first the *Odyssey*, then the *Iliad*, then the plays of Sophocles. (It was not until later, with Reg Snell, that I attempted Aeschylus, and with him too I read some Euripides and Aristophanes.)

When the eggs supplied us by Nicholes, the neighbour who rented our field for his cows, were commandeered for the army, we decided to keep hens, and gave up the tennis court (scene of many family foursomes, especially when Uncle Humphrey came to stay) to make a run for them. We acquired eight Rhode Island Red pullets, which started laying at once, and from harvested fields we gleaned a whole chestful of corn for them. (The chest I think had been a tuck-box belonging to my brothers, converted in wartime Taviton Street into a haybox to save fuel, but now, with the Aga, no longer needed.) Vivian made a coop for the broody hens when he was home for a fortnight's leave from Orkney, and their delicious creamy eggs more than compensated for the job of cleaning out the henhouse. We did not ask Purton to do this, but 'Learn to kill a hen with quick despatch', as the advice booklet put it, was something we funked doing, and left to him. It was not till later that foxes gave us trouble: this happened when the hens took to roosting in the spinney where we could not coax them down to shut them up at sunset, and they were an easy prey.

After the success of the Battle of Britain, our nights were quieter; but December brought the Japanese attack on Pearl Harbor, then the disastrous loss of our battleships in the Pacific, and the fall of Singapore. Matt in the naval base at Colombo was told that it would not be defended in the event of a Japanese attack, and he should send his family back to England. This was of course a naval secret, and he could not do more than hint to Edward that Bertha and their baby son might not be safe. In the event they decided to stay (Bertha taking David to a cottage in the hills), but Matt cabled to ask whether Jan and the children could be given a home at Ringshall End, and whether the food supplies would be sufficient – to which of course the answer was Yes. It seemed fortunate that Vivian and I had decided that Jane and I should go back with him to Orkney after his next leave, and we made the journey in mid-April (1942). We took the night-train to Inverness, in a carriage full of soldiers who smoked all night. Jane became so restless on my lap that we hoisted her into the luggage rack, where she was invisible through the haze of smoke but did go off to sleep; then we flew on to Stromness, the only passengers in the small mail plane. It was a very noisy flight, and Jane began to howl as we left the ground, not stopping till we landed three-quarters of an hour later.

Vivian had found us lodgings in Kirkwall in the house of the vet who serviced all the islands, and he and his wife Hetty made us very welcome. Mrs Johnson confided to me afterwards that she had dreaded having to share her kitchen, but in fact we got on very amicably: I had the sole use of two gas burners, and could use her oven for occasional baking. We had a room on the second floor of their tall house, overlooking a fine vegetable garden, and I was allowed to put Jane's carry-cot in the boxroom next door to it. Mrs Johnson had intended us to eat in a small, windowless room next the kitchen, but it was pervaded with such a rancid smell that I preferred to carry our meals up the two flights of stairs to our wholesomer, sunny bedroom. (Just before we left, they took up the floorboards of our downstairs room, and discovered a lake of foul-smelling water from a blocked pipe.) We grew fond of the Johnsons and they of us: they invited us to supper soon after we arrived, and he intrigued us by reciting the whole of Burns's 'Tam O'Shanter' after-wards.

VAB's diary tells me that we only spent two-and-a-half months in Orkney, but I find this difficult to believe, so settled and pleasant our existence there became. Vivian had made a number of friends (all called Shearer or Smith, it seemed), and we were invited to their houses. I was struck by their interest in the arts, lively even though it did not seem very discriminating – whether Mozart or 'The Desert Song', all was 'right good'. And when I handed over my papers to obtain ration books at the local food-office, the woman behind the counter asked whether I was the Anne Ridler who had edited *A Little Book of Modern Verse*. Also, the weather was wonderful, and I had never seen such cloudscapes. Jane was not at all shy, and was much fêted: she had quite a large vocabulary, and crawled everywhere, pulling herself upright, but showing no inclination to walk. She slept so well that we could leave her at home, not disturbing the Johnsons, while we went out after supper. We would be invited to coffee, and then at about 11pm would be offered all manner of indigestible cheese-snacks: perhaps this derived from their Scandinavian inheritance, which showed itself so strongly in the cadence of Orcadian speech.

Vivian was often free during the day, as he worked on a day-night-shift rota, and one day we went by bus to visit the Linklaters, Eric and Marjorie, who lived out in the countryside with their infant son, Magnus. Marjorie (née MacIntyre) had been an admired Senior when I was at Downe: she was evidently anxious lest her guests might bore Eric, and warned us that he would probably retire upstairs directly lunch was over. We were therefore amused, and rather gratified, that he stayed downstairs talking all the afternoon, and pressed us to stay to tea. I asked him about the fields of beautiful blue lupins we had noticed as we came, and he said that they were planted to improve the soil for agriculture. (Their wolvish name derives from their thrusting roots.)

Kirkwall Cathedral is a magnificent twelfthth-century building of red sandstone, so powerful in its atmosphere that it seemed to demand a more dramatic ritual than the quiet Presbyterian liturgy performed there. It had a fine organ, and we made friends with the organist and his wife and two-year-old daughter. He was a north-countryman called Croft Jackson, who became quite well known later on as a concert-organizer and occasional composer. I took organ lessons from him, but had only just begun to use the pedals when we had to leave. (After that I accompanied services in Little Gaddesden church, with a village boy for blower.) His wife too was a pianist, and they performed duets together, he playing with arms immobile, as at an organ-keyboard. 'I don't allow our Ann to use baby-language' he would say in his strong north-country accent, and seemed surprised when I pointed out that 'Bye-bye', as used by both little girls (and indeed by Croft Jackson himself) *was* baby-language.

The end of our happy time came as cruelly as the storm that in Purcell's *Dido & Aeneas* breaks in on the hunting scene. Hetty Johnson and I had taken Jane for a picnic tea to a beach facing Scapa Flow, where Vivian was to join us when he came off duty. I had been watching for him, and went to meet him as he walked down the hill: when he came near I saw that he was close to tears, as he uttered the one word 'Overseas'.

Hetty Johnson was very upset, and could hardly believe it. We never met again, but kept contact by notes for some years, and I heard from her when Tom and Jean Griffiths met her in Orkney a good while ago.

Vivian was to go on leave and await orders. I telephoned to Mother, and we had till the next morning to pack up and depart, by boat this time across the Pentland Firth, dreaded for its rough seas. Luckily it was a calm day, but the boat did toss a little as we met the tide race, whereat Jane shook her head and shouted *No*. Of course we were welcomed back at Ringshall, but I think Nellie and Mother must have felt rather dismayed at the addition to the house party, for meanwhile Jan and the children had arrived, after a tedious, dangerous journey. Matt had gone with the Naval Staff to Kilindini in East Africa. Dan was now aged nine and Diana six and a half: Father gave them lessons in the mornings, and till the winter they and their mother stayed with us, except for brief visits away.

After all, Vivian was not summoned at once for overseas, and hoped he might be able to qualify for a photographic course instead: meanwhile he went back to camp in Orkney. Disappointingly he didn't achieve the course, and in late October he was summoned to Blackpool to assemble for an unknown destination overseas. I was pregnant with Alison, as we had decided to start another child while we could. So that I could go up to Blackpool for two nights to see him off, Mother and Jan looked after Jane – no doubt with Diana's help. We had bed-and-breakfast with a kind woman whose house was converted from a shop, and we ate behind a large uncurtained plateglass window. It was a bitter-sweet week-end. We strolled along the dreary wind-swept esplanade, and gaped at Epstein's enormous statue of *Jacob*, advertised as Ten Tons of Sensation, between a display of erotica and an oyster bar. And we bought a string of red amber beads, which gave the title to a poem I wrote about a year later: 'Beads from Blackpool'.

Vivian had been given an inoculation against yellow fever, which made us think that he might be bound for the Far East, so it was a relief when a month later I had a cable to say he was in West Africa – actually in the part known as the White Man's Grave from its humid atmosphere, where he was with a Belgian mobile fighter squadron, engaged in building their own airfield at Ikeja outside Lagos (now the main Lagos airport). The inoculation must have been faulty, for he and others developed jaundice, their recovery from which was not assisted by the medical officer, who kept them working in the broiling sun till several of them collapsed. Luckily Vivian was transferred the following spring to Kano, equally hot but much drier, where they provided a staging post for planes intended to support General Montgomery's advance from El Alamein.

A fortnight after I had returned from Blackpool, Matt rang up from London to say that he was safely back from East Africa, having travelled via the Cape and South America to Glasgow, in command of the naval draft on board the cruiser *The Duke of York*. (Their sister ship was torpedoed off South Africa just ahead of them.) After a joyful time with us (not shared by Dan, who had started boarding at a prep school), he went off to join the staff of the C in C Western Approaches at Birkenhead: he and Jan found a house to rent in that neighbourhood, where the children joined them at Christmas. Diana had then been with us for six months, and we all missed her.

By this time we had had to give up the car altogether for lack of petrol, and got about by bicycle and bus. I went to help with the school dinners in Little Gaddesden, and to wash up at Ashridge House, now in use as a military hospital. Charles Williams's wonderful book on Dante [*The Figure of Beatrice*] came out this autumn, and at the time when I went to Blackpool I was struggling to review it for *Time and Tide*. Looking back on our Orkney days I wrote the short poem called 'Kirkwall 1942' which was published the following year in *The Nine Bright Shiners*, but most of the poems in that book were of earlier date.

A pleasant feature of that winter was the presence of the Melvilles in one of the Ringshall cottages – Alan coming down when he was off duty from the London Fire Service. Clarissa was close to Jane in age, and we had many walks together on the common, meetings for tea, and singing. Alan to my delight was a great admirer of Robin's songs. I see from VAB's diary that Clarissa and Madeline came to Jane's second-birthday tea (4 Feb. 1943), by which time she could sing the end word, in tune, of seven nursery rhymes. Mrs Gray, our kind Little Gaddesden neighbour, was also present, and Robin, who had bicycled over from Downe. Nellie made a chocolate cake, using some of the thirty-two eggs we were getting weekly from the hens.

Just before Alison was born on 10 April, we had a week-end visit from

Enrica, who had been evacuated with her Sevenoaks school to Pontesford in Shropshire; and David (Bland) came for one night. He was, I think, about to go on active service as a navigator, not as a pilot as he had hoped, because he had had an unlucky accident while training in Texas. 'Unlucky', I wrote, but actually he had barely escaped with his life, when he hit an overhead cable while bringing a plane in to land, and for a week they feared that he had lost an eye. As it was, the American surgeon skilfully reconstructed his cheek, and although his appearance seemed at first quite unlike himself, we soon got used to it.

Then at 9pm on Friday 9 April I went down to a Berkhamsted nursing home, and Alison Kate was born at 11 o'clock the next morning.

CHAPTER VI

It seems that I had a whole fortnight in The Grange nursing home, to relieve pressure on them at home, and afterwards at Ringshall, in those pampered days, had first Nurse Morty, a friend of Nurse Tookey, for a week, and then a week of Nurse Tookey herself. Jane, surrounded by her usual carers, showed no signs (outwardly at any rate) of being jealous of 'Tinybaby', but breast-fed her dolly in imitation. Also, we had lately acquired a white kitten, Snowflake, which she enjoyed showing off to visitors. 'Would you like to come into the drawing room, because Pussy is just about to purr?' Ted Wager warned, however, that 'There'll be wigs on the green with these two later on: O, bound to be.'

It seemed an age before I knew that Vivian had heard of Alison's birth. Our cable never reached him, probably because he was in hospital with malaria, and he had the news by letter, cabling an answer which reached me in mid-May, and, soon after, his new address in Kano. Mother's entry about this is one of the last in her diary for, meeting the entries written from the other end of the book (recording life at School Field), she ended her fascinating record – or, if she resumed in another book, it has alas not survived.

Alison – or rather Kate, her second name which she adopted in adult life, and which I suppose I should use to avoid confusion – was a very equable baby: in fact I wrote in the book of early records I kept for each of our children that 'in disposition she was unbelievably placid, only crying in a reproachful, offended way if one handled her clumsily or startled her by a sudden noise'. (But from Jane she would suffer all sorts of bumps and bangs uncomplainingly.) Enrica and I, looking at her, would wonder whether so sensitive, gentle a child would be able to stand up for herself later on. (How wrong we were, fortunately!) Enrica was her loving and much-loved godmother, and came to stay for her christening in the early summer, performed by Ted Wager in Little Gaddesden church. Neither of her godfathers could be present: Lumsden Barkway was now a bishop in Scotland (of St Andrews, Dunkeld & Dunblane), and David, alas, was a prisoner in the notorious Stalag Luft 3. He had been shot down over France, and had been at large for two days before being arrested. Kathleen Raine, Kate's other godmother, came down from London, and was with us for tea, but unluckily had mistaken the time of the train and so missed the service.

Kathleen came to stay later in the summer for a week-end while HCB and VAB were away on a short holiday, and together we tried over the poems we intended to read at an event at the Wigmore Hall planned for September. Apart from Edith Sitwell and Lady Dorothy Wellesley we were the only woman poets invited, and public poetry readings were much more unusual than they are now, so we did not know what to expect. I sought advice from Nellie Wager on my speaking, and from Philippa on my clothes: she suggested I should borrow from her sister Diana Murray a blouse made from some beautiful material which her husband Jock had bought.

I still have the booklet, *Poets' Choice*, issued by the National Council for Women, who shared the proceeds with Aid to China. There were fourteen poets, and we sat on the platform in a semi-circle, with the chairman Desmond MacCarthy in the centre, flanked by Edith Sitwell and T. S. Eliot. Most of us read three poems, but William Empson, whose reading is the most vivid in my memory, read only one, 'Bacchus', which is two-and-a-half pages long and very obscure. He became inspired as he read, and began to dance on the spot 'like a satyr' as someone remarked. We read more or less in alphabetical order, and I was amused that Stephen Spender, the last to move forward to the microphone, still had not found the place in his book for his second poem.

As the preface to the booklet records, the Chinese ambassador was represented by Mme Wellington Koo, and the poet S. I. Hsiung 'added a chanted version of his poems in the traditional Chinese manner'. I well remember the intriguing sounds he made, and also that he prefaced his reading by some very disparaging remarks about Britain's slowness in coming to the help of China, which struck me as out of place in the context (we were all giving our services free, of course). Cecil Day Lewis complimented me on my reading, and said that he thought I ought to read for the BBC – hastily adding that he had no influence there. TSE gave me one of his delightfully ambiguous comments: 'You couldn't have done better.'

Letters from Vivian came regularly, and apart from his bout of malaria, he enjoyed much of his time at Kano, where he was able to play a great deal of tennis, with coaching, which he had never had before. It is a walled city, and he saw a fascinating native festival, with warriors on horseback, and jesters as in medieval times. Our life at home with the two little girls continued peacefully, and as we used one of their ration books as for a vegetarian, we always had ample supplies of cheese. We harvested rose-hips for syrup, tediously strained through flannel to get rid of the lethal hairs, and laboriously processed the newly-grown sugar beet – hardly worth the bother, for the amount we got. I went to help with the village school lunches, and was impressed by Vicars Bell's ability to quell a babel of voices by speaking almost in a whisper instead of shouting.

At the outset of the war, Martin Browne, the producer of Eliot's plays, had founded 'The Pilgrim Players', a group of actors who dedicated themselves to producing plays around the country, in village halls, churches, or anywhere that could accommodate an audience and mount a drama with the minimum of props. The plays, some of which were commissioned for the purpose, expressed a Christian point of view, though not necessarily religious in subject. A branch of the Players was run by Ruth Spalding and based in Oxford, and Charles Williams wrote several short plays for them to perform, first of all in the University Church, where Dick Milford was vicar and supportive of the venture. (Ruth's sister Anne, a pupil of Barnett Freedman at the Ruskin School of Drawing, kept house during the war in their parents' home in South Parks Road, where she had Charles Williams and Gerry Hopkins as lodgers.) Encouraged by CW, I wrote a short verse play, *Cain*, with these players in mind, and although they never performed it, it was published by Nicholson & Watson in 1943, and as a result had three productions in the succeeding years, by students at University College, London, by a group from St Anne's, Soho (who acted in a hall off Regent Street), and by pupils at St Christopher, Letchworth. This last was important for us, because the producer was Reginald Snell, second master at the school, and was the beginning of our friendship with him. (It took place in the winter term of 1944 when Vivian was back in England, and we managed to get over from Ringshall by bus to see it.)

Nineteen forty-three saw the publication not only of *Cain* but also of *The Nine Bright Shiners* by Faber & Faber. The edition sold out in a month – the only such success I have ever had. One reason no doubt was that people turned to poetry and music in wartime for emotional nourishment, and for lack of other distractions. The book was printed on expensive hand-made paper, which Dick de la Mare cleverly found to eke out his paper ration; for the second printing he used a blueish writing-paper.

As the Allied forces under General Montgomery drove the Germans out of Egypt, the staging post at Kano was no longer needed, and in the spring of 1944 Vivian began his journey homeward. When his ship was steaming up the Clyde during the last week in May, he saw several battleships moving down, about to go south for the Channel assault, and he noticed a number of empty barges in side creeks.

I went down in the car (now brought into sparing use again) to meet him in Berkhamsted, and he sat in the back holding hands with a very silent Jane. Kate greeted him from the security of her high chair, and showed no surprise at the affectionate stranger. He looked well, but his face was yellow as a result of being dosed with mepocrine against malaria, quinine being unavailable. Twice during succeeding years he had short bouts of fever, the result of the malaria he had suffered at Lagos.

D Day, the Channel assault, was on 8 June, and Christopher in the Royal Army Service Corps was involved in the support which followed. To our delight Vivian was assigned to the RAF camp at Westcott, a few miles west of Aylesbury and just within bicycling distance of us when he had week-end leave.

Vivian remained at Westcott all through the following winter, and thus he was able to be at home for the celebration of Mother and Father's Golden Wedding on 17 April 1945, a joyful day, for which Matt and Jan too were with us. Jan had worked a beautiful piece of embroidery surrounding a poem written by Matt which (I quote from memory) went thus:

> All that glisters is not gold,
> But youthful hearts that ne'er grow old
> Declare when all the tale is told
> 'Our love has prospered fifty-fold'.

Mr Deakin of Coppice Cottage on Duncombe Terrace (father of Bill Deakin the writer) put a bloom of his Crown Imperials, which he knew

Mother envied, in a milk bottle at the bottom of the drive, and there were many telephone calls. I heard Matt speaking down the mouthpiece in the hall to an imaginary caller, with the words from Albert Chevalier's 'My old Dutch': 'Yes, we've been together now for fifty years, And it doesn't seem a day too much...' And Father and I each produced a poem, mine printed later in *The Golden Bird*, his too late to be included in the privately-published *Poems* which I had selected and typed and Uncle Humphrey had had printed in 1942. Later in the summer, Reg Snell brought his 'miniature opera' group over to perform Dibdin's 'Tom Bowling' to our local friends, crammed into the drawing room.

After the German surrender in May 1945 Vivian was busy round the clock (and 'mentioned in Dispatches') guiding the aircraft which brought back our troops. VE Day was celebrated on 8 May, and we went out to see bonfires lit on Ivinghoe Beacon and Whipsnade Hill.

The joy of the peace declaration was followed a week later by the great sadness of Charles Williams's sudden death in Oxford, after a minor operation in the Radcliffe Infirmary. He was only fifty-eight, but had lived a life of such intensity that he had 'worn his thread almost through' as his biographer (Alice Mary Hadfield) put it. I had only seen him twice since Jane's christening, once in Oxford and recently for a brief café talk in London, but through letters we had still been close. His influence on me, especially in matters of religion, remains indelible, nor have I ever wished to reject any of his teaching.

He was buried in St Cross churchyard, where I stood in a bewilderment of grief with several of those whom we used to think of as the 'household' of Taliessin, his poet-persona – notably Charles and Alice Mary Hadfield. It was some solace to me to have, almost at once, the task of editing his short plays for the Oxford University Press.

Later in the summer Vivian went on a week's course as a trial for a commission in the Intelligence, from which he joined the girls and me on a visit to Robin and Kirstie, now again living in their house on Red Shute Hill. He was depressed because he thought he must have failed to be selected, having performed rather badly in a mock assault which involved leaping over barbed wire into a ravine of unseen depth, while loaded with pack and rifle! (He particularly remembered sitting in a downpour taking notes of some discourse, while the words on his pad were instantly washed out by the rain.)

This was the Downe House visit where on our walk through the woods up to the main house (where concerts were taking place) we used to pass a shed where a restless donkey was confined and looked out over a half-door, a sight which obsessed Kate, who kept enquiring: 'Why was the donkey kicking his door?'

Robin and I were collaborating on a radio play, *The Mask,* for the producer Edward Livesey, based on the theme of the folk-song 'Shooting of his Dear', and on a recurrent tune from a musical box, for which Robin composed enchanting music played on a glockenspiel. The play was broadcast on the Midland Region network, and though I later adapted it for the stage, I think the radio version worked better, because of the music.

Vivian's pessimism was unfounded: he was duly awarded his commission in Intelligence, and after a short course at Caen Wood House (near Ken Wood), where he learnt about the Japanese and so expected to be sent to the Far East, he was posted to Herne in the Ruhr, and spent the winter there, inspecting German factories for armaments which England wished to acquire, and guiding visiting officials about the area.

Jane attended a morning class at the Rectory under the care of kind Nellie Wager, where she was happy but inclined to be lethargic, we were told. A remedy was suggested, and 'I take iron pills', she announced to a visitor. Then when she was five, she started at the village school, mornings only, and rapidly learnt to read, and to chant finger-rhymes with an accurately-reproduced Hertfordshire accent, not used in her ordinary speech. I would ride to meet her on the Little Gaddesden road, and I remember that once I had got right to the Church field before she appeared, saying: 'O here I are at last! I *couldn't* get off.'

After the success of Eliot's *Murder in the Cathedral* before the war, Martin Browne was determined to foster the development of poetry in the theatre, and to ensure that poets acquired the necessary knowledge of theatrical technique. He leased from Ashley Dukes the small Mercury Theatre in Notting Hill, where *Murder* had started its London run, and planned a season of 'Plays by Poets' there, in which Robert Speaight was booked to take part, for the winter of 1945. I had been up to see Martin in London, and as a result I wrote a verse play, *The Shadow Factory*, in which the part of the factory manager was designed for Robert Speaight.

The Mercury season started in the autumn of 1945 with Norman Nicholson's play about Elijah, *The Old Man of the Mountains*, and continued with Ronald Duncan's about St Anthony, *This Way to the Tomb*. Mine was to be the third, and was to last over the Christmas season, as it partly had a Christmas context. The idea for the play sprang from a school visit I had paid from Downe to Huntley & Palmer's biscuit factory which I never forgot: such dismay I felt at seeing people engaged all day in totally mechanical work. Set against this emotional response was the reality which Vivian showed me, having experienced factory work himself: that there are satisfactions in such a life (provided that the conditions are good) which are not apparent to the uninformed outsider.

I went up to the actors' read-through, and then to daytime rehearsals during the week before the first night, which were enthralling for me. The excellent cast were mostly old friends of Martin's, some of them from his Pilgrim Players, and one in particular, Alan Wheatley, became a great friend of mine too. The setting for the first scene was striking. The Director's office, with his desk, is placed in front of a white screen, on which are cast the shadow of a large wheel and of three figures, seated at drills, which move at intervals. During the play a loud-speaker intervenes occasionally with directions and a slogan which Vivian composed for me: 'The piece-work way Means better pay. Keep up your output every day.' He also composed a most effective piece of mock-jargon for the 'Progress-chaser', which the actor delivered at top speed. Alan Wheatley took the part of an artist engaged to paint murals which are supposed to glorify the whole enterprise, but which when unveiled are shockingly satirical. These are described but not seen, of course, by the audience. The shock produces a change of heart in the arrogant and insensitive Director, well delineated by Robert Speaight. I think the dialogue is pretty good: the actors thought so but the theme was probably too ambitious for my technical capacity.

It was a severe disappointment that Vivian could not get leave from Germany to see the play. Christopher, however, was back in England, and he, Mother and Father were all able to come to the first night on 17 December. T. S. Eliot was also going to attend, and I decided that I would sit next to him after the interval if the play was going well, and sit for the first half next my parents. The play did go well, and the applause was warm as I went up to take a curtain call, greeted there by a beaming Alan Wheatley. TSE said 'I congratulate you on a success', and my godfather Kenneth Swan was enthusiastic: 'So full of good things, my dear.' Beverley Baxter in the *Evening Standard* , who had praised the other two plays, was also enthusiastic, saying to his readers 'I am very much afraid you will have to go again to the Mercury Theatre.'

It was a great help to have Christopher at hand to help me entertain Robert Speaight and Alan Wheatley after the play, and we took them to Prunier's in St James's, to eat scallops and discuss the evening.

Although the play continued to draw good audiences for the remainder of its planned season, alternating after the first week with the other two, it has only been revived once – by amateurs but never by professionals, as was also the case with Nic's play – but Ronald Duncan's was taken on to a small theatre in Paris and has been once revived in London, though with no critical success.

During the spring of 1946 Edward and Bertha and their two little boys returned to England. (Edward was appointed to be head of the Teachers' Training College at Eastbourne, and later to St Paul's College, Cheltenham, where he remained for the rest of his working life.) I visited them with Jane and Kate at Yotes Court, whence they took me to Glyndebourne to see Britten's *Rape of Lucretia*. (His *Peter Grimes* at Sadler's Wells had been the great musical event of the previous summer, and as Alan Melville trained its chorus, Vivian and I were involved in the excitement, and had gone up from Ringshall for the first night. I also saw, though he did not, Laurence Olivier's wonderful Oedipus and Hotspur in his seasons at the New Theatre.)

Vivian was demobilized in June 1946, and we turned our thoughts to finding a home in London, where he planned to work as a freelance typographer. Mrs Gray strongly advised us not to go back to Bloomsbury but to try leafy Hampstead Garden Suburb for the sake of the children, and this we decided to do, in spite of opposition from John Hayward, who wanted us to come to Chelsea where he was about to set up house in a flat with T. S. Eliot. 'The grocer will perform introductions', he wrote, and we should be swallowed up in suburban society. We found a house in a suitably leafy road, 54 Southway, with a nursery school close by, and were able to buy it without a mortgage, thanks to Father's sister, Aunt Mick, who made over her capital to me, keeping only an annuity for herself.

Before moving, we went on holiday, renting a house at Trebetherick, above Polzeath in south Cornwall, which belonged to Eda and Albert David – the ex-headmaster of Rugby, now Bishop of Liverpool. This was the girls' first seaside holiday: a beach-bathing holiday, not attempting the rocky creeks they came to enjoy later. I found a surf-board in the house, and experienced that pleasure for the first time. Arriving by train on our return, I remember Kate, aged three, addressing me as we went down a long flight of steps: 'Jane can go down these steps, because Jane bigger, but I can't, because I are only a littul gairl' – all the while descending quite successfully.

Also on a visit this summer, she announced that she did not like so-and-so: 'I can't do anything about it I'm afraid.'

Hampstead Garden Suburb was the brain-child of Canon Barnett and his wife Dame Henrietta, familiar and much-satirized figures to my Bradby relatives when they lived in the Dock House, East London. It was inspired by the garden-city movement which had Welwyn Garden City as its pattern. The houses were leasehold, and their owners had to sign an agreement which interfered in a governessy way with their habits. I summed up its aspirations in my poem 'The Golden Bird'.

> Here man is to be orderly, genteel and prosperous,
> Fecund, a lover of flowers, and keep no fowls.
> Here is High spire, Low dome, and Quaker garden,
> But there is no public house
> And no class feeling, for here there is only one class
> And one design for living.

I could have added that this rarefied atmosphere was luckily coarsened by the plentiful supply of children.

Our house was one of the later developments, built I suppose between the wars, with sunny rooms and a small back garden opening into a long communal one where all the neighbouring children played; but Southway itself, sloping up to St Jude's at the top (near which was a large house belonging to Harold Wilson), was even more used, for there was very little traffic and they could ride their tricycles. Opposite to us lived a barrister (later a judge) Neil Lawson and his lively wife Gwen, with whom we spent many convivial evenings; and opposite also were the Archers, who like us had two young children.

It was very exciting to possess our first house and garden, though mixed with anxiety, because of post-war shortages and the difficulty of getting any help in the house, or in transforming the neglected garden. We all felt the wrench of leaving supportive Ringshall End, but perhaps Jane most of all. We could still pay week-end visits, but only occasionally, as of course we had no car. Moreover it was just then that Father began to suffer from the cancer of the long bones that finally killed him. He only came once to Southway, for tea, after we had taken him to see Geoffrey Keynes (an Old Rugbeian from School Field) on John Hayward's suggestion, for a diagnosis.

Ben was conceived during our Cornish holiday, so that I was feeling sick during our weeks of settling into the new home. Then we endured one of the coldest winters of the century, and soon learnt the badly-planned lay-out of our plumbing, as icy or (once) scalding water cascaded down the walls and we clambered to cut off the outflow from the tank. The Suburb was not an easy place to get to for our friends, but many of them managed it (even John Hayward once), and some came to stay: Robin and Kirstie, Reg Snell, Enrica, Audrey. It was a fifteen-minute bicycle ride to North Finchley for the tube to central London, and Vivian went this way for his weekly day of teaching typography at the Royal College of Art (an innovation there), and his visits to Lund Humphries for design work and to the magazine *Contact* for which he was art editor. He had his own study for work at home. Jane was able to start at once at Miss Mulliner's nursery school, and got on well there, though the regime was much more bossy than that of the village school. Miss Mulliner insisted, for instance, that you must be able to tie your own shoelaces by the time you were three years old: Kate, starting after Christmas, passed muster on this score, luckily.

Ken Wood was an easy distance away, but we did not often take the girls into central London. One day, though, I took them to spend a day in Chelsea at the College of St Mark and St John with Janet Roberts (née Janet Adam Smith) and Kathleen Raine: Janet's husband Michael, who had been head of the college, had just died.

Martin Browne still had the lease of the Mercury Theatre, where he revived *The Family Reunion* and some of Yeats's short plays, and he arranged Sunday read-throughs of some new verse plays he was hoping to put on. This included my *Henry Bly,* which was planned with Alan Wheatley in mind, but Cyril Cusack took his part that day, I think. Alas, Ashley Dukes then returned from post-war work in France and re-claimed the use of his theatre, so that Martin had no base for putting on plays by poets, and turned his energies into the work of the British Drama League. *Henry Bly* has never been put on a stage, though it was published by Faber with two of my other plays in 1951. One of these plays was the result of a suggestion by Martin, who was a close friend of Sybil Thorndike and her husband Lewis Casson. They wanted something to be performed in a church (St Luke's Chelsea I believe), with parts designed for themselves and two other of their friends.

I set to work and wrote *The Missing Bridegroom,* finishing it and sending it to the Cassons just before Ben was born. I had nice letters from them, but it was not what they wanted: however, it was performed twice in the 1950s, once by the Unnamed Society (gifted amateurs) in Man-chester, and once by professionals at the Watergate Theatre in the Strand.

Geoffrey Keynes had given a verdict of 'not proven' on Father's cancer, recommending an exploratory operation, but our Dr Phillips quite rightly refused to put him through this ordeal of doubtful value, though he continued to keep him alive by injections of thyroid. When the endless-seeming winter began to give place to spring, Father asked him to discontinue the injections, and after this his life waned rapidly. Ben's birth was expected at the end of May, and on our wintry visits to Ringshall I was vividly aware of the two movements, 'waxing or waning into a new place... ebb and flow In a life persistent as the green under the snow.'

It turned out that Father never saw his grandson, for he died when Ben was about a month old, just as we were planning to travel to Ringshall. I did, however, get a precious token: a verse written in pencil when he heard of Ben's arrival:

Vivat ille Benedictus
Bonis omnibus addictus
Neque unquam mundo victus.

As Father had directed, his ashes were scattered (by Matt) in the churchyard at Little Gaddesden, so there was no gravestone, but later on a plaque was placed in the church. (It was designed and cut by Mr Forrest, the art lecturer at St Paul's, Cheltenham.) Ted Wager gave a fine tribute at the funeral, saying that Father was the most loving man he had ever met.

Through Diana Murray we had heard of a Swedish girl who wanted to work in a family to learn English: this was Kerstin Widelius, our first and dearest au pair. She arrived two days before Ben himself, bringing her shining Swedish bicycle, and we cycled together to the local Food Office to get her ration book. The birth was to be at home, and after much difficulty we secured a prize, an excellent cheerful nurse from a religious agency. As I wrote in the book I kept of his sayings: 'Ben was born at 7.15 pm on Wednesday May 28, 1947, in our bedroom at 54 Southway, a hot evening with children rapping at the door for Jane and Alison to come out. At four o'clock I had ridden my bicycle to meet Vivian and send him for some eye-drops [wanted by the nurse], and brought Jane back from school on it. She and Alison were driven to Ringshall by Mother shortly afterwards.'

This was before the days when fathers assisted at their children's births, but at least Vivian, waiting in his study next door, was for the first time able to see his baby's first moments in the world, and all went happily. The girls returned after a week or so, and I had provided a cradle for their dolls as a counterweight to Ben's. Kate showed no jealousy of him directly, but she was very difficult with Kerstin at first. She was devoted to one of Jane's contemporaries at Miss Mulliner's, though, and this was helpful. (Caroline Hogarth was the daughter of a delightful American, Grace, who lived in the Suburb while her husband, Billy, was abroad: both of them had connexions with the OUP.) And now we were given the chance of a seaside holiday, and a much-needed change for Mother, by Kenneth and Millie Swan, who offered to lend us their house at Littlestone in Kent.

Caroline was to come with us, and of course Kerstin: we had Mother's car, and Grace Hogarth took some of the party in hers, though she did not stay. The Swans had built their house close by the seashore, with golf-links at its back, and I had stayed there as a child with Mother and Father. Kerstin was in her element by the sea, as she was used to spending much of the summer on a small island possessed by her family: she would pick up and cook tiny crabs which we should never have thought of eating, but which proved quite tasty. I enjoyed the unfamiliar flora and fauna – viper's bugloss and horned poppy on the marshes; linnets singing on the telephone wires by the house; sea-mice at low tide with sunset colours in their hairs. And we had delicious vegetables from the Swans' kitchen garden, looked after by a girl gardener, who was company for Kerstin.

Vivian had to return to London after some days, but before he left we visited Rye, and saw Henry James's house there. Mother enjoyed it with us, and never for a moment let her grief cloud the holiday.

She was with us at the end of July when Ben was christened in St Jude's (by John Knights the curate), his godparents being John Christie, Reg Snell, Rhoda Miller and Madeline Melville. Only Rhoda and Reg were present; Alan and Clarissa Melville had to represent Madeline, who just before setting out had burnt in ironing the skirt she meant to wear, and was too upset to come. Christopher too was with us, but not Bip, as they had by then parted company. Jane and Kate made crosses on Ben's forehead beforehand, and attributed his good behaviour to this. Our small group (with the curate who had a good voice) made a fine show at singing 'The King of Love' to the St Columba tune, but I cursed my thoughtlessness in having chosen it, for we had sung it at Father's funeral, and it brought tears to Mother's eyes.

Ben's babyhood continued peacefully, and as he was so contented I did not realize that he was being underfed. I always had plenty of milk for the other babies, but whether from the effect on me of the shock of Father's death, or minor anxieties, he was being short-changed. With supplements he soon put on weight again; but we did have rather a troubled time when Kate, hurtling down Southway on her tricycle, tipped over and fractured her left elbow. We encountered an unsympathetic doctor next day at the hospital, who treated her callously, and as he decided to bind her arm to her side rather than putting it in a splint, we had to be very careful that she did not fall, and she could not go out to play. It was a relief when after a month we were sent to another hospital, and had the sympathetic treatment of Lawrence Page, a friend of David Bland and Vivian.

David by now was back at Faber's, and able to tell us of his hair-raising experiences at the end of his imprisonment, when they were marched by their guards before the advancing Russians – the guards being in even worse shape than they were – eating stray cats or whatever else they could find. Some time during the winter he introduced me to Mary, now a most efficient secretary to Eliot and quickly learning to share all David's interests. A year or so later Vivian was their best man, and they made an ideally happy marriage.

Our course seemed set fair for life in this London suburb. But then came an offer which deflected it. The offer, or rather pressing invitation, came from Charles Batey at Oxford, who had now succeeded John Johnson as Printer to the University. He wanted Vivian to come back as his assistant, on the understanding that Vivian would succeed him as Printer in ten years' time. This presented us with a difficult decision, because it meant that Vivian would have to give up the freelance design and teaching which he enjoyed so much, and go back to factory life. The prestige of being Printer meant very little to him; on the other hand, as TSE said when I spoke to him of our doubts, 'Vivian will be in a position to influence all the printing in England.' And, of course, we thought Oxford would be a better place than London in which to raise a family, much as we should miss our friends. Charles Batey came up for an evening to press his case, and after long hesitation Vivian accepted. He gave a term's notice to the Royal College, and agreed to start at the Press the following April, 1948.

We set about selling our house, and for the only time in my life (so far) I undertook the distasteful task of exposing one's home to the critical eyes of purchasers. The place always seemed to be full of rampaging children when they came: once there were shrieks from the kitchen, and I found that Kate had plunged off a chair and broken the radius bone in her *other* arm: only a greenstick fracture, luckily, but sufficiently disturbing.

Mother went over to Oxford to explore house agents, and picked out two houses for us to visit, one modern one at Yarnell's Hill off the Botley bypass, and the other in East Oxford, Victorian, larger and with a fine big garden. The price asked for both was more than we wanted to give, but Vivian interviewed the owner of 14 Stanley Road, who was ill in bed, and managed to get him to reduce the price from six to five thousand pounds, as it had been on the market for a good while. After completing the contract, Vivian told the agent that he thought he had secured a good bargain. 'Ah sir,' was the reply, 'but then you see the house is in a decaying part of Oxford.' We, no doubt, were part of the decay. But we were really lucky in our neighbours. Next door at No. 12 were three elderly bookish ladies, the two Miss Woodgates who were thick with the Cowley Fathers, and Veronica Ruffer, secretary of the local Archaeological Society. They made us very welcome, and never complained later on of the noise from our garden, which soon became an adventure playground for the street. Then, a few doors away lived the Spencer family, of whom more later on.

As we sold the Southway house for, I think, six thousand pounds, we had enough in hand to cover this second move (only eighteen months after the other) and the much-needed decorating. Everything was painted chocolate brown, and the Colmans, who had naturally done nothing to the house during the war years, kept a large pile of scraps outside the kitchen window. There wasn't anything actually wrong with the drains, but the lavatory pans were deeply stained, and we found that coming along Stanley Road at night before the gas-lamps were lighted, we knew from the smell when we had reached our house gate. When they departed, the Colmans carried off one of the two greenhouses listed in the agent's brochure, but left behind their wooden address stamp with the name Don-a-Gore. We planned to have some fun with this, but unfortunately they soon called to reclaim it.

We moved towards the end of March, Kerstin taking Ben to hospitable Philippa for a few days, and the girls staying at Ringshall. A local character called Jones had done the decorating for us, and procured a young carpenter to put up shelves and pelmet boards, who he declared was a fine craftsman: 'you've only got to look at his tools to see that.' George didn't really live up to this encomium, but Jones himself was very thorough, and had the traditional disdain of one painter for another man's work, especially on the greenhouse in the garden, where he tore great lumps of the wood away – 'Just look at that!' He was horrified at our instruction to paint the hideous shiny pink tiles surrounding the fireplaces plain white – such a desecration – but reluctantly obeyed.

Ration cards for curtain material (as well as clothes) were still in force, and the tall Victorian windows presented a problem. We bought white sheets for the girls' room, and decorated them by prints from a lino-cut of a dog made for us by a Royal College colleague of Vivian's, pressed on with the foot. Kate and Jane were onlookers, but when we broke off for lunch, Kate stole away and made a smudgy print in an unsymmetrical place herself – impossible to erase, of course, and very annoying, but I think I scolded her more than I should have done.

Mother's sister-in-law, our Aunt Elsie, who lived in Chalfont Road, made dining-room curtains for us from red linen, still in use for the 'shower-room'. Her son Dick Milford had only recently left the University Church, and his wife Margaret was helpful with advice. Through her we registered Jane and Kate for the Crescent preparatory school in North Oxford which she had helped to found with her friend Elsa Crawshaw, and she suggested that Canon Collins (of anti-war-marching fame) who lived in East Oxford would like to share a daily taxi for his and our children.

Vivian started work at the Press on 1 April, designated at first as Works Manager, for it was not until he had been introduced to the Delegates and they had confirmed Batey's choice that he could be officially appointed as Assistant Printer. A nasty surprise was that he had to be there at the factory hour of 7.30 am, but still more unpleasant was the situation he discovered concerning the composing-room manager, Peakman, an ambitious man who had hoped he might become Batey's successor, and did his best to undermine Vivian's authority. He managed to make things so unpleasant that Vivian began to think he had made a great mistake in coming, and would sit gazing into the fire in the evenings in a way that was so unlike him that I was seriously worried. Batey had known that Peakman would be jealous, but had wishfully thought that Vivian would win him over; however, after a six months' trial he realized his mistake, and Peakman was quickly packed off, to a job elsewhere. The Personnel Manager, John Hall, was a devoted and tireless support, and Vivian soon began to relish the idiosyncrasies of some of the department managers and men. He invariably went round the works first thing in the morning after examining the post, and although it was a large concern, employing 900 people at its zenith, he was kept well aware (by various sources) of what was being said and done. ('E's all right', he overheard one man whom he had found mending his bicycle say to another: and the reply 'Yes, when e's out the bloody way.') The remarks of various characters would be repeated to me at home; in particular from those first days I remember those of a progress-chaser called Plaister, who took a dim view of everything connected with Oxford, its climate and its people.

The Crescent School nursery class was based in the house of a distinguished Balliol don, Sandy Ogston, and Kate was able to start there at once. Sandy and Liza were our friends thereafter; one of their daughters, called Dervorguilla after the foundress of Balliol, was in the class, and their little boy Walter, too young to be a regular member, was in evidence. Because he was not quite house-trained, and also often wore a bathing cap (why?), Kate was under the impression that his name was Water. The class, under Kay Sawtell, was for mornings only, and Vivian would bring her home to lunch (which he always had at home) on the carrier of his bicycle.

During that first summer, although I worked quite hard at sorting out the neglected garden, as well as at editorial work, and poetry-reviewing for the *Manchester Guardian*, I felt as though I were a holiday tourist, exploring the town. It was thrilling to wake up to the sound of the clock-bell from Magdalen tower, and to get the scent of balsam-poplar from I knew not where (actually from the lane off the Iffley Road by the football ground). I investigated the various college chapels with their pictorial Flemish glass, as well as the gardens so generously open to visitors, above all the Botanical Gardens, and that first year I saw a kingfisher there on the Cherwell, though never since. Then there was the pleasure of the river close at hand. There was only a footbridge then over the Thames at Donnington, so that we could undress in the bushes, and I used to tow the girls across in a motor-tyre raft. We could get a punt or rowing boat there, and one weekend we rowed all the way up to Nuneham Courtney. A thunderstorm struck as we were finishing lunch, and we rowed back in a downpour, with two locks to negotiate, the girls sitting in the stern with their bathing-caps on, trying to keep tiny Ben dry under a rug, from which he kept wriggling out. Next day at the Press Vivian was greeted by the porter with 'You must have got wet yesterday, sir.' He had seen us, still dry, on our outward journey – Vivian's first intimation that wherever he went in Oxford, someone from the Press would be sure to see him.

Kerstin left us at the end of May, much missed, when her year was up, and suggested a Swedish acquaintance to replace her later in the summer. Barbro was an intelligent but very selfish girl, and we were glad to see the last of her after only six or eight months. Luckily we had some cleaning help from a Treasure, Mrs Rymills, who had worked for Uncle Humphrey when he lived in his Bijou Residence off the Cowley Road, and was devoted to him. She lived close to us in Henley Street with her husband and adult daughter, and was a support for all our early years in Oxford. She found an elderly gardener for us, Mr Flint, who was one of the old school, treating me with indulgent patronage. 'I had a young leddy at the last place I worked for, and *she* liked to puddle about with a bit of seed.'

We had found an old indoor bath in the shed which had served as a laundry (together with a copper tub, useful for plants), and he sank this into the ground to serve as a paddling pool. We had brought our climbing frame with its aluminium slide from London, and this made a fine water-chute. We had visitors all through the summer holidays: Vivian's mother (Bristol Granny) as well as mine, Nellie with her sister, Alice Pennant with her children, Margaret Milford with Phillida (who stayed on alone, and got on so well with Jane that poor Kate was miserable), Clarissa and Giles Melville, the latter so homesick that he clung to me, and I could not go to post a letter without taking him too. And soon after we arrived we made the acquaintance of the Spencers (mentioned earlier) in a suitably dramatic way. We were walking back from the river, and had reached the bottom of Fairacres Road, when a child on a tricycle descended at speed and deposited herself at our feet. This was Mary, pursued by Seymour, who characteristically began at once to explain that she had fallen because the unexpected sight of us had distracted her. He was then a consultant at the Warneford, specializing in the treatment of students and young people. We soon met Margaret, and Ben's contemporary Michael, and exchanged tea-visits.

Margaret was a delightful friend, with ready sympathy and a great sense of humour. In speaking of Seymour, her stories portrayed him with loving ridicule, her way of preserving the balance of her marriage to a dominant and tactless, though devoted, husband. During the years that we were neighbours, our families were very close, and Margaret had a special feeling for my mother; Mary was a lively companion for the girls, and Ben's early stories centred round a composite figure, 'a little boy called Michael-and-Ben'.

Indeed, we never lacked company, but the one kind of companionship missing for Vivian was that of his peers in printing and typography. He made up for it later on by membership of the Double Crown Club, but at first he did miss his former cronies. Charles Batey, though a good judge of standards in printing, was not a typographer.

My own connexion with the Press, socially speaking, was not onerous, but there were occasional duties, such as the pleasant one of handing out presents from the tree at the annual Christmas party for the children of Press employees. (Mrs Batey – Topsy – disliked social appearances, so the Assistant Printer's wife took her place.) While waiting to distribute cups at the Fire Brigade competition, I found it hard to keep a judicial face, as the men raced in gumboots to be the first to aim an uncontrollably bucking hose at a target, and I was then appealed to by the secretary, Aubrey Beasley: 'Now Mrs Ridler, criticize our drills.' There were dinners for the various societies, a Pensioners' Party in the summer, and Staff Outings, though after the first year or two I ceased to join in these last, finding that there was very little social mixing involved, for everyone kept to their own partner for the day. A letter to my parents describes my first experience of an outing.

We started out at 7.30 am from Walton Street in 3 charabancs, in glorious sunshine, and had a v.pretty drive over the downs to Newbury and on to Winchester by 10. There it began to rain intermittently, and my discomforts began, for the day had looked so fine that I'd brought no mac or brolly, and my shoes leaked. V and I and nice Mr Wheeler of the Bibles and Prayer Bks Dept walked down to the Cathedral (a good quarter hour from the bus park), but had to come back at once, as we only had a half hour altogether. At Bournemouth we lunched off corned beef and blancmange (96 of us!), and came out to find the rain pouring down, which it continued to do without a pause until we got home. We all split up into twos and threes. V and I went to the Public Library and spent the afternoon there. At 5 we were supposed to return, but the bus drivers kept us waiting 20 minutes in the rain in the bus park before they arrived with the buses. We stopped at Winchester for a v.good supper, where Batey made a little speech, but again had to wait for the buses, so that we left an hour behind the schedule, and then we had to wait 35 minutes at Newbury while the drivers had another drink, so that we didn't arrive at Walton St till 11.15 pm! A bicycle ride home in the rain was quite a relief after that. Mrs Batey wisely didn't come, but Batey put a gallant face on it all, and his secretary John Hall – such a nice fellow, who sings in St Mary's choir – had taken such trouble over the arrangements that one had to try and look as if one were enjoying it – though V. did allow himself to say 'Make yourself miserable this wet, expensive way' at one point!

We soon began to enjoy the Playhouse, then under the management of Frank Shelley, and struggling as always to attract a large enough audience to be financially viable. I remember that we took Mother to see Strindberg's grim play *The Father*, that first summer. The autumn brought the delights of Subscription Concerts (then in the afternoons, so Vivian could not come with me): Beecham brought the Royal Philharmonic to play in the Sheldonian, and once a brilliant young German baritone called Fischer Dieskau gave a recital there to a mere handful of an audience.

Then I joined the Bach Choir, founded by Sir Hugh Allen and made up of both town and university singers: my aunts had sung in it, and Edward when he was an undergraduate. It was now under the conductorship of Thomas Armstrong, 'Choragus' and organist of Christ Church. I was auditioned for it by Mary Archer, music mistress at the High School, who accepted me, and finding that I was a good sight-reader invited me to join a few people who met to sing madrigals or carols, generally at Thomas Norrington's house (more of him later). In the Bach Choir we were practising the B Minor Mass, and had the whole winter to learn it, as it had not been sung since before the war. Normally of course the conductor would have been able to count on a nucleus in the choir who knew it well – indeed one of Tom Armstrong's stories concerned a lady who sang nothing else, and by heart, whatever the set piece. I was to sing it eight times altogether, and it remains one of the great experiences of my life: I was lucky to sing it for the first time under a conductor who felt and conveyed the full glory of the work. (We sang the Mass again the following year under Adrian Boult's professional but not very inspiring beat, to mark the third centenary of Bach's death.)

In those days it was customary to give two performances of any big work, early in the summer term; at the end of term some of us, 'the Little Bach Choir', would go to sing in one of the neighbouring churches, such as Dorchester Abbey or Tewkesbury, and Tom Armstrong always made these into festive occasions, sometimes ending up with round-singing out of doors. I used to sing 2nd soprano, along with Mary Evers and Lorna Symonds (met again after early Rugby days), only changing to 1st alto (under Sydney Watson) in my mid-fifties.

The girls were eager for the autumn term to begin at the Crescent School, and Kate's class was now also included in the house in Norham Gardens. It backed on to the University Parks where they went to play organized games; for break they had its own large garden. It was a very cheerful school, with just the right balance between freedom and discipline – though Philippa, when later on Lucilla joined the school and suffered from the attentions of little boys, thought that there should have been more supervision in 'break'. The majority of the pupils were dons' children: Jane was deputed to be protective to a shy Jonathan Cecil, Lord David's son. Ben and later Colin both started in the nursery class under Kay Sawtell, with her praise-full reports ('Colin is sensitive, but he is also brave'), but first they went to a morning nursery round the corner from us in the Iffley Road. Here, according to the end-of-term report, Ben 'learnt to use scissors in a matter of minutes'; the only serpent in the paradise was an aggressive boy called Royston. 'Did you tell Royston you would knock his block off if he teased you?' Vivian enquired one lunch-time. 'O no, I forgot' was Ben's reply.

Nineteen-fifty saw the publication of my three verse plays, and in March of the following year two of them (*The Mask* and *The Missing Bridegroom*) achieved a London production at a little 'art' theatre off the Strand, the Watergate, leased by two enterprising ladies, Velona Pilcher and Elizabeth Sprigge. Elizabeth had translated Strindberg's 'Ghost Sonata' and planned to put it on; she was also an actress, and had as co-producer a clever young man called Billy Jay, who afterwards left the London theatre to work with the Indian dancer/musician Ravi Shankar. The Watergate enterprise included a choice restaurant, and after

Wedding day: Vivian and Anne, 2 July 1938.

Philippa Kingsbury (née James), late 1930s.

Honeymoon: Anne and Vivian at Talloires, French Alps, July 1938.

(*Left*) Anne with Jane,
portrait by Vivian.

(*Below*) Jane, Vivian and
Alison (Kate).

Colin and Ben at Portholland, Cornwall. A prize-winning photograph by Vivian which appeared on the cover of *Amateur Photographer* in 1961.

Four generations: clockwise from left, Karin, Anne, Jane and baby Imogen, summer 1997.

Poet and master printer: Vivian demonstrates the workings of his Cropper platen press in the 'printing house', 14 Stanley Road, Oxford, while Anne looks on. Photo © Judith Aronson.

Family group 1997: (back row) Toby Wilson, Kate, Ben, Neil Scott, Katharine Ridler, Colin; (front row) Oliver and Dan Wilson, Jane, Vivian, Isobel Ridler, Anne.

Family group 1998: (back row) Oliver, Neil, Richard Wilson, Katharine, Colin, Pippa Länge-Underwood, Andrew Hillier, Will and Richard Länge-Underwood; (seated) Kate, Juliette Hillier, Vivian, Anne, Karin and Genevieve Länge-Underwood, Jane with Imogen Länge-Underwood and Emily Hillier; (front row) Alice Hillier, Isobel Ridler, Charlotte Hillier.

Anne in the garden at 14 Stanley Road, a photograph taken by Christopher Barker for his book *Portraits of Poets*, Carcanet Press, 1986.

watching a rehearsal I had supper there with Velona and Elizabeth, and tasted avocado pear for the first time. The production was very much to my taste, and Billy and I saw eye to eye about the verse-speaking, which was only marred by the mannerisms of one quite well-known actor called Antony Nearey.

Before the first night I went up and had tea (scones and guava jelly) with Jack Isaacs and his wife in Hampstead, and met their two beautiful daughters – just about to launch away from home, which he found devastating. 'There's a lot of delicate stuff here,' he said, scanning a page of *The Mask*: 'I hope you have a producer who can handle it.' I always sent him my books as they came out, feeling such gratitude for his early encouragement, but I only saw him once again before he died; alas, during his final years, his wife told me, he had been sunk in a deep depression.

TSE could not come to the Watergate, as he was in a nursing-home for treatment, but Frank Morley came, and was appreciative – as was John Rothenstein, on the first night, my only meeting with him. Best of all was the reaction of the girls, as I was able to take them to a Saturday matinée: eight-year-old Kate began to plan how to perform *The Mask* at home. The plays did in fact have two more productions that year. *The Mask* was done by the Oxford University Church Union in the Dean's garden at Christ Church, directed by Roy Porter, chaplain of Oriel (the shooting of the swan produced an explosion like a mortar, and Vivian said he expected the Cathedral windows to fall out). And *The Missing Bridegroom* was done by The Unnamed Society of Manchester, with an ingenious device of lifesize cardboard figures for the cocktail party scene which is described by one of the characters.

Altogether it was an interesting year for us. *The Golden Bird* was published by Faber; and we all went up (twice, so as to include the Amusement Park) to the Exhibition on London's South Bank, which marked the centenary of the Great Exhibition under Victoria and Albert. It seemed a moment of great hopefulness, with post-war austerities finally banished, and exciting features promising (to quote Auden's pre-war poem) 'New styles of architecture, a change of heart.'

With the next year, 1952, came a new joy with the birth of Colin, and for this I must begin a new chapter.

CHAPTER VII

At this point it seems best to abandon a chronological narrative and focus on different aspects of our life: events connected with Vivian's work or mine, our family concerns, holidays and so on. But first, Colin's far from orderly arrival in the world.

He was due in mid-March, his birth at home to be attended by the district nurse, and Mother arrived at the beginning of the month to spend a few days with us before taking Kate and Ben to stay at Ringshall – Jane having elected to stop with us to avoid missing school. The day after Mother arrived, however, my pre-birth waters broke, and she had to go off with the two children. The next morning, when I telephoned the district nurse, she insisted that I should dose myself with castor oil, and though I had warned her that as this was my fourth child it would probably arrive very quickly, instead of coming at once when Vivian summoned her, she went off to pick up a student nurse and took forty minutes on the way. Luckily Margaret Spencer was at home when Vivian called her, and delivered Colin expertly just as the nurses appeared – delaying, as Margaret scornfully remarked, to put on their gowns. Vivian also telephoned to Dr Fraser, who arrived after Colin and without her bag – just to complete the confusion of the day – but fortunately did not need it. He was born at 4 pm on Sunday 2 March, while Jane was at Sunday school.

After all this excitement, Colin was a seraphic baby, though being a fortnight premature (with downy hair on cheeks and back) he had to be fed every three hours for a while. The 'monthly nurse' we had planned for was able to come, but I still had to suffer a daily visit from the student nurse to wash me – and to complain each time that she could not count me as 'a case' because of her late arrival! The other nurse's help was welcome, because poor Jane went down with chickenpox, and our German au pair, Martha, slipped when she was leaving the Playhouse after a performance of *Hamlet* and sprained her shoulder.

> The bairn that is born on the Sabbath Day
> Is bonny and blithe and good and gay.

Colin lived up to the rhyme prediction, and he travelled a smooth road through his infancy (as far as that is ever possible in this mortal life), with two sisters to cherish him, and Ben as role model. (I don't remember, however, that he passed through the coal-heaver macho role that Ben briefly adopted, using a rich Oxfordshire accent and dropping his aitches.) He was ready with his smiles from a month onward, and would bestow one on a 'self-portrait' painted by Jane which hung on the wall of our bedroom, and showed a great array of white teeth.

Colin was christened when eight weeks old by Ted Wager at Little Gaddesden, where Mother had decorated the font with cherry-blossom. His godmother Audrey Wheeler came to stay for the occasion, and often looked after him during his babyhood, as she came to Oxford to add a Health Visitor's certificate to her nursing qualifications. His other godmother, my Downe House friend Jean Thomas, was not able to be there; one godfather, the Little Gaddesden headmaster Vicars Bell, was present, but not the other two of his lavish supply of three. One was our old friend, the artist Lynton Lamb, the other, John Read (nephew of Dorothy, my piano teacher at Downe) we had come to know during his post-war ordination training in Oxford. (He had been a banker in Singapore when the Japanese struck, and had vowed during his imprisonment to take orders if he survived.)

Alison was anxious that Colin should be taught to help with household tasks like washing-up from the beginning, 'so that he doesn't make a fuss like we did'. He was a favourite with the neighbourhood children, and Angus Alton would knock at the door rather too soon after lunch for my liking – 'Is Colin coming out?' So he was quite ready to start aged two years and eight months at the nursery school round the corner, after which he followed the others to the Crescent School, and then on like Ben to the Dragon. As a contemporary local playmate he had John Conmee, from an Irish Roman Catholic family who were caretakers at an RC primary school in Stanley Road. Once they took Colin with them to Mass at St Aloysius in North Oxford, from which he brought the following report: 'Those that were old enough got bread, but we didn't, because we were too young. And they went up to the altar while we sat at the back, and the priest went round giving them bread, and while he was giving it he said: 'Yum-yum, chum, yum-yum, chum!''

After the Conmees had left there was Bobby Purnell from the house opposite us, who shared a 'den' in our garden shed, and there initiated Colin into the forbidden pleasure of smoking. Except for the secrecy, this held no attraction for Colin, and he didn't continue, but later on Vivian made it the subject of a film, 'Nought for Behaviour', where Colin is supposed to retch at the sight of a plate of bacon put before him at supper.

Colin learnt to read without setbacks, and enjoyed long books read to him from the time of his fifth birthday, Mother's *The Enchanted Forest* being a special favourite, as it has been with all our children, grand- or great-grandchildren. A taste for anthropology seems to have dated from about then: 'I'm so excited: it's Monday and we're going to hear about Early Man.'

And aged just six, he enjoyed Rex Warner's paraphrase of the *Iliad*, and became frenzied when the Greeks were being beaten. 'I'm glad I'm six', he remarked one day: 'being four was the worst part.' Another day, when Vivian was putting him to bed: 'I *had* thought of being nasty in my bath to-night, but then I decided not to.' And (calling out from bed): 'I'm thinking about the word *gorgeous.*'

'A choice was killed by every childish illness', W. H. Auden wrote in analytical vein, and I can imagine that true of myself, but I see Colin's early years as not much marked by such setbacks until, perhaps, a very unlucky Lent term at the Dragon when he was nearly ten, starting with a bad attack of measles, followed by influenza and then German measles, caught directly he had returned to school. After this he seemed to catch every cold that was in the air, so I took him for four days to Brighton to recover, driven down by Sid Church (the Press chauffeur and a great friend to the family), and returning by train. Here it rained or snowed every day , and as we battled our way in a hailstorm along the sea front Colin enquired rather doubtfully: 'Do you think this is doing me good, Mummy?' What *was* beneficial, he was sure, was our daily afternoon visit to the cinema (when we had exhausted the Pavilion and the Pier), starting with *The Guns of Navarone*.

I mentioned Martha, the au pair who was with us when Colin was born. She was I think the only one among our foreign girls who regretted her decision to come to England, not surprisingly, as she had come with a prejudice against the English to start with. (She startled Vivian one day by snatching the drying-up cloth from his hands, saying 'That's not a job for a man!') Mostly I think the arrangement was mutually profitable, and I felt that in return for the freedom the girls gave to Vivian and me (for evenings out and, when the children were older, some short trips away), we had a responsibility for making their stay useful to them. Mother used to tease me about having 'Magnall's Questions' at mealtimes, as I laboriously explained syntax or history to them. I used to imagine what Henry James would have made of the nuances of family situations with a resident foreigner continually present: something on the lines of *What Maisie Knew*. As our girls grew older, it was much easier to integrate the foreigners into family life, and some of them became valued friends. Certainly they made a difference to our lives.

I always used the definition of (and payment for) a Mother's Help rather than Au Pair, as I expected them to do light housework and some of the cooking (we had reliable Miss Lewis one afternoon a week for scrubbing and polishing); but they had time to go to lectures in the afternoons, and in the evenings unless Vivian and I both had to be out. I engaged them for a year, and paid their fare to England. Several have come back to visit us, and we exchange news at Christmas; and Kate spent part of her Long Vacation from Oxford in Sweden with Kerstin, our first. Annelou Perrenoud was very musical, and taught us French-Swiss, Romansh and Italian songs which she would accompany on her ukulele. Her delightful mother came to stay with us, and Annelou, who settled in Colorado, came a few years ago en route for a visit to Switzerland. And Charlotte Lange, who had met Rolf while they were both learning English, was the means of Jane's introduction to him.

We had some failures, of course. German Irene absconded with a week's advance pay and my precious Faroe Island sweater while we were visiting Ben at Clifton; and once we tried an older German woman, Serita, who had described herself on her CV as 'Guiltless Divorced'. We soon felt sure that the guilt must have been on her side, as she was quite the most obviously selfish and grasping person I have ever met. She would openly boast of having cheated her way into the best seats at the cinema, and tried to borrow various items from kind Veronica Ruffer from next door, who had invited her to tea. When after a fortnight she began to demand more pay, I was thankful for the excuse to give her notice. I was hard put to it to compose a truthful reference: as a London employer soon took her off our hands, I hope it was not too misleading.

Christa Steinmann, who came to us while Ben was a baby, was one of a German family (recommended to us by Isabel Ashcroft) who had had to flee before the advancing Russians. She became very proficient in English, and went to work for an import-export firm in Egypt, where she married a Frenchman (now divorced from her) and had two daughters, both of whom we have entertained when they took English courses in Oxford. She too has visited us, and always writes for my birthday.

Another success, though of a very different kind, was Margaret Heaney from Northern Ireland, whose sojourn gave us a glimpse of the Irish Problem. She had been a sympathetic carer for Aunt Mick in an old people's home in Merthyr Tydfil, but was booked to be housekeeper to a Roman Catholic priest in North Oxford (to be like a Thekla who cared for St Paul, as she imagined it). There was some time to pass before he needed her, so Aunt Mick suggested that she came to us. Resentment towards the English race was indelibly printed on her soul, but fortunately she was inconsistent, and did not include us among the enemy. Only, we occasionally caught a glimpse of the depth of Irish prejudice when some mention of politics made her livid (literally) with fury: a victory for Hitler in the war, she would exclaim, would have been much better for Ireland than the English success.

She had, admittedly, experienced anti-Catholic prejudice in Ulster, and her family was very poor. Our housework was child's play to her, and on the whole she approved of us, though she thought I spoilt the girls; Ben on the other hand could do no wrong, and she would spruce him up to be carried off in his push-chair to visit Mrs Rymills of an afternoon – a short walk to Henley Street. She always said the first thing that came into her head, and on her first arrival, as Jane and Kate waited shyly on the stairs to greet her, she exclaimed: 'O she's got red hair, and I don't like red hair!'

The running of the house was carefree for me while Margaret was with us, but after eighteen months her North Oxford priest claimed her, and she departed. Mrs Rymills visited her once or twice, and thought that the supplies of Communion wine there must be considerably depleted, but I had never noticed that she drank while with us.

After Margaret we continued to employ foreign helps until Colin was old enough to be left alone of an evening; then we still had weekly help, ending with Violet Webb (passed on from Philippa) who still visits as a friend.

In 1958 Charles Batey retired, and Vivian succeeded him as Printer to the University. Vivian had virtually filled the post for several years before that, as Batey was seriously ill for many months – though not before he had set in train various expensive improvements to the Printer's office, and instituted a Museum of print, for which he engaged Harry Carter, the distinguished scholar-typographer, as curator. Another expense, and this time incurred by the Delegates against Batey's advice, was a costly new papermaking machine at Wolvercote, with a Manager (Roderick Henderson). The machine proved unable to cope with the paper required by the Press, and was ultimately a white elephant.

Although Vivian does not regret his decision to leave his congenial work in London and come to Oxford, he took over the Press at a difficult period for the industry. Almost at once the Press was caught up in a strike which lasted for many months, and all through the 'sixties and 'seventies the unions caused difficulties. Vivian was determined to keep abreast of improvements in technology, and it was galling to have a newly-acquired machine stand idle for months because there was union branch disagreement as to who was entitled to operate it. These 'chapels' were each represented at the Joint Works Council by their 'Father', or shop steward, and the head shop steward (Imperial Father) at this time was a power-hungry man called Fulton, who caused endless trouble. (It was appropriate that in the annual pantomime which the workers put on for the children at Christmas he used to play the part of the Demon King.)

In the constant battle to keep the Press profitable (and the workers in employment) Vivian was exposed on the other hand to a conflict of interest with the publishing side of the business, which was free to use other printers and could take advantage of the low wages paid in the Far East. This inevitable clash was a serious weakness in the constitution of the Press; and of course the Delegates of the University had to be satisfied too. Their Finance Committee – the equivalent of the board of directors of a business – covered publishing as well as printing, and met once a month. Vivian and the head of the Clarendon Press (the Secretary) always attended this; the London publisher more rarely.

Set against these disadvantages was the tradition of excellent workmanship which those at the Press inherited, and there was a prestige in belonging to it which everyone felt. Some of the books produced while Vivian was Printer, under his guidance and inspiration, were as fine as any in its history. Some books, such as the Coronation Bible (produced while he was Assistant Printer), he designed himself; others followed a traditional design, or were designed jointly with the reliable Ken Stewart, head of the Lay-Out department, who also trained a brilliant young typographer, Bernard Crosland. The members of the select Roxburgh Club, who each had to produce a book, left the design to the Press, and Vivian was particularly pleased with his design for Walter Oakeshott's edition of Hans Burchmeier's wood engravings.

About seven years before his retirement Vivian designed a book which demanded all his ingenuity: the reproduction of the manuscript of T. S. Eliot's great poem *The Waste Land*, edited by Valerie Eliot, showing the marginal comments of Ezra Pound and Eliot's first wife Vivienne, together with the author's own corrections, clearly displayed and distinguished. (This MS, originally given by Eliot to his benefactor John Quinn, had disappeared after Quinn's death, and turned up in the New York Public Library some years after Eliot died.) While the book was going through the Press, we had Valerie Eliot to stay for a night two or three times, and were both impressed by her determination to decipher every illegible word, even under six lines of crossing-out, and solve every conundrum. We might stay up till midnight poring over the manuscript, and Vivian (having risen at 6.30) sometimes found it trying. But Valerie much appreciated his care, sent us a bottle of the best champagne for our Golden Wedding, as well as tickets to see the production of *Cats* in London preceded by lunch with her, and wanted to be sure that Vivian would still be Printer when Eliot's Letters were ready for publication. (But the first volume was not assembled until some ten years after his retirement, and was printed by Clay's.)

The routine of Vivian's day did not change after he became Printer in 1958: he continued to arrive at the Press at 7.30 am, thinking that he could not expect his Department Managers to keep to this hour if he did not.

He only drank a cup of coffee before setting off by car and picking up Mr Clifford, a disabled employee, en route. (As I have said, he came home to lunch unless he had a business engagement.) Two or three times a week he would go round the works and would talk to individuals, asking them about their work. Thanks to this usually welcome care, he was not at all a remote presence to the large force under his control (900 at its maximum), and we learnt after his retirement how much his involvement was valued, and remembered nostalgically because his successors did not practise it.

The Printing Works closed at 5.30 (except for overtime working), and Vivian usually left his office at 6.15. In later years we took to having high tea soon after he got home, which suited our au pair girls if they were going out, and gave us a pleasantly unbroken evening.

Until Mother died in June 1956 we had a second home at Ringshall End, followed by the house on Hudnall Common (on the outskirts of Little Gaddesden) to which she moved for the last three years of her life. This was a pleasant semi-detached house on the edge of the escarpment above the valley of the river Gade which leads to Hemel Hempstead. It was hard to leave Ringshall End where we had all been so happy, but its remoteness and the size of the garden had become too much for Mother and Nellie, and at Hudnall they were close to a bus route and village life, with K. Talbot and Dorothy Erhart at the Manor House, and Rhoda Miller a few doors away in Hudnall itself.

The house very soon took on the character of its owner, with the 'Canaletto' of St Mark's Venice over the fireplace in the sunny sitting room, and a forte-piano there to replace the Broadwood Baby-Grand. The small garden was well established, with a flourishing quince tree and a white peony which now grows in our Oxford garden. We spent three Christmasses there, being lent a bedroom by Miss Waters, the adjoining neighbour, and followed the traditional programme of tea at the Manor House on the day after Boxing Day, with special games, and charades for which their genuine spinning wheel was brought into use.

Mother continued as active and involved in life as ever (anaemia kept at bay by injections) until her last and mercifully brief illness. I do not remember that she was at all deaf, and she still drove her car, though a minor mishap brought an official hope that she would 'keep off the road as much as possible'! We had celebrated her eightieth birthday in 1951 by meeting Matt, Jan and Christopher for lunch in London before seeing Laurence Olivier and Marilyn Monroe in *The Prince and the Showgirl*, a good vehicle for their acting talents, and later made into a film.

Three times Mother came to share our summer seaside holidays, the first time, I think, being at Broadhaven in Pembrokeshire, when it rained virtually every day for the week that she was there, and she walked every morning from her hotel at one end of the sea-front to our lodgings at the other, to play with undaunted cheerfulness games of Word-Making and Word-Taking or Head, Body and Legs with the children. The next year, 1952, she arrived at Broadhaven to find a telegram summoning her to Oxford, where Uncle Humphrey died a few days later. (Aunt Rose behaved very strangely thereafter, rebuffing all Mother's attempts to maintain contact, though she kept up with us. It was almost as though she was jealous, after his death, of the closeness between brother and sister.)

Two Cornish holidays in Audrey Wheeler's neighbourhood were happy ones: the first at a guest-house in Gerrans, where blancmange featured largely at the pudding course – passed on by us to Vivian's plate in such quantities (to avoid giving offence to the waitress) that Mother said she expected him to foam at the mouth. The second holiday was with a rather temperamental landlady at West Portholland, the next bay to East Portholland where Audrey had her sea-merged dwelling:

> The fourth wall no scale can measure,
> 　The fourth wall is the sea.
> Sometimes it is close, enormous, glassy,
> 　Sometimes rolled away,
> Sometimes troubled and towering comes
> 　Into the room to impart the storm.
> We sit – or swim – the sense is doubtful where
> 　We in the sea's life share.

Mother shared in all our picnics, and sat sketching while we bathed; the best of company always in wet or fine.

During the Easter holidays of 1956 she had seemed to tire easily, but planned to come over with Christopher for the first night of my play about Thomas Cranmer, due to be given in the University Church on 7 May. When the day came, she was too ill to make the trip, though insisting that Christopher should come. I was tied to the play for the rest of the week, but Vivian and I drove over on the Sunday evening, taking with us a film he had shot of the dress rehearsal which she was able to watch from her bed. (It was his very first film, and also showed Colin and John Conmee struggling to prop a plank on some steps.) She was very weak, but anxious to hear all about the play, and happy at its success. Hopeful as always, she told me to look in her drawer to admire the new green 'twin-set' she had recently bought on a visit to London.

Dr Phillips feared cancer of the stomach, and arranged for her to go almost at once into Guy's Hospital, travelling by ambulance with Nellie. I went up to stay with Christopher, and found the doctor at Guy's doubtful of the success of an operation, though Mother wished for it. When I suggested bringing the girls up to see her she said: 'Not when I am like this;' obviously not – or at any rate not consciously – feeling that death was imminent, and not wishing to talk of it, though she was happy to have Campbell Milford, whom I asked to come and give us Communion on the Sunday. I read to her: Wordsworth's Immortality Ode (my choice) and *Pride and Prejudice* (hers); and when I was leaving her for the night – only her fourth night in hospital, I think – she said: 'Now don't go and think about me all the evening: find something else to think about.' These were her last, and typical, words to me, for soon after midnight, she died, and I woke about seven to hear Christopher answering the hospital's call to say so.

He declined their offer for us to see her, which I rather regretted, and when I had collected her few things I caught a late-morning train back to Oxford. I found Kate sitting at my desk just finishing a letter to her much-loved Granny, which made the shock of the news all the worse.

All my brothers were able to come to the funeral, taken by Ted Wager at Little Gaddesden, and I suppose her ashes were scattered there like Father's, though I only remember that we had her name added (by Harry Carter's son Matthew) to the plaque commemorating HCB. My brothers and I went through the rooms at Hudnall taking it in turns to have first pick in each – Matt very positive about what he wanted, Christopher expressing no preference, but then, disappointment. Our only disagreement was over the 'Canaletto' (now ascribed to his brother-in-law, as I have said), which Edward and I would have liked to keep in the family: when sold it fetched only £500, which we divided between us.

Vivian and I took the children for another short holiday with Nellie at Hudnall before the house was sold, and then she moved into a ground-floor flat in Little Gaddesden at the gates of Ashridge Park, where she lived very contentedly for a few more years. I forget the date of her death, but she was certainly able to come over for Jane's marriage to Rolf Länge in 1961.

After that our connexion with Little Gaddesden continued with occasional visits until Rhoda Miller moved to London and Ted Wager died. He with his wife Nellie kept their vivid interest in our children until a year or two before his death, when his mind failed. At that time she sent me a little poem beginning 'I have lost my life's companion And gained a dear, dear child...'

Major Boxer, the purchaser of Ringshall End, who saw my poem 'Leaving Ringshall' in *The Listener*, wrote to invite me to visit the house, but knowing that they had altered it considerably I never wanted to go back, though Kate has visited it with Richard.

As I have already mentioned, my cousin Dick Milford (eldest son of Mother's brother Theodore) had been Vicar of the University Church (St Mary the Virgin) in the High Street until the year before we moved to Oxford, and I was already familiar with the church from Jane Christie's christening there, which I attended as a godparent. So although I experimented with one or two of the churches nearer to us, and the girls once or twice attended Sunday School at 'Cowley Dads' in the Iffley Road, we found St Mary's more congenial, both liturgically and theologically. During Dick's tenure he had encouraged the Pilgrim Players to produce Charles Williams's short plays in the church, and now Dick's successor Roy Lee was anxious to mark the fourth centenary of Cranmer's martyrdom by putting on a play in the church where his trials and final dramatic 'recantation' had taken place. He asked me if I could undertake to write such a play; and at the same time (I forget which came first) the BBC Third Programme – then an exciting innovation – commissioned me. I thought that St Mary's really ought to revive CW's brilliant Canterbury play of ten years earlier, but Roy insisted that he wanted the action to focus on the scenes in the church; so with some misgivings at treating a subject which CW had made his own, I agreed to attempt it.

A sustained effort of this kind was not easy at home, but on this occasion I was lucky enough to be able to leave the household to the care of Rosmarie Bandi, our excellent Swiss au pair, and go with four-year-old Colin to stay at Hudnall for several days, where Mother kept him happy in the mornings and Nellie provided our meals.

In planning the play I had much help from Roy Porter, the chaplain of Oriel, who was to produce it – very likely it was he who had suggested me to Roy Lee, as he had produced my verse play *The Mask* in the Dean's garden at Christ Church the previous summer, with a student cast. He was a historian as well as a theologian, and the theatre was his hobby – I think he had acted quite a lot as an Oxford undergraduate. Probably I also consulted him about the cast, which was to include professionals, but I am sure the choice of Frank Windsor as Cranmer was mine, for Vivian and I had seen him act the part of Bolingbroke in *Richard II* with the 'Young Elizabethans' when they came to the Playhouse, as well as Long John Silver in *Treasure Island* there, and had been impressed by his magnificent voice. (He later became well known in the television series called *Z Cars* and its sequel *Softly, Softly*, but it was a disappointment to us that he didn't continue on the stage in Shakespeare, and never went to act at Stratford.) Derek Hart, who played the Witness – the equivalent of a lone Chorus – also became well known on television as an announcer. The third distinguished actor was Antony Jacobs, Bishop Bonner. He too deserted the stage for radio – I remember his fine verse-speaking in Chapman's *Bussy d'Ambois* – for the reason that on a stage he always seemed impelled to re-plan his movements at each perform-ance, to the confusion of his fellow-actors.

Liza Ogston, who had trained at RADA, was Mrs Cranmer: she was the wife of the Balliol don A. F. (Sandy) Ogston already mentioned, and their whole family became much involved in the production. Smaller parts were taken by their daughter Flora, and by members of the university dramatic society (the OUDS), one of whom, Ian Lowe, became an Assistant Keeper of the Ashmolean. And for the Crowd scenes we had a notable Chorus, of academics and their children.

As I attended all the rehearsals, I felt I knew the actors quite well by the end of the week, although they only once came to our house, for tea in the garden, and went more frequently to the Ogstons close by in Mansfield Road. One day I had to make an emergency trip to London to search the theatrical costumiers for copes and other Elizabethan gear: we ended up by borrowing most of it from the Stratford Memorial Theatre. The raised stage we hired (paid for by my fee from the Third Programme broadcast of the play), and we made use of the pulpit for the tower of Bocardo, Cranmer's prison, as well as for Bonner's declamations, and of the organ loft for the Witness's description of Cranmer's martyrdom.

The hired stage was in place for the dress rehearsal, and the actors grumbled that it felt very insecure. However, Roy Porter brushed aside their objections and the rehearsal proceeded to the ending, where Cranmer and his accusers were to hurry to the East End (to be lit for the final conflagration), followed by the yelling crowd. Roy was dissatisfied by the crowd's shouts of Rhubarb, and leapt on to the stage to pursue them – whereupon it collapsed, and he disappeared like Don Giovanni to the depths! Luckily he climbed up unhurt, so our satisfaction could be freely indulged.

Although I owed a lot to Roy in the planning of the play, and agreed with his ideas for the production, so that our dealings remained amicable, I didn't experience any of the warmth that I have generally found generated by working with others in drama or music, and such as I felt with the actors in the play. Perhaps he liked the play less as we went on. I remember once saying mildly that I thought something might be better said while facing rather than with back to the audience: to which his response was: 'Anyhow that always seemed to me to be a very *bad* line!'

The first night went off without mishap, and the play was well received locally. The view of Cranmer (which was consonant with Professor Pollard's interpretation of the historical facts) did not appeal to some Roman Catholic critics, or to Denis Arundell, who took part in the Third Programme production, but Hugh Lloyd Jones congratulated me on the amount of actual historical record I had managed to bring in. The witness to Cranmer's bravery in the fire (quoted in Foxe's 'Book of

Martyrs') whose words I used, is the more trustworthy in that he belonged to the opposite camp.

(There have been three revivals of Cranmer over the years, though the text is now out of print. One was in Bristol Cathedral, another in Dorchester Abbey, and the most recent was here in St Mary's in 1989, directed by Paul Ranger, a critic and teacher of drama and a member of the congregation. This had a fine performance as Cranmer by a gifted amateur, Freddy Madden: his wife was Mrs Cranmer, Brian Mountford was the Gaoler, Richard Jeffery the Witness, and Vivian and I joined in the Crowd.)

Pleasure in the play's success was quickly submerged by the sorrow of Mother's death, and we resumed our lives as best we could. The girls were both at Oxford High School now, Ben at the Dragon and Colin at The Crescent. During Ben's last year Colin had moved to the Dragon Baby School, portrayed in a film by Vivian entitled 'A Dragon's Life'. They both profited by the celebrated Dragon acting productions of the classics master L. A. Wilding, first singing in Gilbert and Sullivan Choruses, and then taking spoken parts. Ben made a hit as 'Sergeant Willis' in *Iolanthe* and later as Fluellen in *Henry V*; Colin hated playing the part of the Grandmother in *Lady Precious Stream* (though I described him in a letter to Audrey as 'acting delightfully, in pink kimono and pink slippers, his nails varnished, and a stately dark bun-wig surmounting his friendly boy's ears'); later at Magdalen College School he was excellent (and very moving) as Hamlet.

Rather different acting qualities were called for in the story-films that Vivian made during their boyhoods. These were planned by him to record places and family doings in a more interesting way than the usual sequence of picnic or domestic scenes. He plotted the episodes beforehand on a storyboard, and gave them a professional editing after they had been printed. The longest film ('The Fortune-Hunters'), known as our Epic, was started in the summer after the Cranmer production, and finished the following year. It describes the adventures of a small boy who sets out from a humble home (we showed the doorway of a cottage in Combe, from which I waved goodbye to Colin), and fishes up from the lake at Blenheim Park a bottle containing a map illustrating the place of hidden treasure. Unseen, a robber (Ben) observes the finding of the map, and tracks Colin through his wanderings (which include Wychwood Forest and the river at Rotherhithe where Christopher and his Jane greet him) to the goal at St Anthony's headland in South Cornwall. Here the treasure (a suit of plastic armour and 'gold pieces') is hidden in a cave below the cliff. There is a cliff-top battle in which Ben is pushed over the edge into the sea – reluctantly wearing all his clothes. I refused to have him 'drowned', and we can suppose that a ship seen in the distance has picked him up, as Colin walks triumphantly up the path carrying the sack of treasure.

Both boys became expert in rapid cameo-performances, responding to commands from the director (aware of precious film speeding on) to 'hurry up', and they were patient in repeating their actions, Colin only complaining at the shock of washing his face in snow after a supposed night of sleeping out of doors.

About five years later, when Enrica and Colin's friend Nicky Vernède were staying with us in Pembrokeshire, we made a ghost story, 'A Voice from the Past', its theme taken by me from Kipling's short story 'The End of the Passage'. The setting was the cliffs and bay below St Ishmael's, where we stayed in Edward and Bertha's holiday cottage. We only discovered later that there is a local tradition of a ghost who walks on the particular path down to the cove where our ghost frightened the boys (Colin and Nicky). Ours was a monkish hooded figure (played by Ben's Clifton friend Douglas Allford), clad in the costume of 'Friar Lawrence' from the Stratford production of *Romeo and Juliet*. This had been borrowed for the summer vacation by Kate's undergraduate troop, who took the play to Israel, but for some reason did not need the Friar's garb.

Nicky Vernède was the hero (or villain) of a short comedy called 'The Thirteenth Candle' filmed at Colin's thirteenth birthday party (finished off a week later), where Nicky substitutes a firework for one of the candles on the cake, and the resulting explosion shoots several of the guests on to the top of the kitchen cupboard. Another of the most successful comedies was 'Slipped Disc', where Vivian, alone in the house, puts on a record of Cliff Richard with The Shadows, and tries to imitate the movements of the Twist which he has watched the boys performing – including a French boy, Gaby Villeroy de Galhaud, here on an exchange visit. Vivian ricks his back, and hearing the family returning from a shopping trip, hurries into the garden and pretends to be digging, to account for his crippled state.

Alas, this and other films which depend on the sound accompaniment, made on a tape recorder which could be linked to the film projector, are now unplayable, as no one can now repair the out-of-date mechanism. Even the projector itself is now unreliable, and we are gradually transferring to video a few of the most precious films, including 'The Great Exhibition' (of 1851), made from the wonderful series of lithographs which recorded it, and borrowed by Vivian from the John Johnson collection. To shoot the film he rigged up a frame on which the camera could be moved from side to side and the picture raised and lowered by a Meccano motor. I put together the script, impersonating Queen Victoria as I read aloud from her diaries of the time.

Another story-film, made in the mid-sixties, recorded Katharine Ross and the St Mary's Sunday School which she ran, and also provided an excuse to film the curious stone figures in the crypt of the church (originally from the tower), which acted as a depressant on our children during the rather brief period when they attended the Sunday School. (Jane later taught there for a while, and Ben directed a short Tolstoy play.) Andy Vernède, Nicky's elder brother and a talented actor, played the part of a fugitive holed up in the church tower, who is fed by some of the children from the Sunday School: we finally see them acting 'The Prodigal Son'.

During the ten years following the Cranmer production I always had some editing work in hand which required research, and I was very lucky to have the Bodleian Library at a bicycle ride's distance. (We did not own a car until after Vivian's retirement, having the use of the Press's Rover for holidays and in the evenings, though at first Charles Batey did not sanction my using it unless for joint expeditions, so that I had to use my bicycle for the Bach Choir practices.) The first of these projects was *The Image of the City*, a volume of Charles Williams's uncollected essays and reviews, with a long critical-biographical introduction. I was commissioned by Geoffrey Hunt, in charge of religious books at the Oxford University Press, and it had the blessing of CW's widow Michal (also of his son Michael, in so far as he took any interest in his father's work); but the situation was not as simple as it sounds. Raymond Hunt (no connexion with Geoffrey), who had attended all the City Literary Institute lectures, and had, with CW's approval, taken charge of his MSS, was accepted as his literary executor, though I do not know exactly what his legal standing was. I had obtained the typescript of CW's short plays from him when I edited them in 1950, and would have added his name to mine on the title-page, but Humphrey Milford would not sanction this, as I had found it quite impossible to get Raymond to commit himself to any editorial statement on paper. Raymond's reverence and devotion to his guru seemed to paralyse his pen, but also made him jealous of anyone else who attempted to write about CW, and I know he thought I was not reverential enough; moreover he disapproved of any help which I gave to the various research students (chiefly American, and tending to be called Thaddeus) who came hoping to be shown original material. Raymond infected Michal Williams to some extent with this dog-in-the-manger attitude, so that I had to be cautious about giving help; and further I had to choose my words very carefully in writing about the relationships at Amen House. At one point Michal did say that she hoped she would be dead before the book was published, but I think she realized that she was better off with me than with alternative editors, and she ended by giving me an enthusiastic blessing.

Some of CW's most enduring thought is preserved in the pages of the book: in the essay on 'The Way of Exchange' for instance, which explores his doctrine of 'substituted Love', and in the poem 'The Parable of the Wedding Garment' which vividly dramatizes it. The essay on the Cross can be said to sum up his thought on the problem of evil in a universe supposed to have been created by a loving God: the paradox of 'God Almighty and ills unlimited' as it has been phrased.

I was able, in a section concerned with CW's poems on the Arthurian myth, to draw together my own recollection of the many, many talks we had on the subject, stretching over several years, with the surviving notes he left, some printed and some not. The Taliessin poems are, alas, out of fashion, but will I am sure survive.

To immerse oneself in the life and thought of a much-loved dead person inevitably makes more acute the sense of loss. The same was true of another commission I undertook, some years later: an account of the life and pioneering achievement of Olive Willis, the headmistress of

Downe House. I agreed to do it rather reluctantly, having no passionate interest in women's education, and not wishing to rake over the ashes of my own emotional growth, but in the event I enjoyed the research involved; and the letters and records of my Bradby aunts (who were among the first scholars of Lady Margaret Hall) gave me some primary material to use. Also the story of the school is indeed remarkable, starting as Olive did in 1907 in Charles Darwin's old house in Kent with one pupil and a staff of five, with no financial backing or influential friends. As I put it in the blurb for the book: 'Olive formulated no theories and used no publicity; although she had a sense of the dramatic, she was entirely without self-importance ['Headmistresses have large faces so that they can be seen at a distance' was one of her sayings]. Yet because of her rich personality, her high ideals and her genius for personal relations, Downe House played its part in shaping the educational developments of half a century.'

The book was published by John Murray, with an introduction by Elizabeth Bowen (an early pupil), and soon sold out its first edition. After that for a while the second edition, financed by the Old Seniors, languished because the then headmistress refused to have copies on sale at the school, not wishing, she said, to have her pupils look back, but forward, 'to a bright new future'. Fortunately her successor took a different view, saw that the book was stocked at Downe, and often quoted from it. Not that the sales affected me, as I was merely paid for writing it.

Two books published in 1963 represented several years of editing work. One was a second World's Classics edition of critical essays on Shakespeare, continuing from the year when the first volume left off, 1935, and including work up to 1960. The selecting was greatly helped by the Shakespeare Survey, an annual which published new essays from all over the world on 'Shakespearian Study and Production'. The focus of Shakespeare criticism had changed a good deal since the years covered by the earlier book, as I explained in my Introduction, and I only included one contributor (Wilson Knight) who was represented there. I had wanted to include Eliot too, but he felt his later work was inferior, so I did not. Both these collections seem to fill a need and have been many times reprinted.

Two other books of this time involved textual research, and both used material which we owe to the skill and diligence of the bookseller Bertram Dobell (1842–1914) both as editor and collector. The first of my two books, *Poems and Some Letters of James Thomson*, was commissioned by J. M. Cohen of the Centaur Press, who had been our neighbour in Southway. He published it in 1953 at the price of three guineas in his series of Centaur Classics, among such varying titles as Golding's translation of Ovid and *The Myths of Plato*. Thomson (or BV, the pseudonym which distinguishes him from the author of *The Seasons*) is chiefly remembered by his long poem 'The City of Dreadful Night', which owed its publication in book form, some two years before Thomson's death from alcoholism, to the enterprise of his friend Dobell. Eliot acknowledged a debt to the poem in his visions of London, the 'unreal City', and Helen Gardner included extracts from it in her *New Oxford Book of English Verse*. Of equally striking quality is the poem 'In the Room', a dialogue among the pieces of furniture in a dismal lodging-house, which reveals only gradually that the occupant they are discussing is lying dead upon the bed.

The original plan for my book had been a Collected Poems, but Thomson wrote a good deal of indifferent pseudo-Shelleyan verse, and I thought it inappropriate to apply strict scholarly editing – with MS variants duly recorded – to so much dross. So I got Jack Cohen's agreement to my making a selection, and as I wrote in my Introduction: 'I have tried to choose favourable specimens at every stage from early to late, opening the door a little wider than my judgement would approve, in order to admit some examples of his late love poetry.' I had not edited texts from manuscript with a critical apparatus before, and I had a good deal of useful advice and comment from Simon Nowell-Smith, who had by then retired from the librarianship of the London Library and was living in Headington.

During Thomson's final drunken bout, the manuscript of the 'City of Dreadful Night' had found its way to America. I collated the printed version with it for the first time, using a micro-film from the Pierpont Morgan Library, and noting variants from two MS drafts which are in the British Library. (I was fascinated, when I consulted these in the Manuscript Room, to find with them a note signed 'T. J. Wise', recording the date when he had examined the newly-purchased scripts. Wise was the trusted scholar who circulated faked editions of nineteenth-century works, and actually purloined leaves from MSS in the British Library to fill up missing pages in his own collection – then leaving directions in his will that the BL should be given first option on bidding for the collection after his death!)

Research for the biographical sketch of Thomson in my Introduction was very enjoyable, as it was the first time I had encountered the byways of the nineteenth century trodden by the Secularists, Freethinkers, and rebels such as Charles Bradlaugh. I found the pages of *The National Reformer*, Bradlaugh's weekly paper which was Thomson's chief literary outlet, fascinating reading, combining (as I wrote) 'the tone of habitual opposition which is familiar to us in journalism of the extreme Left, with the parochialism of a parish magazine [with touching attempts at substitute liturgies to provide for freethinking funerals and baby-namings] and the naivety of a crank health-periodical.'

The Poems and Meditations of Thomas Traherne was the second of the two books I have just mentioned, again owing much to Bertram Dobell, for there would have been no extant poems to edit but for him. The existence of Traherne's poetry was unknown until the chance purchase of an unsigned manuscript book from a second-hand bookstall in 1898 by a man of letters called W. T. Brooke, and it was Dobell who identified the author as Traherne, hitherto only known by a polemical work and some essays posthumously published. Later, Dobell acquired the even more wonderful 'Centuries of Meditation', and published both books in modernized spelling.

The Oxford University Press published a fine edition of Traherne made by H. M. Margoliouth in its Oxford English Texts, and my edition, for the Shorter Oxford series, was based on his, but I collated the text with the manuscripts, held in the Bodleian and the British Library, and made some changes. (Margoliouth was an old man when he made his collation; mine, published in 1958, was probably the cause of my taking to spectacles for reading shortly afterwards.) My one claim to a discovery resulted in the removal of some poems from the canon, and this happened with the help of our great friend Margaret Crum, who was then compiling a First-Line Index of the MSS held in the Bodleian.

Margoliouth had published, among material taken from the note-books, two Meditations in rhymed couplets which I thought were quite unlike Traherne. Accordingly, I gave Margaret the first lines of the two poems, and one morning she rang me up to say that she had identified them as belonging to a collection of 'Meditations' by a lawyer of Lincoln's Inn, William Austin. An exciting moment! The poems are very fine, and Traherne had admired them enough to copy them into his book, possibly by heart, to judge from the slips he made. Four other short pieces, lacking his initials at the bottom, I identified as being among the 'Emblems', often borrowed for epitaphs, by Francis Quarles.

It is strange to me that I do not owe my discovery of Traherne, one of the formative experiences of my life, to Charles Williams, for Traherne is a great master of the Affirmative Way, which pursues perfection through delight in/adoration of the created world, and this was a doctrine at the heart of Charles's teaching. Yet I do not recall that I ever heard him mention Traherne, though Dobell's edition of the poems came out in 1904 and of the Centuries in 1908. Moreover Dobell's Introduction to the Centuries is eloquent on the subject of Traherne's ecstatic praise of creation, and quotes the lines which of all others came to me as a liberation from doubt and anxiety in spiritual matters. Let me explain briefly what I mean.

When I first read, as the epigraph to T. S. Eliot's 'Ash Wednesday', the quotation from St John of the Cross: 'Hence the soul cannot be possessed of the divine union until it has divested itself of the love of created beings', and read some of St John's writings, I felt a painful conflict of ideals. How could it be right or necessary to deny the most precious outgoings of the soul, in order to love God? Now Traherne pointed to a resolution of the contradiction, with his great passages on Love in the second Century. 'You are as prone to love as the sun is to shine... He that delights not in Love makes vain the universe'... *and* 'Never was anything in this world loved too much' but 'Many things have been loved in a false way, and all in too short a measure.' Surely such passages must have delighted CW, yet I never heard them from his lips.

Another preoccupation of the 'sixties was my membership of a panel appointed by the Council of Churches to work on a modern translation of the Bible, to be published by the 'Privileged Presses' of Oxford and

Cambridge Universities. The translation from the original classical Hebrew, Aramaic or Greek was made by one or more scholars, and passed to a Literary Panel to check the style and contemporary idiom. The decision to make a new translation had been taken just after the end of the last war, and the New Testament, prepared under the chairman-ship of C. H. Dodd, had been published in 1961. The Old Testament translation, chaired by Professor Godfrey Driver, had progressed as far as the Book of Judges when I was invited by Peter Spicer to join it with another new member, John Carey (now Goldsmith's Professor of English Literature). We were replacing Helen Gardner, who had been eased out of the committee, probably by mutual agreement: I know that they found her too dominating and talkative, however brilliant. The other members of the Literary Panel were Roger Mynors (the most brilliant brain of them all), Dr H. T. P. Williams, Bishop of Winchester, Professor Basil Willey from Cambridge, Canon Adam Fox from West-minster Abbey (a distant cousin of mine), and the Dean of York, Milman, who had originated the service of Nine Lessons and Carols during his time in Cambridge. Dr Dodd was often present too, also Thomas Norrington or Peter Spicer, with a secretary to record the proceedings, representing the Oxford Press. When the secretary was not there, tea-making fell to my share.

Each member had been sent a copy of the translated text to be revised, and the chairman would read a few paragraphs of this at a time for our comments and corrections. John Carey and I had I suppose a special responsibility for spotting out-of-date expressions, and I remember that at my very first meeting (before he had joined) I had to point out that 'he went into her' was not a contemporary way of describing sexual inter-course. On my first objecting to the phrase someone kindly explained to me what it meant, and when I said that I did know the meaning there was a pause, till Basil Willey said: 'I think Mrs Ridler is right.'

Our task was in some ways an impossible one: to replace a literary masterpiece, written at a time when the English language was at its richest, by a text using the impoverished speech of the present day, to be comprehensible to the common man, yet retaining enough dignity to sound well when read aloud in church. Moreover, our chairman Godfrey Driver insisted that the translation should be serviceable for students of the Hebrew Bible, so that key words must always be translated by the same English word. As English is rich in synonyms and Hebrew is not, this considerably cramped our style.

It was a privilege to hear Godfrey Driver talk about the various books we were working on. His familiarity with the subject had a few drawbacks: he was hard to convince that when the Lord said 'My storms will blast your sycamore figs' the present-day reader might be unmoved at the prospect. And it was commonly said that though he knew every detail of the lay-out in a Hebrew dwelling, in a freezing winter he did not know where to find the coal in his own house. But he was a wise and delightful man, showing total patience as we groped for a phrase.

One of the revelations I had from his exposition was the uncertainty in so much of the wording of the Psalms, due to the fact that the Hebrew alphabet possessed only consonants, and 'vocalization' by the Scribes in the fifth century was responsible for the meaning available to the early translators. The best piece of Driver lore that I encountered was a script which he circulated to us entitled 'Farewell to Queen Hussab'. Unfortunately I can't find the original of this, and can only record here its proof that this warrior queen in the Book of Amos (who has perhaps figured in many a sermon) owes her existence to the misreading of a past participle: 'she was lifted up'.

A small Oxford group met for an afternoon every fortnight in term-time under Professor Driver to work on the Psalms. The fact that Roger Mynors was one of the group made it enjoyable, but it went much against the grain with me to tamper with Coverdale, whose version is used in our Prayer Book. (The Authorized version is nothing like as graceful, we found.) We had to discard Coverdale's inspired coinage of 'loving-kindness' for the word which expresses the mutual love of God and his people, and I was sad to find that we had to alter the phrasing of the Christmas psalm (85), where God's mercy and his justice towards men are reconciled ('Mercy and truth are met together; righteousness and peace have kissed each other') to a slightly different phrase: 'Love and fidelity have come together'. However, the second part, 'Justice and peace join hands,' does keep the suggestion of reconciliation.

For the London meetings, which involved staying for a night, I got the Press to pay my subscription to Enrica's club in Bryanston Square; and as the place where we met was in the City, I used to go for lunch to Dick and Margaret Milford in the Temple, where he was then Master. Once a year, in May, we met in Cambridge, and that was particularly enjoyable, as some of us stayed at the Garden House Hotel on the river, and we all dined at Basil Willey's college, Pembroke, where we ate off gold plate. It was the season when the Backs were especially beautiful, with scarlet tulips under the white-flowering cherry-trees.

When both the Apocrypha (under the chairmanship of Professor McHardy) and the Old Testament were finished, Thomas Norrington was responsible for checking the draft, and he asked me to join him, with Peter Spicer and Roger Mynors, in going through some of the text for consistency and occasional second thoughts about phrasing, working in his study in Trinity College where he was President. The New Testament was then revised to make it consistent with the rest, and the whole Bible was published by the two University Presses in 1970.

When the decision to publish a new translation was first made, Vivian had met his Cambridge counterpart, Brooke Crutchley (a good friend), to discuss how to divide the work. It seemed obvious that Oxford, with its rotary presses suitable for printing large quantities at a time, should undertake the popular edition, while Cambridge would be responsible for the limited ('Library') edition in a bigger size. In designing the popular edition Vivian's problem was to find a typeface easily legible in a small size, enabling him to produce a comfortably readable text in the minimum number of pages. He thought of a type called Goudy Catalogue, in which the large-looking letters were mounted on a very small body, so producing a great many words per page. He had already used this type for a single Gospel which he had printed for the Bible Society, and it proved to be exactly what was wanted for the new Bible.

Now the rotary presses were set to work round the clock (on 'treble shift'), and produced the whole Bible in good time for the planned date of publication. It was to be dedicated in Westminster Abbey, and Vivian as Printer took part in the service, but not in the procession at the beginning where the members of the various Panels followed the clergy up the Nave. I remember remarking to one of the vergers that I thought I should be the only processor without a gown, but there must have been someone else, for he said to me afterwards: 'You see Miss, you weren't the only one in civvies.'

In 1961 when the New Testament was dedicated, Vivian had been introduced to the Queen in the Jerusalem Chamber, where some of the printing plates were on display, and had been impressed by the intelligent questions she asked, and her easy conversation with various bishops.

Needless to say, the translation was much criticized. Thirty years later, it is in regular use, and no one has improved on it, though Ronald Knox's single-handed New Testament translation has some stylistic advantages. If beauty were identical with truth, as Keats's Grecian Urn proclaimed, the advantage of greater accuracy would carry the day, but unhappily it is not so. The visionary passages suffer most in the new version; however, some successes can be claimed for modern diction: the word 'love' for instance, rather than 'charity', in 13 Corinthians; and 'the darkness has never mastered it' in the beginning of St John's Gospel, instead of 'comprehended it'. There remain some problems that just can't be solved: I am glad it has not yet been my turn to read the lesson in the Book of Revelation: 'With two [wings] he covered his face, with two he covered his feet, and with two he flew'! I should alter the words, I am sure, but I haven't yet thought of a good solution.

For family doings during these years, and for Vivian's time as chairman of the Master Printers' Federation, I will take a new chapter.

CHAPTER VIII

Until nearly the end of the 'fifties our family party living at 14 Stanley Road, with an annual change of au pair girl, continued unaltered. Vivian's mother, known to the children as Bristol Granny (though she would have preferred 'Trelawney Granny' after the name of the road she lived in), used to stay with us annually for a summer visit, and Vivian was generally able to see her when he went to Bristol for meetings of the printers' South-Western Alliance. Our children were a great pleasure to her, though her deafness made communication difficult, and outings were slightly complicated by her nervous inability to get ready anywhere near the time for setting out – which had been Vivian's despair as a schoolboy.

I couldn't have had a kinder or more appreciative mother-in-law, and during these visits she told me quite a lot about her early married life (though not about her brief departure from home, taking the children, which Mildred remembered though Vivian did not; only returning when Bertram, their sociable father, promised not to invite friends for meals so frequently). As she had been obliged to leave school early when her father died (killed by a farm accident), there were some gaps in her education, and Bertram used to suggest books for reading. He recommended Flaubert's *Salammbo* (in translation) for their honeymoon, which suggests an exacting taste: I am not surprised that she stuck in it, as I had done. One of her stories that fascinated me concerned the letters exchanged during their engagement. After her husband's death she thought to destroy them, but could not bring herself to do so; instead, she buried them at the foot of a white lilac that grew in the little garden of 58 Trelawney Road. And (shades of the tale of Pyramus and Thisbe) the flowers thereafter were always coloured purple!

While I was busy during her visits I suggested that she might rub out the lavender which had been laid out as usual on a dust-sheet for drying, thinking that this would be a soothing occupation. She did not take to it, and used to start guiltily if I came into the room and found her not doing it. Vivian laughed, and said that I ought to have set her to scrub the kitchen floor, which she would have found much more acceptable. Hard work had certainly been her lot all her life, for when Vivian was nine years old his father had been incapacitated by a stroke, and she had been obliged to take in a lodger to help eke out his pension, managing it so well that her children were never deprived of school outings (such as a visit to Paris) while they were growing up.

In her last days she had grown increasingly isolated, in spite of the efforts of some local friends to keep in touch, and it was merciful that her last illness, in the summer of 1954, was a very short one. Cancer had been diagnosed and she was taken to hospital, where Vivian and I drove down to see her. She was very cheerful, telling me that she had been enjoying the food – 'chicken, Anne!' – and the comfort: she died a day or two later. Her name was added by a local carver to the stone which Vivian had had designed for his father by Eric Gill, in the cemetery at Westbury-on-Trym.

I return to our life in the 'fifties at Stanley Road. Jane and Kate bicycled to the High School in the Woodstock Road – something I should hardly countenance with to-day's traffic; Ben (and from 1959, Colin) travelled virtually the same distance to the Dragon School, by bus, or conveyed home to lunch by Vivian, or sometimes by Sid Church. A Dragon parent reported to me that her son had said: 'Colin Ridler's quite rich – he's got a Sofa.'

The High School was not at all inspiring – except for the singing, taught by Mary Archer (who was also Secretary to the Bach Choir), and English, while Dorothy Bartholomew was there, but she left to become a headmistress elsewhere a year or two after Jane started. As one would expect of an Oxford school, the intellectual level among the pupils was high, and both the girls made good friendships there. Though Shakespeare plays were acted by the pupils, there were no expeditions to see professional productions, and although the headmistress (Miss Stack) welcomed me cordially when I once went to read my poetry to the English Club, the only letter I ever had from her was a complaint because we had taken Kate to Stratford (with the agreement of her form mistress), and so caused her to be late with handing in a prep – not even missing it.

Thanks to the efficient teaching, O Level was not a bugbear, and Jane would have taken A Levels in French and Geography, but timetables would not allow the combination, so she left at Christmas 1958, before her eighteenth birthday. She had always been quite clear about what profession she wanted to follow, that of a nursery school teacher, and she planned to take the two-year training the next autumn, first spending three months abroad to learn French, and to take the one necessary A Level in the summer.

The engraver Reynolds Stone, whom we knew slightly, strongly recommended a French family living in Avignon, and Jane set off to join them in the New Year. It should have been an excellent plan, but alas, the slight sore throat which she had when she arrived, worsened after a walk when the Mistral was blowing, and turned into pleurisy. So poor Jane acquired an unwelcome acquaintance with French medical terms during miserable weeks in bed, and was not strong enough at the end of her three months to go and stay with the de Galhauds at Nancy on her way home as we had planned. (The eldest boy, Emmanuel, had stayed with us the previous summer, and he and Jane had become fond of each other. The two families kept in touch: later on another son, Gaby, made an exchange with Ben, who became very fond of Madame, and Kate became friends with their daughter Elisabeth.)

Back at home, Jane took some coaching from our former neighbour Jeannine Alton and achieved her French A Level, while gaining some teaching practice at the Crescent nursery department under Kay Sawtell, the kindly teacher who used to give such glowing reports of Ben and Colin.

That year (1959) we spent our summer holiday in Olive Willis's cottage at Aisholt, while she herself stayed at the upper cottage with her housekeeper Miss Angus: we shared some of their delicious meals, and they shared some of our doings. One day we went over to Porlock, meeting Mildred there and poring over the many Ridler tombs in the churchyard. Mildred had been doing some research into the family antecedents, and had found the interesting coincidence that their forebear Christopher had been the village schoolmaster just at the time when Coleridge and the Wordsworths were living in the Quantocks; moreover, he had some responsibility for customs supervision. Was it not possible, even likely, we thought, that *he* was the 'person from Porlock' who is supposed to have prevented the completion of 'Kubla Khan'? (Not that I believe in Coleridge's story, for I don't think the poem is incomplete.) We have suggested this possibility to one or two experts, including Richard Holmes, but none have been disposed to be interested.

The name Ridler (not a rhymer, but one who riddles an oven) is still common in the neighbourhood, and Mildred called on one prosperous farmer, but all she could learn about her and Vivian's ancestor is that he took to the bottle and lost his land: hence the emigration across the Bristol Channel to Cardiff some time during the nineteenth century, where the family settled. Vivian has visited his birthplace, 13 Elton Road, Cardiff, which had the advantage to him of being within sight of a railway cutting, where trains carrying pit-props used to pass. When he was five years old his father was appointed to the important job of Superintendent of the Avonmouth Docks, and the family moved to Bristol.

To return to the narrative of Jane. She went in the autumn to the training college at Kingston-on-Thames, where she lived in term-time during the next two years. It was a good training, involving some teaching experience in schools as well as theory and general education, and she made a lasting friendship with Christine Hulse, her companion in trips to London and overnight queuing for Wimbledon.

Jane had made the acquaintance of Rolf Länge in Oxford through our au pair Charlotte (called Lange but no relation), and now towards the end of a Christmas term he suggested a meeting on Waterloo Bridge when he was en route for Germany, having finished his English course. Jane went at the appointed time, and waited for more than an hour in a bitter wind; caught a cold; and heard nothing from Rolf to explain why he had not appeared. Typically, he had missed his train from Oxford, and had been defeated by the difficulty of framing a letter of explanation. Nevertheless, after more than six months of silence he wrote to ask Jane to come and spend the following Christmas at his home in Münsingen, South Germany. She, having still a tendresse for him in spite of her hurt feelings, was anxious to accept, but Vivian and I were most disinclined to let her go, fearing further muddles. However, I said that if she received a formal invitation from Rolf's mother, we would agree to it; and this was duly sent – composed by Rolf in English as far as I remember, but signed by Frau Länge.

Jane went, and was happy. And Rolf, with the courageous persistence that is a counterbalance to his waywardness, determined to come and work in England and persuade her to marry him. Before pursuing their story, I return to the narrative of Kate, the next to leave the nest.

Kate did quite a lot of acting during her High School days, and scored hits as Juliet in Terence Rattigan's *Harlequinade* and in various scenes from Shakespeare: 'O what a lovely Shrew!', her form-mistress exclaimed to me after one performance. She spent one summer holiday at Antibes on an exchange visit to a French family with whom Jane had stayed earlier. Kate's opposite number, Claude, was a great deal more congenial than her elder sister, who had continually made 'odious comparisons' between France and England. 'In France we 'ave BIG stroberries', and 'I do not like this weather. I think in France my perrents 'ave a beautiful deh.' Claude was good at drawing, and interested in the sights of Oxford; nevertheless she and Kate did not keep in touch after her visit.

Our joint family holidays had continued through the decade: apart from Aisholt, we spent them chiefly in Pembrokeshire, as already described, and in South Cornwall. While Audrey was living with her parents at St Mawes, opposite Falmouth, we stayed at a cottage she found for us on St Anthony's headland, which could be reached by a row across the bay in their dinghy. Its lovely position made up for the fact that it had only an earth closet, and no hot water laid on: we threw our kitchen waste into the surrounding field to be gobbled up by a sow in attendance. To get to our favourite bathing-place on the headland we crossed fields full of cows viewed apprehensively by Ben (Colin, still an infant, was in a carry-cot). One day, as we were passing the herd, Ben said delightedly: 'Golly, Daddy, that one smiled!' It was later, when Audrey had gone to live at East Portholland, that we stayed in lodgings at West Portholland in the next bay.

In 1957 we rented Robin and Kirstie's cottage at Lyme Regis, while they stayed with their friend Norah Ford in her big house near by – a delightful arrangement, which meant that we saw a lot of Robin (Kirstie worked daily at a bookshop), and played tennis with him on Norah's hard court. (It was delightful to see the change in Robin when a game was under way, his habitual aspect as the old man he liked to think himself, quite forgotten as he leapt about the court.) The cottage had a wonderful view over Lyme Bay, until some years later when the callous owner of the field below them sold it for building plots, blocking out the view of all the overlooking houses, and giving them no chance to buy at least part of the field themselves.

At the bottom of that same field was a large pool fed by a stream, where for more than an hour I watched a kingfisher diving for fish from an overhanging branch. A cruiser, HMS *Grafton*, was anchored off Lyme for several days while we were there, and we were able to go over it; the popular hit-song 'Last train to San Fernandez' was playing on board at full volume, as we all remember vividly. Vivian made his film entitled 'Corn on the Cobb', about a supposed surfeit of pink Candy Floss, sited on the Cobb and its steps (down which Louisa Musgrove took her fall in *Persuasion*); one night we watched fireworks over the bay; and we saw the delightful film *The Red Balloon* at the local cinema. I took Colin out before the frightening film which followed, and we were rewarded by a marvellous complete rainbow arching over the sea. At the end of our fortnight Vivian went back to Oxford, and we stayed on at Seatown (below Golden Cap) whose boulder-strewn shore with its rather gloomy atmosphere inspired my poem:

> Rocks at the cliff's foot seem dead souls
> Bound in these boulder-shapes, with headless
> Torsoes, rounded thighs and shoulders…
> Prone upon a forlorn shore
> Until as small shingle all
> Under the grinding tide are rolled.

In 1960 came the break with our tradition of undivided family holidays. Vivian and I took the girls and Enrica by car to the Dordogne, stopping for a night at Chartres and another at Bourges on the way. Ben meanwhile was with a French family in Paris and Brittany, and Colin went by train to Cornwall to stay with the Wheelers.

In the Dordogne we found by sheer luck a wonderful place to stay: a guest-house converted from the abbey at Carennac where Fénélon had been abbot, the village being on a hillside above the river, broad and swift-flowing at that point. Each evening from our windows we could watch the cows being brought up the village street from the fields for the night, and there was a fine pile of their manure in the courtyard outside the entrance to the abbey church. We breakfasted on a flat roof overlooking the tree-clad slope to the river, and ate our delicious dinners in the former refectory, which was over the nave of the church. (Ben and Allan Cumming were to visit Carennac nearly forty years later, finding motor vehicles, not cows, filling the streets, and the guest-house now a museum, but still with its fine view over river and church.)

Enrica of course was the perfect companion on all our explorations – in the caves at the Gouffre de Padirac, in the pilgrimage church on the hill at Rocamadour (where she and Kate ascended with the throng on their knees up steps to see the black Madonna), and best of all, at Lascaux, where the cave-paintings were still open to the public. I think they were closed a year or two later, except to small parties, for fear of damage from the breath of crowds.

Ben had enjoyed his time only moderately, as he and Aymar, his boy exchange, had not much in common, but Colin had had a blissful visit to the Wheelers, wearing Dr Wheeler's yachting cap most of the time. When I opened his suitcase to unpack it on his return, a most evocative smell of fish came wafting up from all the shells he had brought back. Audrey's uncle, whom she called Puncle, found a firm place in Colin's affection by giving him every threepenny bit he collected during their stay.

It must have been the following year that Aymar came with us to Wales near Carmarthen, where we stayed at a family farm. The young farmer, Dic Jones, who had taken over its management on the sudden death of his father, was to become famous as the wearer of the bardic crown, and had already begun to win armchairs as prizes for his poetry – which of course I could not understand, and I don't think I showed him any of mine. We were surprised, when we first arrived, at the number of armchairs in our rooms, and wondered what they would do with them all if he continued at the same rate of success. 'Give them away to my friends,' he said. I envied him his useful function as the local wordsmith, to be called on for epitaphs and other inscriptions: the only taste I had of something like it was when Tom Armstrong would ask me to translate a carol to be sung at 'The Mayor's Carols', which he made such a feature of Christmas in Oxford.

Colin fell in love with the affectionate Corgi dogs at the farm, and Aymar enjoyed the rock bathing, for he was an accomplished swimmer and diver (Vivian made a film exploiting this talent), but he was happier back in Oxford, where I took him round the colleges.

Until nearly the end of the decade we had Colin at home with us, as he moved on from the Dragon to Magdalen College School, a short trip down the road on his bicycle, and back in time for a cosy tea with me by the Baxi fire of logs from the garden (now replaced by gas-coal, an excellent labour-saving imitation, but useless for toast or roasted chestnuts). Perhaps I have a rosier recollection of those teatimes than he, for I had no obligation of homework hanging over me. Magdalen College School provided very well for his chief interests of music and history, in addition to the opportunity for acting. It was not until near the end of his time that he acted again, having been disillusioned (as I have said) by the experience of *Lady Precious Stream* at the Dragon. He went somewhat hesitantly to audition for a part in *Hamlet*, and was surprised (and slightly alarmed) to be picked for the Prince. In the event, the production was an outstanding experience during his time at school, and all our friends who saw it agreed in finding his performance extremely moving. He brought out the vulnerability of Hamlet's situation in a remarkable way, and spoke the verse beautifully. Vivian's film of the dress rehearsal records the look of the performance, but alas not the sound.

In Colin's last year or two he belonged to the joint music club of Magdalen College School and the Oxford High School for Girls, grandly called The Bach Gesellschaft, which used to meet at our house and use our piano. During summer week-ends he went to excavate with Conant Brodribb at a Roman villa called Shakenoak, north of Oxford; and I remember one delightful outing when we took our bicycles by train to Charlbury, whence we explored Bourton-on-the-Water and the Christian Maze at Wick Rissington churchyard not far from there, which was entered beside a giant redwood.

Two or three times a year we would visit Ben at Clifton (where he had won a scholarship in 1960), sometimes staying with Mildred at the house in Trelawney Road, and sometimes at a guesthouse overlooking the gorge. We enjoyed his various successes: directing a short Brecht play in a competition, acting as Gertrude in *Hamlet* and Prospero (with white hair) in *The Tempest*; and singing the tenor recitative in Bach's *Christmas Oratorio*, at the thrilling moment where the choir comes in with 'Break forth O beauteous, heavenly light!' Only his cricketing promise (as a left-handed slow bowler) had been cut short by an unlucky fall in some slippery-soled shoes, when he tore the cartilage in his knee.

During the spring and summer of 1963, while Rolf was living with us and working at a local bakery, Jane fulfilled the practical part of her teacher's diploma by working at Headington under Miss Bennett. She became engaged to Rolf, and in November they were married in St Mary's by Tom Griffiths, with Kate as maid-of-honour, Martin Wilkinson as best man, and Jonathan Dillon (Jane's godson) as page. We held the reception at Corpus Christi College, conveniently close by, where Vivian had dining rights: Nellie came over from Little Gaddesden, Enrica from Sevenoaks, Edward and Bertha from Cheltenham, and Jan from Wiltshire.

After a week-end honeymoon at the Garden House Hotel in Cambridge (my suggestion, as it was not the time of year for a seaside holiday), they set off for Germany. They rented a flat in Mannheim, where Rolf was to work in a patisserie, and Jane in a kindergarten.

According to a bibliography of my work sent me by an American Jesuit, Fr Feeney, I had three books published that year (1963): a play called *Who is my Neighbour?*, and two pieces of the editorial work which I have already described: *Shakespeare Criticism* and the *Poems* of James Thomson. *Who is my Neighbour?* and another play, *Witnesses*, (never published), were commissioned by Pamela Keily, an older contemporary of mine at Downe, when she was producing religious drama in the northern diocese. She had learnt her craft with Martin Browne's Pilgrim Players during the war; now she had trained a group of amateurs whose work reached a professional standard, performing in a Leeds theatre, and sometimes in Manchester Cathedral. *Who is my Neighbour?* was based on an episode I read about in the newspapers: an incident of what we should now call 'Road Rage', where a quarrel in a car park led to a man being attacked and killed, and, as the news report put it, 'no one answered his cries for help'.

Vivian and I drove up to attend the first night of the play (in 1961), and stayed with one of Pam's neighbours in Sheffield. It was given at the Leeds Civic Theatre for a week, and was 'warmly received', as the book's blurb put it. But it hasn't ever been revived, as far as I know. It is of course strongly derivative from Eliot, even to ending with an incantation as *The Family Reunion* does. The dialogue seems to me pretty good, as I look at it again, but I never possessed the secret of imbuing invented characters with life – the secret which Tolstoy possessed to such a degree that even when he is writing about a horse, the animal steps from the page as an individual. A short play, 'How bitter the bread', about a refugee, which was printed in the same volume, was written at the suggestion of Oliver Wilkinson for Toc H amateur performance, and did I believe prove useful. Vicars and Dorothy Bell put it on in the school hall at Little Gaddesden, and we went over to see it. Another verse play, *Witnesses,* concerned the rebellion against Hitler of the group called 'The White Rose', and was given by Pam's players in Manchester Cathedral. But the greater realism of the 'kitchen sink' type of drama, and perhaps that of television, killed the taste for verse plays, and no more commissions came my way. A substitute arose in the form of libretti for opera, and translating foreign libretti into English, but this came later, in the 'seventies.

In the spring of 1964 I went to stay for a few days with Jane and Rolf in their flat in Mannheim, and saw the kindergarten where Jane taught. Although the Germans had been pioneers in employing the ideas of Froebel in the education of young children, this particular school was anything but enlightened, and Jane disagreed with much of the discipline she was obliged to enforce. The children were not allowed to try to sign their own names at this stage, and in 'break' they had to walk sedately down the paths without straying on to the grass. In displays of drawing and handicraft, most of the work was actually that of the teachers. But Jane learnt many ingenious ways of making Christmas decorations, by which we all profited later on, at home.

After my visit to their pleasant flat, I crossed the Alps (the long train descent into Italy memorable as always) to stay with Kate in Florence, where she was spending six months, learning Italian and supporting herself by teaching English to students. She had found a most delightful flat on the far side of the Arno, on the three top floors of a house where the painter Filippino Lippi was born. (His father Filippo had absconded from Sta Maria del Carmine, close by.) Kate's large sitting room had windows looking towards the Cascine Gardens on one side; my bedroom above it was octagonal, and I could see the Palazzo Pubblico in the distance across the river. Kate had furnished the flat by picking up pieces in second-hand shops here and there, and had fixed a bookcase above her bed by some very precarious-looking nails, the thought of which, poised above her head, used to give me nightmares after I returned home. (I had given her money to get it fixed, but suspected it would be used for something else.)

I met a number of her friends, and visited all my favourite places: San Miniato of course, and Fiesole where we picnicked. Spring was well under way in Italy, and we found Kate's favourite grape hyacinths growing wild in the countryside.

Ben also enjoyed a stay at this flat during the summer, after some weeks in France at Villeurbanne to work as a 'stagiaire' with Roger Planchon at his Théâtre National Populaire. Ben had stayed on at Clifton for the Easter term to be head of the school – rather reluctantly, as he had already secured a scholarship for the following autumn at King's College, Cambridge. This was to read Spanish, but after his intensive work at the grammar of the language during his school years, he longed for some study of literature, which could not have happened during the first part of his Spanish degree. Accordingly he chose to read English, though urged that more honours were likely to accrue in Spanish. In this respect he was unambitious, and his Cambridge years were productive in the ways that interested him most – of music, acting and general reading – rather than concentrating on exam results. He achieved a 2:1 degree, and then went with his close friend Peter Pelz to teach for a year at a progressive school in the Quantocks.

Although Kate's similar degree in English could have led on to post-graduate research, she felt she had not sufficient enthusiasm to carry her through the years of study, and wanted 'to do something useful' with her life. Accordingly she signed on for a diploma in 'Social Work' at the University of Sussex, and lived for the next two years at lodgings in Brighton. On gaining her diploma she undertook the exacting job of

Probation Officer in Tower Hamlets in the East End of London, and it was here that she found a colleague in Susan Wates, who became close to our family in so many ways thereafter.

During this time too Kate became engaged to Tim Wilson, whom she had met in Oxford. We had made Tim's acquaintance through Donald Allchin and Pusey House, and it was in Pusey House Chapel that Kate and Tim were married in 1968, with small Karin as a bridesmaid – doing her best to tread on Kate's train as they walked up the nave. After a honeymoon at Edward and Bertha's cottage in Pembrokeshire, they took over the flat vacated by Christopher and Jane, high up on the fifteeth floor of John Kennedy House in the East End of London, with a fine view over the Thames. Kate enjoyed finding there some of the furniture she remembered from Ringshall End.

She continued her work in Tower Hamlets, while Tim pursued commissions as a freelance writer, and they looked about for a more permanent home. Kate took out a mortgage on Number 92 Fentiman Road, near the Oval, which was really a bargain in value, as although the interior was in a squalid state (occupied by several families), the structure needed no major repairs.

All our family helped at one time or another in the painting and repair of the house, clearing out all manner of distasteful rubbish, and getting the garden into some sort of shape, but as Tim was at home while Kate kept office hours, he was, rather fitfully, in charge. He was a charming, talented but disorganized young man, whose high ideals for society did not extend to punctiliousness in everyday life. The responsibility for keeping their finances afloat fell on Kate, and she paid for the anxiety with a gastric ulcer. At length she left Tim in possession of 92 Fentiman Road and went to live with Sue Wates; then divorced him by agreement in 1973.

Ben shared in the house for some time while he was teaching in London, and Colin too stayed there occasionally. Tim and his friends experimented with drugs, and once persuaded Ben to try a particularly powerful strain of marijuana, which gave him a very stressful 'trip', and contributed to his decision to leave London and go to live in Wales – of which more later.

When Kate made her happy marriage to Richard Wilson, the house was sold, and Tim left England for America, where so far as I know he still lives.

Our holiday in the Lake District mentioned earlier must have been the first of many, starting with consecutive years at a cottage in Little Langdale. My friend Norman Nicholson (Nic) had recommended to us a painter called Delmar Banner who had a cottage to let, originally the farm-worker's dwelling next to the farmhouse which Delmar and his wife (the sculptress Josephina de Vasconcellos) had bought from Beatrix Potter, then a landowner and sheep-breeder in the district. (They obtained it because they promised to live there, not just for holidays.) High Bield is on a hillside overlooking Little Langdale tarn, about half a mile from the village, and has a stream dancing down beneath Josephina's studio. She was often absent fulfilling commissions, but Delmar rarely left the place, and lived to paint the mountains: when he grew too old to do so any more, he could still walk them in his dreams.

Josephina, who made a portrait bust of Nic, was active in all sorts of ways besides her sculpture. She devised a special carpet, patterned so that disabled people could 'dance' in a beneficial way by following the pattern; and she hired a trawler to be anchored where delinquent children could undergo training. Moreover, she and Delmar had adopted two destitute boys; unfortunately this particular good work turned out badly, and Josephina had to keep changing her address in London to escape their sometimes violent demands for money. She outlived Delmar by many years, and in the year when I am writing (2000) she is still active, aged ninety-seven, and has carved a sculpture called 'Reconciliation' intended for Northern Ireland, following one which is on the Berlin Wall and one in Coventry Cathedral with the same title.

The walls round the top-floor rooms of the Banners' house displayed a panorama of the mountains, geographically accurate, but not entirely satisfactory because it did not convey their ruggedness. Nic used to say that this was because Delmar desired to paint Nature from a Christian viewpoint; for whatever reason, the surface had an unpleasant softness – 'the land under summer grass', Delmar would explain, but to me it was rather 'the land under blancmange'.

HIGH BIELD, LITTLE LANGDALE
For Delmar and Josephine

The stillness of that valley
To town-bred ears is positive as a sound.
At early light the tarn
On dark-green glass re-prints the slaty mountain,
And little grassy hills
With rounded slopes follow each other in canon.

If there is sound, it is sudden:
Flycatcher clacks, robin winds an alarm-clock,
Or flings his chain of silver notes
Out of the yew-tree; then in the distant quarry
A wheel screams, slicing at stone,
Where sombre Wetherlam shows his frown-marks eastward.

Bright image on the remembering eye,
Your mountains go with each of us departing,
And traverse England; so for me
A winter long they loom in summer plumage.

But you, with a remembering brush,
Live for them, set all seasons on your walls, your heart.

I think my poem conveys much of what we loved about the place, but when Delmar had read it, he wrote rather wistfully that he never knew whether we liked his paintings. This I suppose was because we had not bought one, though he knew that we did acquire modern paintings. He never would show us his sketch-books, though we should certainly have bought a drawing; his portraits too were skilful, and included one of Beatrix Potter which is in the National Portrait Gallery. During Josephine's frequent absences Delmar seemed to exist chiefly on baked mince, prepared by his daily and eaten cold, so he enjoyed occasionally coming to supper with us. On Sundays he read the lessons in Little Langdale church, where once or twice I had to accompany the hymns on the hand-blown organ.

Scaling heights has never been one of Vivian's favourite occupations (I always ascribed this to the admirable absence of the thrusting super-ego in his character), so on our longer climbs we generally left him to sit and read halfway up. Over the years Colin and I climbed the main peaks, including Scafell Pike, and Vivian certainly accompanied us to the top of Helvellyn, which involves the dizzying walk along Striding Edge. One year we went in early June with Kate and Daniel (then aged about three), and enjoyed having a nest of spotted flycatchers in the cottage porch. Vivian was able to film them through the window, and recorded their whole progress from hatching to wing-testing, though missing their flight from the nest on the day after we left.

One year we took the cottage for a whole three weeks, and left it for a couple of nights to stay in Hexham and explore Hadrian's Wall. We had our share of Lakeland soakings – one year so often that we returned home a day early. Delmar shared Wordsworth's favourable view that in the Lakes the rain was always hearty, compared with the dismal drizzle of Ireland.

Much later, Vivian and I shared the cottage with Jane, Rolf and their children when Karin was about five, and I vividly remember making the long walk down from Walnar Scar with her hand in mine, as she talked all the way about Tiny-Tears her doll, and the clothes Tiny was to wear for Karin's wedding.

Later still we explored the northern lakes, staying on Derwentwater with Jane and her two girls, in the house on whose walled garden Beatrix Potter based 'Mr MacGregor's garden' in *Peter Rabbit*; and another year at Crookwath Cottage near Dockray above Ullswater with Allan Cumming, Colin and family, when Isobel was a toddler.

On each of our Little Langdale holidays we drove over to Millom to visit Norman Nicholson, living there with his wife Yvonne, in the house where he had been born. Nic had battled against tuberculosis in his 'teens, and survived to maintain himself as a writer, against the odds. His excellent guidebooks to the Lakes were based on his early explorations on foot and bicycle, but he could still visit favourite places by car, and delighted in showing us the gigantic fallen breakwater on the shore at Millom, and the flora of its surroundings which he knew so well. He had made a late and happy marriage to Yvonne, met when she came to teach in the local school, and we liked her very much, though I felt resentful for Enrica, who had been engaged to him for years, always hoping that the time would come when he proved able to break away from his father and stepmother, to marry her. By the time Yvonne appeared, of course, they were both dead. Yvonne's great admiration for Nic was compatible with friendly teasing, and when he began to sport some prominent side-whiskers she said that he hoped to resemble Matthew Arnold.

Nic and I agreed about poetry, and I was at least partly responsible for Eliot's accepting him as a Faber poet. We freely exchanged comments, and I valued his opinion, but conversation on general topics was rather one-sided, for Vivian and I never felt he was interested in matters outside his own concerns. We felt this particularly when he and Yvonne came to stay with us in Oxford – Nic and I having been booked to give a joint poetry-recital. Even the printing press did not provoke a spark of attention.

Yvonne was a devoted carer for Nic, but he outlived her by several years; she died at no great age of cancer, and we wondered whether the proximity of Sellafield nuclear centre had anything to do with it. Nic published his lively autobiography, *Wednesday Early Closing*, in 1975, and his last book of poems, *Sea to the West*, in 1981. We continued to correspond but we did not meet again after his visit to Oxford; he died aged seventy-seven in 1987, and Enrica, who had not seen him again after he broke off their engagement, travelled north to attend his funeral.

During the last years of the 'sixties Vivian was very active in the affairs of the British Federation of Master Printers (or The British Printing Industries Federation, as to his disgust they decided in the 'seventies to call themselves, wishing to appear more democratic). He had already served his turn as President of the South-Western Alliance. and at the conference of June 1967 at Gleneagles was elected Vice-President of the Federation, to serve for a year before becoming President for the year thereafter. It was quite arduous to add this to the work of running the Press, but luckily Vivian enjoyed the job, being admirably suited to it: he was an excellent chairman, skilful at discouraging digressions without giving offence, and relishing the company of his fellow-printers. (A letter from one of them after his retirement, wishing that his year of office was not at an end, commented on his *dignity*.) His public speeches were always very amusing, and I can testify to their quality, having listened to them two or three times a year for a decade. My one contribution to the regular proceedings was to write a new printers' prayer for the Sunday service, instead of a petition which implied that the printers were responsible for the content of the books they printed, asking that they might be 'mindful of those for whom they write'. I find it printed in the service-leaflet for Sunday at the Torquay conference.

Almighty God, through whom each act achieves its own perfection [quoted from Aquinas], help us to bring our best powers to our work, and to find satisfaction in work welldone. And though we cannot fully know the end of what we do, may we in all our dealings keep in mind the image of thy love and justice...

The annual week-end conferences of Alliance and Federation took us to Scotland, Northern Ireland, Spain and Dublin, as well as to places nearer home such as Weston-super-Mare, Newquay, Ambleside, Harrogate, Sheffield, Stratford on Avon, and Torquay. This last was in June at the end of Vivian's year as Federation President, and we were luxuriously lodged in a bridal suite at the Imperial Hotel, complete with cocktail bar, which had a splendid view over the sea. Kate and Tim were invited, and added a lot to everyone's enjoyment. For one of the outings, at the instigation of Richard Russell (a colleague of Vivian's at the Press), the Federation had hired a train from the Totnes to Dartmouth Light Railway, and had caused the engine (on which Vivian rode) to carry a headboard with the legend 'The Master Printer', now displayed in our printing house. Vivian invited Kenneth Wheare, then head of Exeter College, to be the speaker besides himself for the Saturday night dinner: the pair of them made it a record for amusement.

Being much less sociably-minded than Vivian, I had anticipated his Presidential years with some dread, but I enjoyed the sight-seeing and the friends we made, notably that of the Director Leonard Kenyon, who had a fine sense of humour, and of Philippa Wright, the wife of the Alliance Secretary Sam Wright. I liked Sam, too, though we had not so much in common. He drove us on a number of occasions, very efficiently, and we enjoyed the company of both of them on various sightseeing outings in the Somerset and Devonshire countryside. Other friends were Philip Wright and his wife Brenda: his firm, John Wright & Son, were long-established Bristol printers and publishers.

By the end of one of those rich-feeding week-ends even Vivian looked forward to scrambled-eggs at home – and *he* didn't have to think about varying his wardrobe. Once or twice I got Sid Church to drive me to London for a shopping trip; and I invested in a hair-piece for evening wear. (If anyone could have given me confidence in my looks, Vivian would have managed it, for he is always a total support, but – as Kathleen Raine once surprisingly said of herself – I have always preferred to think of myself as invisible.)

Apart from the conference outings to great houses and other places of interest, there were entertainments on the Saturday evening. During the Stratford week-end we saw *The Winter's Tale*, when the theatre had undergone one of its periodic transformations and was arranged in imitation of the Globe of Shakespeare's day, long before we could experience in London something closer to the real thing. The one drawback to the production, as I remember it, was that the director had decided to emphasize Leontes' jealousy by spotlighting him in blue whenever the pangs were supposed to assail him. Another memorable evening was a guitar and lute concert by Julian Bream; and another, at Sheffield, was an 'Evening with Ken Dodd'. This was a revelation to us, for hitherto we had only seen him on television and thought him rather silly; he needs an audience to evoke his real genius, and teased the printing Federation very amusingly. I was glad I was not sitting in the front row, however, to be a target for his sallies.

Vivian's predecessor as President was Max Bemrose, whom we knew slightly because he and his wife had a house in Ashridge Park. We had nothing in common, and he was an enthusiastic Tory; he invited Ted Heath to be the visiting speaker at his Presidential conference, held at Eastbourne. We were invited for drinks before the Saturday night dinner, and I was much disgruntled with Ted Heath, who held forth about the annoyance of having women in the common rooms at Oxford colleges, 'talking about nothing but children and nappies'.

During the business meetings, the womenfolk were provided with amusements on their own, and during the Belfast conference I was booked to entertain the ladies to dinner at our hotel. The local Alliance President and his wife had driven us out all the previous day, showing us the spectacular Giant's Causeway on the north coast among other sights, and she and I had exhausted all our possible topics of conversation. The wives arrived for the evening at half-past six, and I knew that we couldn't expect the husbands back until after ten o'clock. After allowing an hour for dinner, how *were* we to get through the rest of the evening? Vivian and I had a large television in our bed-sitting room, and I remembered that my Alliance hostess had deplored the fact that she would miss the weekly episode of 'Sherlock Holmes' which would then be showing; so after dinner I shepherded them all upstairs and settled them in front of the television, to my satisfaction, and I think to theirs too, though one or two of them murmured 'O should we really?' Half way through the story, I glanced at my Alliance hostess and saw that she was fast asleep, tired out, poor dear, by her efforts of the day before.

Every three years the European and American printers had an International Conference, and we always met the Cambridge University Printer there (Brooke Crutchley and his wife Diana), which was a special pleasure. In this way we visited Lausanne, Nice, Vienna and Madrid. There was always an opening ceremony of welcome from the municipal authorities, replied to by the International Federation President, a rather pompous speaker who disguised his bald pate with what, according to Leonard Kenyon, was boot-blacking. Each trip had its memorable treat: at Lausanne it was a steamer trip to the head of the lake; at Nice a visit to Monet's garden; at Vienna an evening in the woods to drink the new wine; also a visit to see the Lippizaner horses caracole in time to music. We also went to the opera: to our disappointment it was not Mozart, but Gounod's *Faust*.

During the Nice conference Vivian and I had some delicious bathes from a small off-shore islet, and we enjoyed fireworks over the sea on the last evening, but the evening party itself was rather dismaying, as our French hosts had provided an over-lavish display of food for the open-air buffet, and the printer-guests attacked it with such greedy abandon that whole cheeses and portions of dismembered chicken were strewn on the ground beside the tables.

On each occasion we took the opportunity to spend another few days abroad. From Lausanne we went to a small hotel near Burgdorf, where on the night we arrived there was a wedding party, as I remember, who were lustily singing the 'Chanson de la Mariée' which gloats over the new bride: *she* won't be going out to balls any longer; she will be keeping house while *we* are out enjoying ourselves. From there (on the one or two days when it was not pouring with rain) we could take a chair-lift up the Jungfrau (picnicking beside a glacier), and take mountain walks where the flowers were appearing below the snow-line: golden globe-flowered Trollius, mauve-coloured Soldanella ('Mountain Tassel-Flower'), and brilliant blue Spring Gentian. We took a train to Berne to visit the family home of our very nice au pair, Rosmarie Bandi (left at Oxford in charge of the children). Her sister kindly met us in the centre of the town, and I remember standing in the square while she fluently reeled off information about population numbers as the rain poured down. She and I had umbrellas, and she seemed oblivious of the fact that mine was not really shielding Vivian, while the rain bounced off his shoulder. The sun must have come out later, for I remember eating raspberries for tea in their leafy garden.

After Nice we went to Avignon, driven over by Sam and Philippa Wright, and stopping on the way at Les Eyzies to add to our stock of Santans, the little clay Nativity figures traditional there, to which Enrica had introduced us. The heat was tremendous, and we stifled in a little room at the top of our hotel, but out of doors the streets of Avignon are pleasantly shaded by great trees whose branches meet above.

From there we visited Nîmes (very hot in the Roman amphitheatre), and spent a day in the Camargue, watching from the coach its white horses and water buffalo (of which Vivian had had rather a surfeit in Africa), and bathing in the sea at the port where gypsies annually dip their Madonna.

The conference at Madrid was in mid-September 1970, and unexpectedly cold. I shivered in my evening dress at the alfresco dinner on the first evening, where we waited about till nearly ten o'clock before eating. The usual boring opening ceremony was enlivened this time by a performance of Rodrigo's famous guitar concerto, composed in 1944, but new then to Vivian and me. During the week we renewed acquaintance with an agreeable German printer from Freiburg, Herr Wiebe, whom we had met in Lausanne, and lunched with him in the Plaza Mayor. Vivian delivered a paper on Industrial Training which was voted the best in the conference. Apart from visits to the Prado pictures, the high spots of our time were visits to Toledo in its spectacular ravine, with its pictures by El Greco, and to Segovia with its fairytale castle. The reverse of enjoyable was our tour of Franco's Civil War monument, with its inevitable Fascist swagger.

Ben arrived in time to share the last evening, and next day we set off for Salamanca in a hired Simca. The start was difficult, for the car stalled after a couple of hundred yards, at the first traffic lights. We were rescued from the hooting throng by a saintly lorry-driver, who got the engine going by a spark from his screwdriver, sufficiently to get us back to our hotel, where we rang the agent for another car. (Even this one was inclined to stall, but we all managed to drive it without mishap.)

The journey over the Guadarrama mountains to Salamanca is very beautiful, and in the city we found a third-floor room with a fine view: we spent a couple of days exploring the town, our pleasure much enhanced by Ben's knowledgeable company and his fluent Spanish. He had hoped to hear singing in the streets, and to pick up some folk-songs to add to his repertoire, but in this he was disappointed, even at La Alberca, the remote hill town near the Portuguese border, where there is no wheeled traffic and national costume is worn. The young girls at our lodgings there were delighted to hear Ben play, and recognized some of his songs from the radio, but they themselves had never sung them.

From La Alberca (where the children were just going back to school for the autumn term) Ben lured us to drive up to a mountain viewpoint, whence we took a hairpin descent to a monastery, Las Batuecas, in a deep valley. Here only the males were allowed to enter – which they did, while Anne sat on a rock and fumed. Rather than climb the mountain again we decided to push on from there to Avila, though the road was not marked on our map; a decision we regretted, as we ground along for thirty miles in bottom gear, expecting the Simca to give up at any moment. We reached Avila in the late evening, and the sight of the city walls lit by the rays of the setting sun banished our discomforts. The temperature reminded Vivian of Oxford on Christmas Eve, and I wished for a warm coat, rather than the mac I had brought, during our explorations of the next two days. The market, and the many gold and silver treasures of the cathedral stand out in my memory.

Back in Madrid, Ben was to stay for a few more days, and our last sight of him as we drove off was as he directed a French girl on her way.

Jane had been pregnant when I went to stay with them in Mannheim, and we discussed plans for them to start their family in England. It was easy for Rolf to find a job in an Oxford bakery, and Philippa offered the lease of a ground-floor flat in her house on Hinksey Hill. Accordingly they came over in the spring of 1965, and Karin was born in August, at the cottage hospital in Abingdon. The following year they were able to buy a house in Summertown (North Oxford), where Juliette was born in February 1967, and later still, they moved to the pleasant suburb of Kidlington, where Rolf was a manager in a patisserie. While the children were small, Jane ran a play-group locally, in which of course they were included, and later she taught for the local authority, first in Summertown and then in Wolvercote, where until her retirement she ran the nursery department with great success, helped by a colleague, Margaret Auty, who became a close friend. For several years Vivian was roped in to act as Father Christmas at the end of the autumn term.

It was delightful for Vivian and me to have the children close at hand during their early years: we saw the family for Sunday lunch most weeks, and they always enjoyed being read to (Mother's *Enchanted Forest* and *The Happy Families* were favourites); or they would sing at the piano and play their recorders. At Christmas, we went to them for dinner on Christmas Eve, the rooms beautifully decorated by Jane, with some of the ingenious constructions she had learnt to make in Germany; and they would come to us for Christmas Day. We sang English carols to the piano, and German ones (also folk-songs) to the accompaniment of Rolf's accordion. As I have said, we shared some Lakeland holidays, and Juliette tells me that according to her memory they went *every* year to the Lakes with us. She retains a recollection of a picnic, when she can have been only three, where as we sat in a moorland field (rather wet, it surely must have been), Vivian delivered a disquisition on sphagnum moss!

I find it difficult to cover the divergent family fortunes from the second half of the 'sixties in anything like a consistent narrative. Vivian's sister Mildred, who had returned to live in the Trelawney Road house after a period of training as a social worker, fell ill with cancer in 1965, and died aged only fifty-four in the Homeopathic Hospital (not far from where she had grown up), after a few months of illness. It was a sad end to a life that was in some ways unfulfilled. Her engagement after the war had been broken off by her young man, and later she had a nervous breakdown and spent some time in the Park Hospital in Oxford, before going to live for nearly a year with Aunt Barbara Hammond (lately widowed) at Piccotts End. Aunt Barbara then paid for her to take the social work training, which she completed, though I do not think she ever actually practised. Possibly the war years, when she had worked as secretary to George Weidenfeld at the BBC in Bristol and then in Pershore, had been the most satisfying for her.

I have spoken of Ben's company on our holiday after the Madrid conference. He had come to us from Bristol, where (after his year of teaching at a school in the Quantocks) he was sharing a flat with Werner Pelz, Peter's father, and studying Spanish sixteenth-century song for a doctorate. He had built up quite a large repertoire of songs with the accompaniment of his guitar (besides those in Spanish, there were folk-songs in various languages and some of his own composition), and had hoped to pursue this as a profession. This ambition had to be set aside, because he experienced a serious set-back during his time in Bristol. He sang the leading tenor part in a week of performances by the University Opera Club of an opera by the Polish composer Moniuszko, *Strasny Dwor*, 'The Haunted House', hitherto unperformed in England. It was a success, and Ben's singing was commended as the most accomplished of the company in a review by Andrew Porter. Unfortunately the tessitura of the tenor part is very high, and singing it for a week with an amateur orchestra would have taxed even a professional. Ben was not in touch with a singing teacher at the time, or he would probably have been discouraged from attempting it. As it was, he bruised his vocal chords, and temporarily had to give up singing, to his (and our) great distress.

Ben's voice did recover ultimately, and before that he continued his studies while teaching for the LCC in London, but the blow to his hopes, and other troubles, made him decide to leave his thesis unfinished and go to begin a different life in Wales. There Lotte Pelz was hoping to start a self-supporting community, which should also be a place of healing for others, at Bryn Coch on the lower slopes of Cader Idris. She and Ben were joined for a time by John and Fran Campbell, who helped in building a square living-room on to the eccentric triangular-shaped rooms of the house, originally two combined nineteenth-century cottages.

The commune did not materialize, but after taking a training in reflexology – which Ben also learnt – Lotte discovered powers of healing in her hands, and had patients among the neighbours (and, following a television item, from farther afield) until her illness and death in December 1981.

I return at this point to 1969, and an earlier part of the family story. Colin had left Magdalen College School at Christmas that year, after securing a place at King's College, Cambridge for the autumn of 1970, to read archaeology and anthropology. He spent part of the spring in London (lodged at Fentiman Road) developing his violin playing at a centre organized by Mary Elspeth Milford, Dick Milford's daughter, who had succeeded Frances Kitching as his teacher. In March he went with us on holiday to Greece (Athens, Delphi, the Peloponnese), and parted from us at Nauplion, whence he took ship for Asia Minor, there to be joined by Nicky Vernède, and to spend the summer excavating at both Can Hassan, south of Konya, and in the east, on the Euphrates. From there he wrote some splendid letters, which I later typed up as a collection; and in the autumn I drove him over to Cambridge, where we made the first of our book-laden staircase-climbs, this one to rooms at the top of a house in Market Square.

With the 1970s began my preoccupation with libretto-writing for opera, both original and translated, and with this I will start a new chapter.

CHAPTER IX

One of the joys of our life in Oxford from the start had been the many opportunities to hear music of all kinds, whether orchestras, soloists or choirs in the Sheldonian (where Haydn had conducted his own symphony from the unlikely position of the organ loft – so Thomas Armstrong told us), or chamber ensembles in the beautiful eighteenth-century Holywell Music Room (where Handel himself had once played the chamber organ). And for me, singing in the Bach Choir or in our own madrigal group at home was life-enhancing. So I had often had occasion to think about the techniques of singing; but it was a lucky chance that put me in the way of translating opera libretti. Jane Glover, who was later to become a well-known conductor, had studied the works of the seventeenth-century Italian composer Cavalli for her Oxford doctorate, and in 1971 planned to put on the first performance in English of his opera *La Rosinda* with the University Opera Club. She had intended to make the translation herself with a friend, but with only a month or so before the date of the performance had not progressed beyond a literal translation. She went for advice to one of the music dons, Dr Sternfeld, whom I knew slightly, and he suggested that I might be interested. Jane had heard *The Jesse Tree* at Dorchester, liked the suggestion, and so came to see me. Although I had tried my hand at translating Italian poetry (a Dante sonnet, and a couple of poems by Eugenio Montale), I had never thought of tackling a libretto, and I began by translating directly from the text, but I soon realized that it was necessary to *hear* the music in one's head while making an English version. As I wrote in an article on translating opera: 'because the translator is an interpreter and not a creator, the musical line is always the leader, and he must strive to follow its twists and turns as though he were a shadow, tacked to its heels.'

As soon as I had drafted the first scene, Jane came up to go through it with me, and in the course of several sessions I learnt from her all that I needed to know about the treatment of a musical text: about the difference in the composer's approach to triple and duple time, and what liberties can be taken with the time-values in translating recitative. As I wrote in the article already quoted: 'The pitch-outline, or essential shape of the phrase, is to be followed, but the syllables can be redistributed to make the accents fall naturally in English – a need that would not be felt in French, where the stress can be varied at will.' (In arias, of course, both the syllables and the strophic pattern are important, but not the literal meaning: one should digest the general sense, and then 'write a new lyric to fit the music', as Auden put it in describing his own practice.)

Other technical points I learnt as I gained experience: how much importance to attach to the rhyme-scheme of the original, for instance; and the need to set 'open' vowels for words sung on very high or very low notes. I found that conductors other than Jane had idiosyncracies: some attached importance to the literal meaning, to the detriment of natural-ness in English, and some insisted on keeping all the rhymes – source of shipwreck to some earlier translators. I had a few arguments with Roger Norrington over this: he called me 'the mistress of the half-rhyme', and generally gave way. For quite apart from the fact that certain rhyme pairs (pleasure/treasure; languish/anguish) have become clichés and induce boredom, full rhymes in English tend to draw attention to themselves, which is appropriate in comic verse but otherwise may not suit the tone of the original. So I have found the dissonance and assonance of rhymes used in modern prosody invaluable, especially in the recitative of baroque composers, where the rhymes are often unstressed, but used to knit the phrases together. Another difficulty is the abundance of femi-nine endings in Italian, which can't be matched except by present participles in English. Most directors will agree to a monosyllabic crotchet instead of two quavers, but Raymond Leppard, for instance, would not. Then, I found that often the actual vowel or consonantal sounds of the original carry an emotional charge, so that I tried when I could to match them. I have not found that other translators thought this important, but some singers who had come to the English after singing the Italian original have told me that they found it helpful. The guiding principle, though, is to make a version sound so natural that it will seem to the listener as though the work had originally been set to a text in his own language; and if I felt depressed because too often the audience does not hear the words, it is all-important to the singer that he can believe in them.

I had only a month in which to complete this first attempt, and the singers rehearsed as I progressed, but the result was a success, both for them and for me, and Jane asked me to collaborate in her next enterprise, which was still more exciting.

In 1925 Dr Jack Westrup had produced with the University Opera Club the first English performance of Monteverdi's *Orfeo*, which is considered to be the first true opera, performed in Mantua in 1607. Now, fifty years after their earlier production, the club proposed to produce it again, in an edition closer to the original instrumentation, made by Jane, and a new translation to supersede the one commissioned in 1925, which used a somewhat archaic diction.

For *La Rosinda* of course I had had no recording to listen to, but had to depend on picking out the vocal line on the piano, and to some extent hearing it in my head from the score. For *Orfeo* I had a record, and again I worked through my version with Jane Glover. Her production (in February 1975) with Ian Caddy as Orfeo, Eiddwen Harrhy as Music, and Peter Reynolds (a local architect and experienced amateur baritone) as Pluto, was acclaimed as a success, and Stanley Sadie, reviewing it in *The Times*, said that mine should become the standard English translation. (So in fact it has remained up to now.) Roger Norrington, then in the heyday of his career as conductor of Kent Opera, heard the performance and asked to use my translation for his production, which was to go on tour the following year, though he made his own edition of the score instead of Jane's. With the encouragement of my godson Martin Kingsbury, the text was published by Faber Music, and is still in use.

I heard Roger's production in 1977 at the Camden Festival, with Peter Knapp as Orfeo, and also saw it on television. Vivian and I were able to go to the White City and watch the recording – a fascinating experience for us.

[At this point AR's illness, and other commitments, prevented completion of the full text as planned. What follows is written up by Ben from taped conversations, and then revised by AR herself.]

My collaboration with Jane Glover continued with a number of other seventeenth-century opera productions. In 1976 Vivian and I travelled over to the Wexford Festival to see Cavalli's *Eritrea*, with Philip Langridge in the tenor lead. (Ben had 'ghosted' a prose translation for me, in between joinery sessions at a training centre in Wrexham.) The production was a success, in spite of Philip Langridge having to begin singing whilst lying flat on his back.

My version was also broadcast on Radio Three in March of that year. Royalties and copyright have been the subject of much often tedious correspondence over the years; letters from the time show that on that occasion, I was paid to a measure of £1.25 per minute.

In the same period I translated Act One of Cavalli's *La Didone* for Jane, and I remember going up to London to broadcast a short introductory talk, and watching her through the glass as she recorded her specially prepared performance. We also worked together on Cavalli's *La Calisto* for Oxford University Opera Club, a translation adopted by David Freeman's Opera Factory (with Paul Daniel) in the 1980s, and performed as recently as 1996 at the Guildhall School of Music & Drama.

In 1977 I was also commissioned by the Arts Council to translate Cesti's *Orontea* for Jubilee Opera, which we went up to see performed at a hall in London University. Period instruments were used (as in the productions of seventeenth-century operas already mentioned), and I remember that it was rather difficult to hear the accompaniment of lutes, the oboes etc., given their modest dynamic range. Apart from this the realization was enjoyable.

Before we leave the seventies it is worth recalling two musical undertakings involving not just translation but the writing of fresh libretti. In about 1974 the PCC of St Mary's decided that they wanted to commission a work suitable for the vocal and choral forces available, and obtained funds from the Arts Council to enable Elizabeth Maconchy (composer of *The Jesse Tree*) and myself to proceed. We adapted and expanded a Ruskin tale (itself derived from Grimm), *The King of the Golden River*, and although a highly ambitious project it came to successful fruition. A key agent in this was répétiteur Christopher Tolley, organist at St Mary's and one of the best they ever had. The producer was our friend Katharine Ross, and another friend Sheila Southern (contralto) sang the Schoolmistress, with Peter Reynolds (Pluto in *Orfeo*) as the King, 'alias South West Wind Esq'. Karin and Juliette (aet. nine and seven) were amongst the Children of the Village, and had the task of unfurling a rather splendid golden drape centrestage to represent the River. (Set design and a fine backdrop by Peter Pelz.) The conductor was

David Whittington, who subsequently put on a production in Stockton at the church where he became priest in charge. Vivian, Katharine and I stayed with him when we went to see this; although musically effective the presentation was inhibited by sparse costumes and set, and so suffered by comparison with the original.

The other original libretto of this period was *The Lambton Worm*, an opera in two acts commissioned by the Oxford University Opera Club to music by Robert Sherlaw Johnson. (The story is based on a folk tale of County Durham recorded orally by Cecil Sharp and others.) The composer came and played some of his ideas to me on the piano, and also gave me one or two of his song-settings. The published libretto (OUP, 1979) records that the first performance was given at the Playhouse on 14 February 1978, and I vividly remember the 'worm' or dragon emerging from the well in what was quite a realistic setting. Such was the production's success that a director from East Germany was keen to put it on in East Berlin, though this came to nothing. Sir John Lambton (the baritone lead) was sung by Richard Lloyd Morgan, whom by coincidence Ben has also got to know, their family having a cottage near Llanfachreth.

In March 1981 came the first performance (at the Theatre Royal, Nottingham) of David Freeman's production of *Orfeo*, a production which has been revived many times since at the Coliseum and has become quite famous. I met John Eliot Gardiner in a room above Trafalgar Square in order to accommodate my translation to his new performing edition, and found him very easy to work with. He was not at all captious, and we readily agreed on most matters to do with rhyme. Anthony Rolfe Johnson was the Orfeo, with Patricia O'Neill as Eurydice; we also went to see the production being televised. Anthony Rolfe Johnson went on to sing the part many times, and himself conducted the most recent revival.

At about this time I also worked on Monteverdi's *Il Ritorno d'Ulisse in Patria* for Oxford University Opera Club, in a performing edition prepared and conducted by Professor Denis Arnold. Edmund Tracey and Roger Norrington went over my version of the libretto with me to make sure that everything was up to the mark. I was delighted to see the first, semi-staged performance take place (in May) in St Mary's, with period instruments including a bellows organ; unfortunately the vocal demands were rather too much of a challenge for the student singers available. A caustic reviewer refers to 'a thin spread of vocal talent and an even thinner expenditure of money'; he is also scathing about the arrangement, commenting tartly that 'Professor Arnold conducts his own edition, which in fact leaves him very little to conduct'. Luckily this libretto too was destined to be given much wider exposure at the Coliseum, where it first appeared in November 1989 in a new performing edition by Paul Daniel. The producer would again be David Freeman, with singers such as Anthony Rolfe Johnson, Jean Rigby, Sally Burgess, John Mark Ainsley and James Bowman doing much more justice to Monteverdi's glorious music.

Kent Opera commissioned my only Handel translation, *Agrippina*, from a libretto by Vincenzo Grimani. (The plot involves much 'jostling for thrones'.)

My main contact at Kent Opera was Norman Platt, who has recently sent me a copy of his autobiography *Making Music* – it contains two stills from *Agrippina*, including one of the formidable Felicity Palmer in the title role. We went over for the première at Tonbridge Wells in 1982, and the production (conducted by Ivan Fischer and directed by Platt) was revived in 1985. More recently my libretto has been used as far afield as Manhattan, Indiana and San Francisco.

The useful Appendix to Norman Platt's *Making Music* lists all my collaborations with Kent Opera, which besides *Orfeo* (1976 & 1997) and *Ulisse* (1978 & 1989) have included Monteverdi's *Il Ballo delle Ingrate* ('The Ungrateful Women', 1980 & 1981), Rameau's *Pygmalion* (1986), and Mozart's *Il Re Pastore* (1987). There is by now rather more on this list than I can clearly remember! Many of these had sets by Roger Butlin, a first-rate designer.

In the mid-'eighties we went over to Cambridge (staying with Brooke Crutchley) to see Cambridge University Opera Club put on the first production of my translation of Gluck's *Orpheus and Eurydice*: it was directed in period style by Julia Hollander, who went on to be a staff director at ENO. I was struck already then by the exceptional beauty of Michael Chance's singing as Orpheus; he was still partly pursuing academic studies at that time. Much later, in 1997, when Jane Glover took up my libretto at the Coliseum, I hoped that they might adopt Julia Hollander's production; instead they turned to the American choreographer Martha Clarke as director, and neither Jane nor I (nor many of the critics) were much in sympathy with her ideas. Michael Chance was again the Orpheus, with Lesley Garrett as Eurydice. (She entertained us at one rehearsal with a vivid story of her baby rolling off her lap!) Jane went on soon after to conduct the opera at Bordeaux, and concluded that it was in any case virtually impossible to stage satisfactorily.

Despite our overall reservations, some of the effects, such as the naked male dancers in the Underworld, were eloquent and graceful, and the production was a great success, being revived in the 1998 – 99 season and scheduled again for 2001 – 02. My libretto was also used in 1997 by Welsh National Youth Opera and Opera Atelier, Canada.

It is now time to speak in rather more detail of my collaboration, over a period of some fifteen years, with David Freeman and his Opera Factory – either in its own right, or in conjunction with ENO or Opera North. Working with him opened up for me a fresh world of possibilities. His productions were invariably striking and full of life, and although not popular in all quarters (his love-scenes were challenging for singers and audiences alike), I always found him cooperative and indeed life-enhancing. We agreed on most matters to do with contemporary language. He was a hard taskmaster to his company, requiring them to sing from the most awkward positions; but he was extremely sensitive to words, and to the poetic elements in a text, and it was perhaps this aspect of my work that led him to return to me so often.

On several visits he was accompanied by his wife Marie Angel, a versatile actress as well as a gifted singer (with a 'crème brulée' tone, according to one critic), and we enjoyed giving them a meal in the garden and meeting them *en famille* with their young children. She was Fiordiligi in the ground-breaking *Così* (South Bank Festival 1986), the production which did so much to establish his reputation. A *Guardian* reviewer enthused: 'I am not saying this production will transform the history of theatre. It is just one of the best things of its kind I have ever seen.' It is perhaps no coincidence that this should be the performing text of mine to have achieved the widest currency, right down to the present.

Another key personality in that production and in my relations with the company (and elsewhere) was the Despina, Janis Kelly. We have stayed in contact ever since those early days, and the birth of her triplets gave us an additional point of common interest. (She has also kept up with Kate and Richard when on tour with Opera North at Leeds.) It is remarkable how she has combined a taxing career with a difficult domestic background, hurrying back from rehearsals to fetch the triplets from school etc. Always very fashionably dressed in her private life, she has a stunning and exuberant presence on stage, and managed successfully to make the transition from soubrette roles (Despina, Zerlina) to those of greater stature and sobriety (the Countess in *Figaro*). Most recently she has turned her hand to directing: for her own *Così* at Grange Park Festival (June 2001) she consulted me on adding some macaronic verses to my text, and having the returning 'Arabs' speak the original Italian as a 'foreign' language. These effects, and the production as a whole, were very well received.

The conductor for those early productions (*La Calisto* 1984 & 1986, *Così* 1986 & 1988) was Paul Daniel, who has since of course gone on to even greater pre-eminence at Opera North and the Coliseum. I first met him when he was carrying out some secretarial work on John Eliot Gardiner's edition of *Orfeo*. He could be quite cavalier in his treatment of the text, and we had a good many arguments over wording, not all of which I won. (There was *always* the risk of texts being changed without my agreement, and Edmund Tracey said he liked for this reason to be present at rehearsals of his own translations; but this was not often possible for me.) We were fundamentally in agreement, however, and he was (and is) a fine and confident musician. I remember that he was especially rigorous about my giving singers open vowels on high notes.

There were many others in Opera Factory whom I enjoyed working with and getting to know. Salient amongst them are the tenors Howard Milner (brilliant as Arnalta and Monostatos) and Nigel Robson (Ferrando, Nero), and later the conductor Nicholas Kok (*Magic Flute* 1996), with whom I also worked very harmoniously. The main body of this work was of course translation from Italian: the three Mozarts (*Così* 1986, *Don Giovanni* 1990, *Figaro* 1993) and *Poppea* (1992). Translating from German for *The Magic Flute* (1996) was a new venture, and David Freeman and I split the work between us: he translated the spoken dialogue, and

I the arias and sung recitatives.

At the Coliseum my version of *Così* was given a very different treatment (1994 + revivals) by Nicolette Molnar, who has since gone on to produce the work in Italian. We didn't always see eye to eye over words; and some of her ideas (eg the lovers giving everyone the slip at the end and sneaking off with their suitcases) were only partially successful. But the production was enhanced by a beautiful set (eighteenth-century, with ruins and a staircase), and the revivals testify to its popularity.

One key figure at the Coliseum is sadly no longer with us – Nicholas John, the house dramaturge, who was returning hurriedly from a misty walk in the Austrian Alps (trying to get back in time to give a lecture on music) when he slipped and fell to his death. He had always been such a welcoming personality, and I missed our going out for a cup of coffee together. He is a great loss. An enduring legacy is the series of ENO opera guides which he initiated, and I enjoyed working with him on the Monteverdi volume, published by John Calder. It was through Nick's good offices that I was invited to give a pre-performance talk to the Friends of ENO before one of the revivals of *Orfeo*.

Most of the relevant productions at the Coliseum have already been mentioned. The 'odd' one out, in every sense of the word, was a version I made of Monteverdi's *Combattimento* ('The Duel of Tancredi and Clorinda'), presented in an unusual double bill with Bartok's *Bluebeard's Castle* in March 1993. David Alden, another of today's radical directors, staged most of the action high up on a sofa, but improbably this seemed to work, not least thanks to the superbly idiomatic singing of Paul Nilon as Narrator. We enjoyed meeting Bluebeard himself – Gwynne Howell – after the performance in one of the Italian restaurants nearby.

To close this chapter as I began it, by speaking of my happy association with Jane Glover. She it was (so I learnt after the event) who wrote a delightful and most charitable letter – encomium, indeed – in support of my being awarded an OBE. I also had a most touching letter from her afterwards. It is a great joy to look back to our first collaboration of 1971, and think of all the musical and personal riches that have ensued.

ANNE RIDLER: SELECTED WRITINGS

POETRY

Poems, Oxford University Press, 1939.
A Dream Observed and Other Poems, Editions Poetry London, 1941.
The Nine Bright Shiners, Faber, London, 1943.
The Golden Bird and Other Poems, Faber, London, 1951.
A Matter of Life and Death, Faber, London, 1959.
Selected Poems, Macmillan, New York, 1961.
Some Time After and Other Poems, Faber, London, 1972.
Italian Prospect: Six Poems, Perpetua Press, Oxford, 1976.
Dies Natalis: Poems of Birth and Infancy, Perpetua Press, Oxford, 1980.
New and Selected Poems, Faber, London, 1988.
Collected Poems, Carcanet, Manchester, 1994 (paperback edition, 1997).

Work anthologized in *Ten Oxford Poets*, Charles Brand, Oxford, 1978, and in *Women's Poetry of the 1930s*, ed. Jane Dowson, Routledge, London, 1996.

PLAYS AND TRANSLATIONS

Cain, produced in Letchworth, England, 1943, then London, 1944, published by Editions Poetry London, 1943.
The Shadow Factory: A Nativity Play, produced in London, 1945, published by Faber, London, 1946.
Henry Bly, produced in London, 1947, published in Henry Bly and Other Plays, Faber, London, 1950.
The Mask and The Missing Bridegroom, produced in London, 1951, published in *Henry Bly and Other Plays*, Faber, London, 1950.
The Trial of Thomas Cranmer (music by Brian Kelly), produced in Oxford, England, 1956, published by Faber, London, 1956.
The Departure (music by Elizabeth Maconchy), produced in London, 1961, published in *Some Time After and Other Poems*, Faber, London, 1972.
Who Is My Neighbour? produced in Leeds, England, 1961, published with *How Bitter the Bread*, Faber, London, 1963.

The Jesse Tree: A Masque in Verse (music by Elizabeth Maconchy), produced in Dorchester, England, 1970, published by Lyrebird Press, London, 1972.

Rosinda (translation of a libretto by Faustini; music by Cavalli), produced in Oxford, 1973, then London, 1975.

Eritrea (translation of a libretto by Faustini; music by Cavalli), produced in Wexford, Ireland, 1975, published by Oxford University Press, 1975.

Orfeo (translation of a libretto by Striggio; music by Monteverdi), produced in Oxford, 1975, then London, 1981, published by Faber Music, London, 1975, and included in *The Operas of Monteverdi*, John Calder, London, 1992.

The King of the Golden River (music by Elizabeth Maconchy), produced in Oxford, 1975.

The Return of Ulysses (translation of a libretto by Badoaro; music by Monteverdi), produced in London, 1978, included in *The Operas of Monteverdi*, John Calder, London, 1992, and published separately as score/vocal score *Il Ritorno di Ulisse in Patria*, ed. Alan Curtis, Novello, London, 2002.

The Lambton Worm (music by Robert Sherlaw Johnson), produced in Oxford, 1978, published by Oxford University Press, 1979.

Orontea (translation of a libretto by Cicognini; music by Cesti), produced in London, 1979.

Agrippina (translation of a libretto by Grimani; music by Handel), produced in London, 1982.

La Calisto (translation of a libretto by Faustini; music by Cavalli), produced in London, 1984.

Così Fan Tutte (translation of a libretto by da Ponte; music by Mozart), produced in London, 1986, published by Perpetua Press, Oxford, 1987.

The Marriage of Figaro (translation of a libretto by da Ponte; music by Mozart), produced in London, 1991, published by Perpetua Press, Oxford, 1991.

The Crucifixion Cantata (libretto; music by Brian Kelly), 1993.

Other translations include *Don Giovanni*, 1990; *The Coronation of Poppea*, 1992;

The Magic Flute (excluding spoken word; translation of a libretto by
  Schikaneder), produced in London, Opera Factory, 1996; *Orfeo ed
  Euridice* (translation of a libretto by Calzabigi), produced in London,
  1997.

PLAY COLLECTIONS

Henry Bly and Other Plays, Faber, London, 1950.
The Operas of Monteverdi, John Calder, London, 1992.

EDITED WORKS

Shakespeare Criticism, 1919-1935, Oxford University Press, 1936, second
  edition, 1956.
Walter de la Mare, *Time Passes and Other Poems*, Faber, London, 1942.
Best Ghost Stories, Faber, London, 1945.
A Little Book of Modern Verse, Faber, London, 1951.
The Faber Book of Modern Verse (with Michael Roberts), Faber, London,
  1957.
Charles Williams, *The Image of the City and Other Essays*, Oxford
  University Press, 1958.
Charles Williams, *Selected Writings*, Oxford University Press, 1961.
Shakespeare Criticism, 1935-1960, Oxford University Press, 1963.
Poems and Some Letters of James Thomson, Centaur Press, London, 1963.
Thomas Traherne: Poems, Centuries, and Three Thanksgivings, Oxford
  University Press, 1966.
Best Stories of Church and Clergy (with Christopher Bradby), Faber,
  London, 1966.
Selected Poems of George Darley, Merrion Press, London, 1979.
The Poems of William Austin, Perpetua Press, Oxford, 1984.

OTHER WORKS

Olive Willis and Downe House: An Adventure in Education, John Murray,
  London, 1967.
A Victorian Family Postbag, Perpetua Press, Oxford, 1988.
Profitable Wonders: Aspects of Traherne (written with A. M. Allchin and
  Julia Smith), The Amate Press, Oxford, 1989.
A Measure of English Poetry, Perpetua Press, Oxford, 1991.

INDEX

Milford, Marion 16, 19, 29, 44, 128; death of 128
Milford, Mary Elspeth 210
Milford, Phillida 157
Milford, Philippa (Pippa) 19, 128, 132
Milford, Robin 16, 53, 128, 129, 132–33, 138, 144, 149, 191; engaged to Kirstie 19; death of son Barnaby 133; attempted suicide 133; electro-convulsive treatment 133; *A Prophet in the Land* 80; 'Mass for children's voices' 133; *The Mask* 145; *The Shoemaker* 40
Milford, Rose 170
Milford, Theodore 172
Miller, Rhoda 131, 152, 169, 172
Millom 201
Milman, Dean of York 183
Milne, A. A., *The Dover Road* 50
Milner, Howard 218
Milton, John 29, 70, 82
Mino da Fiesole 66
Missing Bridegroom, The 150, 160, 161
Molnar, Nicolette 219
Moly *see* Ohlson, Miss
Monet, Claude 101
Monroe, Marilyn 170
Mont Blanc 119
Montale, Eugenio 211
Monte Cavo 73
Monte Morello 66
Monte Soracte 74
Monte Subasio 75
Monteverdi, Claudio 219; *Combattimento* 219; *Il Ballo delle Ingrate* 216; *Orfeo* 213, 215, 216; *Il Ritorno d'Ulisse in Patria* 215, 216
Montgomery, General 138, 143
Moray Firth 90
Morgan Brown, Winnie 88
Morley, Frank 98, 105, 107, 109, 120–21, 122, 123, 129, 161
Morris, William 8, 93
Morty, Nurse 140
Mount Grace 17, 38

Mountford, Brian 175
Mozart, Wolfgang Amadeus, *Così Fan Tutte* 217, 218, 219; *Don Giovanni* 218; *Il Re Pastore* 216; *The Coronation of Poppea* 218; *The Magic Flute* 218; *The Marriage of Figaro* 218
Mulliner's, Miss 151
Munich 101
Münsingen 190
Murray, Diana 141, 151
Murray, Gilbert 54
Murray, Jock 141
Murray, John 179
Murray, Rosemary 49
Muskamp 23
Mussolini, Benito 64, 67, 74, 113
Mynors, Roger 183, 184, 185

National Council for Women 141
National Gallery 53
National Reformer, The 181
National Trust 47, 51
Naughton and Gold 99
Nauplion 210
Nazi regime 100, 101
Nearey, Antony 161
Nello (Rome waiter) 64
Nemi, Lake 71, 73
Nether Stowey 59
New Book of English Verse 97, 101
New Oxford Book of English Verse 180
New Theatre 147
New Verse 121
New Yorker, The 111
Newbury 29, 32, 38, 49, 158
Newbury amateur orchestra 53
Newquay 203
Nice 205, 206
Nicholson, Norman 124, 199, 201, 202; *Sea to the West* 202; *The Old Man of the Mountains* 146, 147; *Wednesday Early Closing* 202
Nicholson, Yvonne 201, 202
Nickel, Maria 29, 33, 35, 37, 40, 54, 55